The Politics of
International Humanitarian
Aid Operations

THE POLITICS OF INTERNATIONAL HUMANITARIAN AID OPERATIONS

Edited by ERIC A. BELGRAD
and NITZA NACHMIAS

Foreword by GENERAL SIR MICHAEL ROSE

PRAEGER

Westport, Connecticut
London

Library of Congress Cataloging-in-Publication Data

The politics of international humanitarian aid operations / edited by
  Eric A. Belgrad and Nitza Nachmias ; foreword by Sir Michael Rose.
      p.   cm.
    Includes bibliographical references and index.
    ISBN 0–275–95273–8 (alk. paper)
      1. Humanitarian assistance.   2. Humanitarian assistance—Case
  studies.   I. Belgrad, Eric A., 1935– . II. Nachmias, Nitza.
  HV553.P64   1997
  361.2'6—dc20   96–44677

British Library Cataloguing in Publication Data is available.

Library of Congress Catalog Card Number: 96–44677
ISBN: 0–275–95273–8

First published in 1997

Praeger Publishers, 88 Post Road West, Westport, CT 06881
An imprint of Greenwood Publishing Group, Inc.

Printed in the United States of America

The paper used in this book complies with the
Permanent Paper Standard issued by the National
Information Standards Organization (Z39.48–1984).

10 9 8 7 6 5 4 3 2 1

Copyright Acknowledgments

The editors and publisher are grateful to the following for granting permission to reprint
from their material:

Portions of Chapter 7 appeared in Janet E. Heininger, *Peacekeeping in Transition: The
United Nations in Cambodia* (New York: Twentieth Century Fund Press, 1994).

This book is dedicated to the Nachmias granchild, Nir Tomer, and to the Belgrad grandchildren, Alex, Benjamin, Gideon, Max, and Asher.

May they grow up and flourish in a world free of war and filled with humanitarian concern.

Contents

Part II   Humanitarian Aid Operations:
          Case Studies

Part III   Prospects for Future Humanitarian Interventions

Foreword

GENERAL SIR MICHAEL ROSE

Any work which contributes to an understanding of how the international community can better confront the challenge of creating stability in the face of problems spawned by the fast-expanding economically and politically insecure populations of the world is to be warmly welcomed. *The Politics of International Humanitarian Aid Operations*, focusing on this vitally important area, seeks to draw lessons from the past which will not only be helpful to academic thinking but also highly useful to practitioners in the field.

Neither political consideration nor emotional response caused by vivid media coverage is likely ever to replace the moral imperative as a sufficient basis for developing an adequate international response to the sort of disorder and consequent human suffering which occurred in Somalia and Yugoslavia, and which continue to occur in many other areas of the world. Political motives for intervention will always be tempered by regard to self-interest and perceived cost in human and financial terms, whilst media coverage will always tend to be haphazard and inconsistent in quality. Neither, therefore, should become the sole factor in determining international policy. The response to the moral imperative must lie in promoting a greater world understanding of both the limitations and the aspirations of the international community. Clearly, there must also be provision of an intergovernmental planning and policy-making structure at the United Nations (UN) and regional levels, as well as a specifically agreed-on international doctrine for humanitarian aid operations—what defines their limitations, and how the competing political, security, and aid components of such missions can be coordinated. All participating elements of a humanitarian mission must, therefore, accept the limitations of the mission, and the military element, above all, must understand that the military can act only in support of the civil humanitarian aid delivery mission which is the underlying purpose of the mandate. The principle of minimum use of force to achieve a necessary objective must also be clearly stated, for too much use of military force in what is essentially a humanitarian aid delivery mission is likely to affect the flow of aid, especially where such force is being used against those who control most of the terrain. Anything else will result in mission creep and endanger the success of the mission. In addition, the international community must explicitly accept that because of the very nature of its deployments and rules of engagement, a peacekeeping and humanitarian aid delivery force deployed for humanitarian purposes is likely, in the end, to become a hostage of the situation itself, and that this will preclude the use of military force to obtain political goals. If such a force is to fulfill the object of its mission, it will have to deploy into remote places in small numbers and would therefore be unable to act as a military occupying power capable of imposing political solutions in the region.

The international community must also accept that the consequence of humanitarian intervention can actually be the prolongation of conflict in situations of civil war. Inevitably, in the first instance the warlords will use the aid delivered to sustain the soldiers engaged in the conflict, as well as their families. However, the consequence of not delivering aid to a suffering population will always be far more unacceptable to international public opinion than supplying the armies of the warring parties. Although conflict might be prolonged in this way, at least in the interim the suffering of the population can be alleviated. This is likely to remain an entirely morally justifiable position for the international community to adopt.

The final point which I believe it is important to make is that better coordination in the area of public information policy is necessary. The media always tend to press for vigorous military intervention, which they perceive as a more effective response to the problems on the ground than humanitarian aid. In effect, humanitarian and peacekeeping missions will be criticised for failing to do what they were never asked to do. Yet, there are clear limitations on the use of military force which prevent these missions from engaging in war fighting. Therefore, unless the political and military shortfalls of such missions can be clearly justified publicly against the value of the aid delivery programme, they will lose international credibility and ultimately fail. Bosnia provides a clear example of this happening. The mandate of the mission in Bosnia was simply to sustain the lives of 2.7 million people and, at the same time, to try to bring about conditions for a peaceful resolution of the conflict—both of which the UN achieved in large measure. Nevertheless, the United Nations Protection Force in the former Yugoslavia (UNPROFOR) ultimately stood condemned for not delivering the political aspirations of the many supporters of Bosnia in the international community. It is ironic that those countries which cried loudest over Bosnia were, in fact, the most reluctant to offer the UN actual support on the ground. The message that can be derived from all of this is that the UN and all aid organisations must maintain a coherent and consistent public information campaign in order to justify short-term action in the light of whatever long-term strategy has been agreed-on as necessary to fulfill the mandate.

The solutions to the problems of the world in the next fifty years are probably not going to be delivered from the bomb bay of an aircraft or emerge from the muzzle of a gun. The solutions are likely to come from a better understanding of the processes of peace and how the world can confront the challenges of the future. The analysis contained in this collection of essays will undoubtedly help further international understanding of the processes of peace and, to use the words of Ralph Bunche, add reason's voice in order "to make radical change possible without upheaval."

Introduction

ERIC A. BELGRAD

The end of the Cold War signaled a radical redefinition of the requirements of world peace. Whereas world politics since the end of World War II had dealt primarily with issues of security and related alliance considerations, the end of bipolar competition opened the way to a resurrection and reenactment of ancient historic wrongs inflicted and suffered in parts of the world that had until then been relegated largely to the fringes of Cold War strategic concerns. Internecine struggles now began to take center stage, focused, as they were, by the cyclops eye of the television camera that transmitted instantly to conference rooms and living rooms throughout the civilized world pictures and narrations of horrendous excesses—the seemingly inevitable concomitant of inter-ethnic struggles in Asia, Africa, and Europe.

The United Nations (UN) and individual members of the community of nations, responding to mounting pressures from popular opinion to bring such conflicts to a halt, encountered almost immediately a great number of unexpected difficulties that frustrated their attempts to pacify the combatants and bring aid and comfort to civilian victims. Even when the will to interpose outside forces between participants in these conflicts could be mustered and resources to provide aid could be found, local conditions often nullified attempts at pacification and aid distribution. Indeed, the combatants in such internecine conflicts often made the good samaritans the objects of their rapacity and ill-will.

The editors of this book have attempted to shed light on recent developments in the politics of international humanitarian aid operations by gathering a number of essays that deal with theoretical considerations as well as case studies reflecting recent experience in attempting pacification of what are essentially civil wars and providing aid to victims of such conflicts. Specifically, insights gained in the interventions in Cambodia, Somalia, Rwanda, and Bosnia-Herzegovina have been examined here, and various analytical models defining the limits and opportunities of humanitarian aid policies have been included.

The editors wish to express their appreciation to all the contributors, whose expertise and broad experience are at the very core of this book and justify its publication. They want to thank General Sir Michael Rose for his gracious consent to provide a foreword that effectively defines and illuminates the problems discussed in the essays and Professor Jim Whitman for his valuable intercessions in the face of seemingly insoluble problems. In particular, the editors wish to single out for their thanks Professor Leon Gordenker, on whose encyclopedic knowledge and advice they drew at every stage of preparing this book. The editors also want to thank Gloria M. Belgrad, without whose sage counsel and considerable editorial assistance this work could not have been completed. Finally, they would like to thank James Dunton, Jean Lynch, and Michelle Scott of Praeger for their unfailing patience and assistance. Errors and omissions are the responsibility of the editors, who are well aware that history has not stood still between the composition of these essays and their actual publication. Indeed, all the troublesome quandaries of humanitarian aid operations analyzed by our contributors in their European, African, Asian, and Middle Eastern contexts continue to bedevil policy makers with inherent complexities and internal contradictions.

Acronyms

AHT	Advance Humanitarian Team
ASEAN	Association of South East Asian Nations
CCP	Conciliation Commission on Palestine
CGDK	Coalition Government of Democratic Kampuchea
CRS	Catholic Relief Services
CSCE	Conference on Security and Cooperation in Europe
DHA	United Nations Department of Humanitarian Affairs
DOP	Declaration of Principles
DPKO	United Nations Department of Peacekeeping Operations
EC	European Community
FAO	United Nations Food and Agriculture Organization
FRODEBU	Hutu-dominated party in Rwanda led by Melchior Ndadye
FUNCINPEC	Non-Communist Cambodian party led by Prince Sihanouk
GAO	General Accounting Office of the United States
GATT	General Agreement on Tariffs and Trade
HUMPROFOR	United Nations Humanitarian Protection Force (proposed)
ICJ	International Court of Justice
ICORC	International Committee on the Reconstruction of Cambodia
ICRC	International Committee of the Red Cross

IDF	Israel Defense Forces
IGO	Intergovernmental organization
IMF	International Monetary Fund
KPNLF	Cambodian party of former prime minister Son Sann
NATO	North Atlantic Treaty Organization
NGO	Nongovernmental organization
NMOG	Neutral Military Observer Group (of OAU)
OAS	Organization of American States
OAU	Organization for African Unity
OECD	Organization for Economic Cooperation and Development
ONUMOZ	United Nations Operation in Mozambique
OSCE	Organization on Security and Cooperation in Europe
PDD	Presidential Decision Directive
PECDAR	Palestinian Economic Council for Development and Reconstruction
PLO	Palestine Liberation Organization
QIP	Quick Impact Project
RAO	Refugee Affairs Officer
RDF	Rapid Deployment Force
RPF	Rwanda Patriotic Front, Tutsi-dominated party
SG	Surgeon General (IDF Medical Corps Mission to Rwanda)
SNC	Supreme National Council (Cambodia)
SOC	State of Cambodia
UN	United Nations
UNA-USA	United Nations Association of the United States
UNAMIR	United Nations Assistance Mission for Rwanda
UNAVEM II, III	United Nations Angola Verification Mission(s)
UNBRO	United Nations Border Relief Operation
UNCTAD	United Nations Conference on Trade and Development
UNDP	United Nations Development Program
UNESCO	United Nations Educational, Scientific, and Cultural Organization
UNFICYP	United Nations Force in Cyprus
UNHCR	United Nations High Commissioner for Refugees
UNICEF	United Nations International Emergency Children's Fund
UNITA	Union for the Total Liberation of Angola
UNOMUR	United Nations Observer Mission Uganda-Rwanda

UNOSOM	United Nations Operation in Somalia
UNOSOM II	United Nations Operation in Somalia (1993–95)
UNPROFOR	United Nations Protection Force in the former Yugoslavia
UNPROFOR I	United Nations Protection Force in Croatia
UNPROFOR II	United Nations Protection Force in Bosnia
UNREO	United Nations Rwanda Emergency Office
UNRPR	United Nations Relief for Palestinian Refugees
UNRRA	United Nations Relief and Rehabilitation Administration
UNRWA	United Nations Work and Relief Agency
UNTAC	United Nations Transitional Authority in Cambodia
UPRONA	Rwanda political party led by Prince Rwagasore
USAID	United States Agency for International Development
WFP	World Food Program
WHO	World Health Organization
WTO	World Trade Organization

PART I

Issues and Concepts in International Humanitarian Aid Operations

1

The Politics of Humanitarian Aid

ERIC A. BELGRAD

The juxtaposition of the terms "politics" and "humanitarian aid" in the title of this book was hardly fortuitous. It was designed to reflect a fundamental dichotomy characteristic of virtually all aid programs: The humanitarian impulse to relieve the suffering of the victims of war, famine, disease, or natural disasters tends to run counter to the self-serving motives that normally animate the pursuit of national interests. Indeed, the present work on the infusion of politics into humanitarian aid policies owes its inspiration to the pivotal fact that, since their inception at the close of World War I, humanitarian aid programs have been more or less driven by conflicting needs to reconcile charitable aims with practical and self-interested constraints of politics.

GENERAL CONSIDERATIONS: HISTORICAL ORIGINS

With the end of World War I, programs of humanitarian assistance based on the need to succor innocent victims of the conflict became a matter of concern to Allied political leaders. Because the extent of the suffering of World War I victims was unprecedented, private charities, which would have intervened in earlier times, could not command resources sufficient to alleviate the hunger and disease on the scale circumstances now dictated. The Wilson administration, driven by eleemosynary considerations worthy of the president's humane reputation, determined to put in place a massive rescue apparatus in those areas of Western Europe most ravaged by German war occupation. Belgium, whose vio-

lated neutrality and brutal occupation had been a central focus of Allied propaganda during the conflict, was identified early as most deserving of aid. Belgium,
therefore, became the first beneficiary of a postwar American relief effort headed
by Herbert Hoover.[1] What had been a privately arranged rescue effort headed
by Hoover during the course of the War—enjoying financial support from private
as well as from governmental sources—became, with the end of hostilities, the
first official humanitarian relief effort sponsored and controlled by the U.S. government.[2]

    Unlike most later international relief efforts, the work of the American Relief
Administration achieved all its objectives with a high degree of success in the
short period between the Armistice and the signing of the peace—some eight
months—and was thereupon promptly terminated by Congress. Subsequently,
Hoover organized two new humanitarian aid efforts. The first of these, the European Children's Fund, collected private and governmental donations that made
possible the distribution of food and clothing to some eight million children until
1922. The second, privately organized in the fall of 1921 and known as the
Hoover-Nansen Mission, purported to provide aid to the survivors of the Russian
Civil War.

    In actuality, this latter effort was designed to use the mechanism of humani-
tarian relief as a blind behind which an anti-Bolshevik subversive political program could be carried out. In the wake of the failure of Allied military
interventions to force an anti-Soviet outcome to the Russian Civil War, Hoover
and his associates determined to use, as a Trojan horse—to infiltrate and subvert
the Soviet government—food, medicine, and the means essential for reconstructing the economy.[3] More particularly, by creating a food and medicine distribution system outside the control of the Soviet government, Hoover hoped to
establish an alternative power center through which the loyalty of the recipient
populations, weakened as they were at the end of the civil war by massive starvation and disease, might be turned against the Bolsheviks. Lenin recognized
that ulterior motives inspired these offers of humanitarian aid and refused to
subject his regime to subversive activities mascarading as international relief
efforts. Ultimately, the aid was provided without the original onerous conditions;
it was offered purely to satisfy humanitarian objectives.[4]

HUMANITARIAN AID: GRANTING AND RECEIVING

    When governments decide to sponsor humanitarian aid efforts, they seldom
do so without considering how their own political interests may be furthered
thereby.[5] It may appear to be egregiously hard-hearted and manipulative to use
the misery of others for one's own political advantage. Nevertheless, the pursuit
of what are regarded as legitimate national interests by piggy-backing them on
humanitarian programs is usually defended on practical as well as ethical grounds.
Self-serving motives favoring the giver more than the receiver of humanitarian
aid are bound to be hidden by policy makers. After all, those who offer aid cannot

be expected to broadcast their innermost motives for doing so. Neither public nor private charities would long survive if they had to make public confession of how they expected to benefit from policies that purported to be devoted exclusively to humanitarian concerns.

A defensible test of the validity of any governmental humanitarian aid program might be, not whether the donor will derive some benefit from the program, but whether recipients are likely to benefit as much from the program as the donor. In the case of government-sponsored programs, it is not unreasonable to expect donors to seek some political advantage in connection with succoring those in need.[6] It might even be argued that whether that political advantage is incidental to the aid or is a basic condition precedent to its offer is immaterial. By contrast, the use of aid programs as a blind for infiltrating and destabilizing governments, as was attempted with the Hoover-Nansen initiative in Soviet Russia, would seem to violate any legitimate concept of international aid programs.[7] But it might be argued that in 1921 the United States had not recognized the legitimacy of the Bolshevik regime and had no legal obligations toward it. The Bolsheviks, regarded as international outlaws guilty of the most heinous violations of international law and of human rights, were not entitled to claim safeguards provided by international law and custom. Would the subversion of such a regime by a stratagem involving the use of a purported humanitarian aid program violate international law? Would the incidental benefits to the recipient civilian population clothe the humanitarian aid subterfuge with a degree of legitimacy that would not be achieved otherwise?

Clearly, it cannot be maintained that self-interested motives of the donor nations automatically bring into question the humanitarian bona fides of their aid programs. Every political act is motivated by some form of self-interest.[8] If there is a fine line between legitimate humanitarian concerns and pretense, where is that fine line to be drawn? What to one interpreter is an act of imperialism, albeit disguised by claims of the loftiest of moral intentions, may well be the act of misguided but well-intentioned officials truly concerned to relieve hunger and suffering.

If ambivalence attaches to the donor's motives in dispensing humanitarian aid, the recipients are likewise bedeviled by conflicting sentiments regarding their dependence on the largesse of others. The need for charity must be particularly galling for emerging states attempting to assert their national independence after a usually long and demeaning period of colonial subservience. In a general context the philosopher Arthur O. Lovejoy, commenting on Thorstein Veblen's *Theory of the Leisure Class*, pointed out that "economic values are, for the most part, prestige values; . . . since the desire is not for a particular sum of possessions, but always for *more* possessions than others have, it can never reach a final limit [emphasis in original]."[9]

The ability to render humanitarian aid is a mark of prestige: Those who have surplus resources to give to those in want thereby establish for themselves a high status in the community of nations. Conversely, those whose deprivation forces them to ask for assistance accept lower status and concomitant loss of prestige. Furthermore, those who have wealth and are charitable "aim at approbation as well as attention; at esteem as well as consideration; and admiration and gratitude, as well as congratulation."[10] It follows, however, that the greater the generosity and consequent prestige of the donor, the greater the decline of prestige and the cause for resentment on the part of the recipient.

In any bilateral linkage between donors and recipients of humanitarian aid, the issue of prestige is likely to drive a wedge between nations. Donors, expecting gratitude, will reap resentment instead; recipients will find in their dependent status a galling reminder of recent colonial subservience and will alternately resent donors for allegedly patronizing them or not providing sufficient relief. To paraphrase Adam Smith and adapt his observations to current international circumstances: The more the poverty of less-developed or impoverished nations is noticed, the more these become recipients of humanitarian aid, the more their self-esteem suffers.[11] And self-esteem, more than food and shelter, is what humanity prizes.

This cleavage between donors and recipients of humanitarian assistance has the unfortunate consequence of imposing limits on the extent and duration of any aid that may be provided. The political costs of rendering assistance can be justified domestically only in the ephemeral coin of the recipient's gratitude or the donor's political advantage. The inevitable resentment of recipient nations, therefore, effectively places a cap on the extent to which donor nations may be able to marshall continuing political support for further aid. Furthermore, since the conditions of deprivation that occasion the need for aid tend to be deeply ingrained and not amenable to quick solutions, such a cap may well stop the delivery of aid before the recipient nation can develop the means for autonomous development. This, in turn, is likely to cause the dependence to become chronic, bringing with it a long-lasting condition of low self-esteem, political instability, and internecine violence.

On the other hand, the continuous provision of aid (albeit inadequate to assure ultimate self-sufficiency) may itself encourage chronic economic dependence— a kind of "cargo cult" that leads recipients to develop an abiding belief that necessities will always be provided by the outside world, and that their responsibilities are solely to collect and consume what others have provided.[12]

An unresolved debate centers on whether humanitarian assistance programs may encourage permanent dependence by fueling tendencies toward overpopulation. A recent study appears to establish that the postcolonial population explosion in the Third World was largely engendered by "economic development" aid and reckless lending provided by industrialized nations.[13] The study suggests that humanitarian assistance makes available resources that would otherwise not be available and that encourage population growth, with the net effect that domestic consumption and dependence among beneficiaries increase while production, which would lead to autonomy, decreases.

FOREIGN ASSISTANCE PROGRAMS: A FORM OF
HUMANITARIAN AID

If the end of World War I gave rise to the first U.S. humanitarian aid programs, the end of World War II gave rise to the concept of economic assistance programs which, like those precursor programs, pursued a mix of political and humanitarian objectives. As early as 1943 the Roosevelt administration began to consider postwar needs of liberated areas and sought to put in place mechanisms to meet such needs at the earliest practical time. Among these was the United Nations Relief and Rehabilitation Administration (UNRRA), which depended on annual congressional appropriations and which was therefore subject to intense and continuous scrutiny by lawmakers who needed to be reassured that the money spent not only supported the highest humanitarian considerations but also served the national interest.[14]

Even before war's end, however, UNRRA failed to match political authority with funding authority: The congressional piper was not invited to call the tune. Whereas Congress was expected to provide virtually all funds, the recipient members of the wartime alliance, the UN, played a major, if not decisive, role in determining how and to whom the aid was to be dispensed. Congressional displeasure was palpable and predictable. Congress asserted its intention to rectify this situation by shifting to a program of foreign assistance. In this connection Assistant Secretary for Economic Affairs Will L. Clayton of the U.S. Department of State argued in favor of providing massive assistance for the reconstruction of postwar Europe. Significantly, he did so on the condition that "we must avoid getting into another UNRRA. *The United States must run this show*" [emphasis in original].[15] At a meeting with Secretary of State George Marshall and then Under-Secretary Dean Acheson, Clayton explained the humanitarian and the practical concerns that motivated his proposal:

Millions of people would soon die, creating chaos of bloodshed and disorder in doing so. To organize the great effort needed to prevent this disaster would take time, but it had to begin here and now. Surely the plan should be a European plan and come—at any rate, appear to come—from Europe. *But the United States must run the show* [emphasis in original].[16]

In proposing what came to be known as the Marshall Plan, Clayton's concern was to provide essential humanitarian relief to Europe, but to link the aid effort to the larger requirements of U.S. foreign policy interests. The unspoken premise of Clayton's proposals was that humanitarian aid, as it had theretofore been practiced, was much too decentralized, far too easily exploited by corrupt officials in recipient nations—the example of UNRRA assistance to China, which had been massively looted by Kuomintang officials, was fresh in Clayton's mind—and not properly harnessed to the donor's national interests. Only a much more structured system of economic assistance could provide aid in a rational and controlled manner.

Clayton's views were endorsed enthusiastically by Marshall and Acheson. In a speech entitled "Ethics in International Relations Today," given at Amherst College on December 9, 1964, Acheson sagely advocated the need to reconcile the practical dictates of statecraft with humanitarian aims:

A good deal of trouble comes from the anthropomorphic urge to regard nations as individuals and apply to our own national conduct vague maxims for individual conduct— for instance, the Golden Rule—even though in practice individuals rarely practice it. The fact is that nations are not individuals. . . . This does not mean that considerations of compassion have no place in government decisions. It does mean that the criteria are generally quite different and far more complicated. . . . The overriding guide must be achievement of a major goal of policy—in this case, creating an environment in which free societies may flourish and undeveloped nations who want to work on their development may find the means to do so. . . . The criteria should be hard-headed in the extreme. Decisions are not helped by considering them in terms of sharing, brotherly love, the Golden Rule, or inducting our citizens into the Kingdom of Heaven.[17]

Acheson's views on humanitarian aid were tailored to coincide with his so-called bipolar view of the world. He had come to accept the thesis, then recently proposed by George F. Kennan,[18] that between the Soviet Union and the United States there had developed a deep-seated conflict, encompassing ideological, political, economic, and military considerations. It was this conflict that was to define all requirements to be met by U.S. foreign policy, including those concerned with humanitarian assistance. Although it is true that initially Marshall Plan offers of help were extended to the Europeans in general, including the Soviet Union and the nations under its control, the United States imposed terms of eligibility for assistance that made those offers unacceptable to the Soviet bloc, and for the same reason that the conditions imposed at the time of the Hoover Mission in 1921 had been found unacceptable.

The precursor to the Marshall Plan, Public Law 75, which came to be known as the Truman Doctrine, defined the objective of U.S. foreign policy: to contain Soviet expansionism by building a coalition of like-minded states through assistance programs that reached from the economic to the military. This shift of U.S. policy, from a reliance on the coalition that had been victorious in World War II and that comprised the permanent membership of the Security Council to an anti-Soviet alliance system, was based on the recognition that "the seeds of totalitarian regimes are nurtured by misery and want. They spread and grow in the evil soil of poverty and strife. They reach full growth when the hope of a people for a better life has died. We must keep that hope alive."[19]

Foreign assistance programs of the type represented by Public Law 75 rapidly proliferated. The initial programs favored Western Europe; subsequent foreign assistance was offered to non-European clients. Both the earlier assistance pro-

grams and the later assistance programs shared a number of essential characteristics: Recipient nations became eligible for assistance by virtue of damaged or
undeveloped economies that forced their populations to live in hunger and want;
because of these conditions of deprivation, recipients were deemed to be particularly vulnerable to Soviet aggression, intimidation, or subversion; and
accordingly, U.S. aid was to be offered to recipients who had elected to make
common cause with the United States in resisting Soviet expansion and subor-
dinating their national self-interests to a broader American vision of "Western
interests."

The most successful of such foreign assistance programs, the Marshall Plan,
was predicated on the concept that Western European recipients were to defer,
in favor of "Western interests" as defined by the United States, the exercise of
historic national rights to determine trade and economic policies, to control the
flow of people, trade, and capital within their boundaries, and even to promulgate
their own social policies.[20] Clayton's dictum, that the United States was to define
eligibility for bilateral assistance on the basis of U.S. national interests, was
amended. Except under extraordinary circumstances, all aid was to be funneled
through multilateral instrumentalities, and eligibility for such aid was to be conditioned on whether applicants served "Western interests," as defined by the
United States. The intent was to create multinational groupings, which would
be linked together politically, economically, and, most importantly, ideologically,
in the struggle against the Soviet Union. The infrastructure created to administer
the Marshall Plan and the fundamental objectives of European economic and
political integration, which ultimately gave rise to the birth of the European
Community (EC)—all this is, in a very real sense, attributable to the conditions
imposed upon the European recipients of U.S. aid.

The Truman administration and its successors found it more difficult to exact
compliance with U.S.-dictated standards of eligibility from Afro-Asian nations
then emerging from their erstwhile colonial status. That these nations were being
wooed by both the Soviet Union and the United States heavily influenced
whether they were deemed eligible for U.S. economic aid; the U.S. Point Four
Program was in no position to demand unquestioning support for U.S. positions
in the East-West struggle as a precondition for delivering grants of foreign aid.
The Clayton requirement that aid be linked to consideration of U.S. national
interests could be applied effectively only to those nations deemed most exposed
to Soviet threats of subversion. America's closest allies, which came under that
threat most directly, were held to a much closer adherence to U.S. definitions
of Western interests than Afro-Asian nations, which were under no such danger.
Thus these nations were able to exploit the rivalry between the superpowers and
thereby escape the overly tight embrace of either of them.[21] The Soviet Union
(and later China) similarly made the dispensation of aid dependent upon the
recipients' acceptance of the donor's worldviews. Consequently, the less-
developed nations viewed the aims of all superpowers in offering foreign assistance with suspicion; neither the Soviet Union nor the United States was

consistently able to translate its specific national ambitions into recognizable policy gains demonstrably achieved by the provision of aid. Nevertheless, the attempt to gain advantage by doing good had to be made. Abba Eban pithily articulated the inherently cynical self-interest underlying all foreign policy when he wrote recently, "All governments take their decisions in the name of national interest and then explain them in terms of self-sacrificing altruism."[22]

THE INTERNATIONALIZATION OF HUMANITARIAN ASSISTANCE

The pervasive suspicions attached to the motives of those who offer assistance gave rise to the idea that the only appropriate vehicle for the distribution of humanitarian assistance would be the UN: It was believed that aid offered by the UN would be free from the taint of self-serving motives. But why would states agree to the internationalization of humanitarian relief efforts without specific regard to the furtherance of their own national interests? The reason, in part, may lie in the remembrance of twentieth-century holocausts, from the slaughter of Armenians after World War I to the extermination camps of World War II— memories that leap over narrow issues of national interest and make universal claims on the conscience of humanity. Perhaps, however, the reason is to be found in the rising understanding that human misery cannot be quarantined: that it cannot be kept at arm's length forever; that if it is not opposed there, sooner or later it will descend upon us here.

Beginning in 1949 the UN initiated programs for the benefit of Palestinian populations that had been dislocated from their homes as a consequence of the Arab-Israeli conflict of the previous year.[23] The United Nations Work and Relief Administration (UNRWA), the first UN agency created to dispense humanitarian aid, gradually developed into a large bureaucracy divided into two very distinct groups: a UN directorate composed of a relatively small cadre of international civil servants overseeing, from a distance, and a burgeoning local bureaucracy, which operated with ever-increasing autonomy.[24] Over the course of almost five decades of service, both parts of that bureaucracy demonstrated a virtually unlimited capacity to act in a self-serving manner, generally at the expense of their clients. Furthermore, it was hardly foreseen that, notwithstanding the international character of the proffered aid, these programs—and all others offered through the aegis of the UN—would become mired in political and ideological disputes on the part of donors and recipients alike.

The hope that funneling humanitarian aid through UN agencies would elevate this activity to a higher moral, nonpolitical plane was not realized. Funding for these first and subsequent UN efforts was held hostage to the political and ideological interests of donor nations. It was as if the Clayton rule had now been adopted by all foreign offices and parliaments whose annual task it was to recommend or approve humanitarian assistance budgets.[25]

These funding problems worsened as a result of the expansion of UN responsibilities in the post–Cold War period, and hence, all too often, the number of aid programs the UN wished to conduct was substantially lower than available funding would permit. Complicating matters even more was the fact that in several cases distribution of aid in regions of the world where the need was the greatest was made contingent on pacification of local conflicts, so that the assistance could be made available without placing recipients and assistance personnel in mortal danger.[26]

During the last half-dozen years the increased number of demands for humanitarian assistance placed concerned UN agencies under ever greater strain as available trained personnel and resources were stretched beyond their capacities. At the same time, UN missions found themselves incapable of applying effective controls over waste, corruption, and mismanagement. In November 1994 UN Secretary-General Boutros-Ghali responded to the growing number of complaints lodged by contributing member states by creating the Office of Internal Oversight Services to investigate allegations of waste. Although this office has not been able to stem the hemorrhage of theft and mismanaged funds, the under secretary-general in charge, Karl T. Paschke, stated in his report of June 1995: "Reform in my view is a process, a difficult long-haul undertaking. . . . It is not a quick fix that happens overnight."[27] Paschke concluded, "I have not found the U.N. to be a more corrupt organization that shows more fraud than any other comparable public organization."[28] Not surprisingly, this lukewarm endorsement of the honesty and accountability of UN agencies did not suffice to overcome member states' reluctance to pay their shares of humanitarian assistance costs. Indeed, the United States is well over $1 billion in arrears on its assessed contributions for peacekeeping and humanitarian assistance, and Congress has shown no enthusiasm to vote appropriation measures to make the necessary funds available to the UN.[29]

In recent years Secretary-General Boutros-Ghali has sought to meet the burgeoning need for humanitarian assistance by relying increasingly on UN agencies rather than on traditional bilateral or multilateral arrangements. Others take sharp issue with this approach. The Final Report of the Eighty-Seventh American Assembly, whose 1995 meetings were co-sponsored by the United Nations Association of the United States (UNA-USA), clearly delineated the unprecedented scale of the refugee problem. According to U.S. intelligence estimates, the number of refugees and displaced persons was placed at "more than 40 million people—nearly one percent of the world's population—[who] are in need of and dependent on international aid to avoid large-scale malnutrition and death."[30] Precisely because the demand for aid has grown beyond the resources available to the UN, the American Assembly and UNA-USA recommended that "U.N. development agencies should be reorganized and pared down to focus only on those activities that cannot be performed more effectively by other multilateral or bilateral agencies, nongovernmental organizations and private enterprise."[31] Clearly, although they had long supported the expansion of the UN's role in international affairs, the American Assembly and UNA-USA now insisted that the UN's role in providing long-term assistance be discontinued.[32]

Yet it must be understood that stopgap emergency interventions can have no long-term curative effects. To intervene with food and emergency medical assistance in the face of drought, flood, or ethnic warfare can, at best, solve problems of the moment; it cannot effect long-term solutions, that is, establish the kind of lasting conditions essential for normal life. Indeed, the beneficiaries of today's emergency relief may well be the needy victims of tomorrow if the root causes of their deprivation are not addressed today.

Beyond humanitarian assistance to meet emergencies, long-term solutions require interventions that will build infrastructures and prepare recipients to become autonomous. The building of such infrastructures is ultimately dependent on stable sociopolitical conditions, but these are generally lacking precisely in those parts of the world where most of the clientele for humanitarian assistance can be found. The recent experiment in Somalia is highly instructive in delineating the limits of humanitarian assistance and the dangers of reaching beyond succoring the starving to the heights—or depths—of nation-building.

The intent of the Bush administration in providing food and medical assistance to the starving masses in Somalia was initially quite modest. Because Somali military factions had seized relief materials, which they had then used as assets in their own internecine warfare, the U.S. relief effort came ashore accompanied by armed military personnel charged with the task of safeguarding the supplies that were to be distributed to the civilian population. American troops were in Somalia only to assure that the relief would reach those most in need; they were not there to disarm the Somali warlords or to help the Somali people develop democratic institutions.

From the start UN agencies, which had struggled unsuccessfully to deliver humanitarian assistance while being opposed by the Somali warlords, urged the U.S. military presence to take on a more aggressive role, arguing that the American idea of temporary humanitarian intervention would permit the eventual return of the warlords and, with them, a return to the disaster of the status quo ante, once the U.S. forces were withdrawn.[33]

With the change of administrations in Washington, State Department careerists found a sympathetic ear in the new president. The more circumscribed policy advocated by President George Bush called for U.S. forces to distribute the aid in Somalia and then transfer security functions to UN peacekeeping forces.[34] The Clinton administration, however, determined to disarm the Somali warlords and thereafter set up civilian advisors throughout Somalia as a preliminary step to nation-building, as had been requested by Secretary-General Boutros Boutros-Ghali.[35] The results were, by general agreement, disastrous. Attacks on U.S. forces by the most powerful of the warlords, General Aideed, led to fruitless and costly attempts to destroy the General's power base and culminated in an embarrassing and deadly loss by U.S. forces seeking to arrest the General.[36] The conclusion became inescapable that to mix nation-building and humanitarian assistance requires the most exquisite care because of its explosive potential: "The real lesson of the American experience in attempting to relieve famine in Somalia is that any administration must play out the long-range consequences even of humanitarian decisions because of the complex political and military consequences inevitably entailed."[37]

CONCLUSION

Experience, particularly recent experience, has underscored the dilemma that bedevils humanitarian aid programs. On the one hand, emergency interventions are able to provide no more than stopgap solutions that invite festering, chronic dependence; on the other hand, the root causes of the hunger and disease that evoke the humanitarian impulse can be eradicated only, if at all, by means of long-term processes of nation-building that are politically dangerous. It has also become increasingly clear that the economic, political, and military costs of interventions, both long term and short term, are so great that they cannot be borne by even the wealthiest of nations, especially since their political elites cannot muster long-term popular support and commitment for such expenditures. At the same time, emerging nations patently chafe at their dependence on the largesse of others as a galling reminder of their erstwhile colonial subservience and their current low self-esteem. The internationalization of humanitarian aid under the aegis of the UN has provided only a translucent fig leaf to cover the recipient nations' sense of embarrassment over their weakness and poverty. Adding to this quandary is that the UN has been unable to mobilize world public opinion either to intervene at all or to intervene substantially in some of the most harrowing disasters of recent years, particularly in a number of catastrophes visited upon African or Asian populations, where millions have died of starvation or disease or in genocidal wars, with little more than superficial, ephemeral, and generally ineffective intervention by the world community.[38]

When viewed against this background, the replacement of the UN presence in Bosnia-Herzegovina by North Atlantic Treaty Organization (NATO) forces has profound implications for the future of UN humanitarian interventions. The UN's failure to halt the civil war among Croats, Bosnians, and Serbs; its apparent impotence to prevent ethnic cleansing and the displacement of hundreds of thousands of civilians; and its ultimate abdication in favor of those whose credible military threats could separate combatants long enough to permit the flow of humanitarian assistance to those most in need of it—these developments would seem to presage a diminution in the future role of the UN as the front-line protector of refugees, of the starving, and of displaced millions who have come to count on the world body as their ultimate protector.

Yet there are more hopeful straws in the wind. Growing concern over the fate of the millions who are displaced and starving, and notably the recent precedent set by the UN Security Council in defense of Kurd and Shiite populations,[39] appears to point to a gradual evolution toward a more comprehensive and humane order, one that substitutes, for the traditional definition of national self-interest, a broader definition that encompasses common humanitarian interest—that is, a definition nurtured by a keener awareness of the universality of human misery, even when it occurs in remote corners of the world with which no common bond would have been experienced before the age of television and instant communications.

The cause of humanitarian assistance may yet come to be defined as a responsibility for the entire human race, and not just that part of it which is sufficiently vigorous to nourish and safeguard its own population. The words of one of the most unequivocal defenders of Darwinian survival of the fittest may well be prophetic:

It is possible that yet another unique quality of man is a capacity for genuine, disinterested, true altruism. . . . [E]ven if we look on the dark side and assume that individual man is fundamentally selfish, our conscious foresight—our capacity to simulate the future in imagination—could save us from the worst selfish excesses. . . . We have at least the mental equipment to foster our long-term selfish interests rather than merely our short-term selfish interests. . . . We can even discuss ways of deliberately cultivating and nurturing pure, disinterested altruism—something that has no place in nature, something that has never existed before in the whole history of the world.[40]

NOTES

1. In applauding British intervention on behalf of Belgian neutrality, which had been guaranteed by England, Theodore Roosevelt stated that he "[took] this position as an American . . . who endeavor[ed] loyally to serve his own country, but who also endeavor[ed] to do what he [could] for justice and decency as regard[ed] mankind at large." Roosevelt to Sir Edward Grey, letter, January 22, 1915, quoted in Hans J. Morgenthau, *Politics Among Nations*, 5th ed. (New York: Alfred A. Knopf, 1973), p. 13. Morgenthau's discussion confirms the concept that the political realism espoused by Roosevelt must, by its very nature, accommodate political as well as ethical considerations, and this duality can be found, to one degree or another, in almost all humanitarian aid programs since World War I. It must be noted, at the same time, that the very existence of dual and often conflicting considerations has occasionally led to an excessive concern for one of these *desiderata* at the expense of the other—as, for example, when the pursuit of national interests has blocked the initial generous impulse that inspired a particular humanitarian aid program.

2. During the war Hoover controlled the Commission for Relief to Belgium, which used funds advanced by the governments of the United States, France, and England. After the Armistice Congress set up the American Relief Administration which, under Hoover's leadership, extended the aid that had been afforded Belgian civilians during the war to include, ultimately, some twenty-three nations, which benefited from $1 billion worth of food and other supplies.

3. See, for example, Nicholas V. Riasanovsky, *A History of Russia*, 5th ed. (Oxford: Oxford University Press, 1993), p. 488, which pictures Russia at the conclusion of the civil war as a charnel house, a land in which entire districts had been depopulated by

famine and disease and in which industrial capacity had been reduced to 20 percent of its prewar level, while agriculture had declined to 37 percent of the levels in 1914.

4. George F. Kennan, *Russia and the West under Lenin and Stalin* (New York: Mentor, 1960), p. 131. Kennan condemns the cynicism of offering food to the starving as a mechanism to achieve political subversion: "The idea of using food as a weapon . . . appealed to some of the most dangerous weakness in the American view of international affairs, and had, in my opinion, a most pernicious influence on American thinking." In particular, Kennan decries this method as one that "is made to contrast favorably with that evil and awful thing called 'power politics' " (p. 133).

5. Indeed, aid to Russia was held hostage to political considerations as early as Woodrow Wilson's Fourteen Points. The sixth point appeared to be a magnanimous proposal of assistance to the Russian people, which had suffered more than any other during the war; in fact, the offer was made contingent on the return to a democratic form of government, preferably the Provisional Government, which had gained the recognition of the Western democracies and had recently been overthrown by the Bolsheviks. See George F. Kennan, *Russia Leaves the War* (Princeton, NJ: Princeton University Press, 1956), p. 243.

6. In a groundbreaking article, "The Evolution of Behavior," *Scientific American* 239, no. 3 (1978): 176–92, John Maynard Smith examined how altruism can be explained from an evolutionary perspective. Smith pointed out that in all orders, from bacteria to primates, it can be shown, by such analytical tools as game theory, that natural selection favors species practicing altruistic behavior over those that behave selfishly (p. 184). In baboon societies, for example, reciprocal altruism benefits both the giver and the receiver of aid over a given period of time.

7. Raymond H. Anderson, "Americans Played Role in Early Economic Development of the Soviet Union," *New York Times*, November 1, 1967, credited the Hoover relief effort with ultimately saving the lives of ten million people, more than one third of them children.

8. The utilitarian aspect of charitable work done for political purposes was investigated in as early a classical sociological analysis as William E. H. Lecky's *History of European Morals*, 3d ed. (New York: D. Appleton & Co., 1913), vol. 1, pp. 6–75.

9. Arthur O. Lovejoy, *Reflections on Human Nature* (Baltimore: The Johns Hopkins Press, 1961), p. 209.

10. Ibid., p. 201, quoting John Adams.

11. Adam Smith, *The Theory of Moral Sentiments*, 6th ed. (1790), pt. 1, sec. 3, chap. 2:

The poor man . . . is ashamed of his poverty. He feels that it either places him out of sight of mankind, or that, if they take any notice of him, they have . . . [little sympathy for his plight]. . . . [T]hough to be overlooked and to be disapproved of are things entirely different, yet as obscurity covers us from the daylight of honor and approbation, to feel that we are taken no notice of, necessarily damps the most agreeable hope, and disappoints the most ardent desire of human life.

Quoted in Lovejoy, *Reflections*, pp. 214–15.

12. See, for example, Dan Jorgensen, "Cargo Cult: Strange Stories of Desire from Melanesia and Beyond," *Pacific Affairs* 67, no. 4 (1994).

13. Virginia Abernethy, "Optimism and Overpopulation," *Atlantic Monthly* 274, no. 6 (1994): 84. In a subsequent issue (275, no. 3 [1995]: 14), Stuart J. D. Schwartzstein, a correspondent, asked rhetorically whether "Gaza's through-the-roof rate of population

growth (about five percent a year) [is] attributable to the handouts of the United Nations Relief and Works Agency and to a strong belief among many Palestinians that Israel will cease to exist and that they will soon have a much expanded niche?"

14. Dean Acheson, *Present at the Creation* (New York: New American Library, 1969), p. 186.

15. Ibid., p. 309.

16. Ibid.

17. Dean Acheson, *This Vast External Realm* (New York: W. W. Norton & Co., 1973), pp. 133–34.

18. George F. Kennan, the State Department's acknowledged expert on the Soviet Union and the head of its policy planning staff, published his famous X article in *Foreign Affairs* in July 1947 under the title "Sources of Soviet Conduct." Its thesis was at the very core of the Truman Doctrine and the policy of containment.

19. Speech by Harry S. Truman to Congress, as quoted in William Reitzel, Morton A. Kaplan, and Constance G. Coblenz, *United States Foreign Policy, 1945–1955* (Washington, DC: Brookings Institution, 1956), p. 115.

20. Reitzel, Kaplan and Coblentz, *United States Foreign Policy*, p. 120.

21. Robert L. Rothstein, *Alliances and Small Powers* (New York: Columbia University Press, 1968), p. 247, points out that "nonalignment is possible for a Small Power only so long as it is not threatened by a Great Power; once directly threatened, it is difficult to avoid alignment with another Great Power."

22. Abba Eban, "The U.N. Idea Revisited," *Foreign Affairs* 74, no. 5 (1995): 51.

23. Nitza Nachmias and Eric A. Belgrad, "Five Decades of Humanitarian Aid: The Case of UNRWA," *Towson State Journal of International Affairs* 29, no. 2 (1994): 1–13.

24. See Nitza Nachmias's chapter on humanitarian assistance to Palestinians.

25. Throughout the history of the UN, member states, wielding the power of the purse, have delayed payments of their financial obligations to the world body to express displeasure with UN policies. Currently, the United States is more than $1 billion in arrears, in large measure reflecting congressional demands that perceived extravagances in UN spending be reined in. *The* [Baltimore] *Sun*, September 26, 1995, p. 12A.

26. See, for example, Joseph R. Rudolph, Jr.'s, chapter on the additional costs of giving aid in Bosnia in the face of a three-cornered ethnic conflict.

27. Quoted in Christopher S. Wren, "Surprise! U.N. Auditors of Peacekeeping Mission Find Waste," *New York Times*, October 29, 1995, p. A18.

28. Ibid.

29. "U.S. Demands Blueprint for a Leaner U.N. by Next Year," *The* [Baltimore] *Sun*, September 26, 1995, p. 12A. In this article Secretary of State Warren Christopher was described as "showing a touch of impatience with the slow pace of change [in increasing the accountability of UN expenditures and] warned that only effective reform would help sustain broad U.S. support."

30. "U.S. Foreign Policy and the United Nations System," *Eighty-Seventh American Assembly, Final Report* (Harriman, NY: Arden House, 1995), p. 9.

31. Ibid., p. 11.

32. Paul Kennedy and Bruce Russett, "Reforming the United Nations," *Foreign Affairs* 74, no. 5 (1995). Although the views of the American Assembly and the UNA-USA were generally endorsed here, in recognition of "donor fatigue" (p. 62), the authors proposed far-ranging measures to provide the UN new funding sources that do not directly

depend on contributions from member states and would therefore free the UN from fiscal vetoes by member states (pp. 68–70).

33. The miscalculations inherent in turning the Somalian exercise from humanitarian assistance to aggressive nation-building is eloquently described by John R. Bolton, "Wrong Turn in Somalia," *Foreign Affairs* 73, no. 1 (1994): 57–66.

34. UN Res. S/794 (December 3, 1992).

35. Bolton, "Wrong Turn in Somalia," p. 62.

36. Ibid., p. 63.

37. Ibid., p. 66.

38. Christopher S. Wren, "U.N. Is Cutting Back on Its Peacekeeping Ambitions," *New York Times*, November 12, 1995, p. A14, in which the UN secretary-general is reported to have complained that "the money spent for five days in Bosnia could finance a year's peacekeeping in Liberia, another victim of civil war."

39. UN Res. S/688 (1991) for the first time limited the exercise of sovereign authority of a government over its own territory and population. In this instance the measure was designed to safeguard Kurd and Shiite populations that were being hunted down and killed by the Iraqi government.

40. Richard Dawkins, *The Selfish Gene* (New York: Oxford University Press, 1976), p. 215.

2

Military Risk and Political Commitment in UN Humanitarian Peace Support Operations

JIM WHITMAN

Nearly a decade after the UN was freed of the constraints of the Cold War, we now have a constellation of peacekeeping activities with, appurtenant thereto, much confusing terminology, new conceptual frameworks, refined legal criteria, the dedicated attention of military planners—and humanitarian disasters in number and on a scale to daunt any amount of unalloyed goodwill. This chapter takes as its starting point the incontrovertible assertion that the principal determinant of the coherence and potential effectiveness of any UN humanitarian peace support operation is the nature and quality of the political commitment of the participating member states.[1]

Understandably, because a government's decision to place its troops in harm's way is widely regarded as its highest expression of political commitment, attention thereafter usually shifts to the operational particulars of the mission. The epithet "lack of political will" is reserved for refusal or inaction and is rarely applied qualitatively. But the fact of military risk easily obscures the strength and quality of the political impetus behind it. Once empowered, however nominally, it is the UN which carries the burden of success or failure, and matters of political commitment are overtaken by considerations of operational competence. There is a pressing logic in the concentration on operational matters, since further peace support operations will almost certainly be undertaken. The circumstances—size, urgency, tasks, and conditions—vary enormously; and insofar as a discernible pattern can be traced, the variables are increasing in number almost as quickly as demand. Yet the decision to deploy troops for such purposes is the political threshold, not the arena, and the reduction of commitment to authorisation does as little justice to political realities as simple faith in military capacity–building does to practical ones.

The importance and immediacy of actions which follow the fact of a political commitment to deploy troops do much to inhibit awareness and analysis of the larger political domain. But the structural determinants of peace support operations—the nature of "emergencies" themselves as well as institutional and resource particulars—are operative on both sides of the decision whether or not to engage.

That peace support operations are intermittent, that the rationale is inconsistently applied, that the action is sometimes framed to accommodate the needs of the participating states as much as the victims and usually delimited in a manner which provides against "entanglement" or open-ended commitment— are considerations none of which fits within the frame of assessment of active operations, however much they loom over them. There are a number of reasons for this. First, although the particulars of judging and balancing the military and political risk of a prospective peace support operation are a thematic constant, it is perhaps in the nature of public affairs that the decisions themselves will always be more visible than the interests which inform them. Second, the dangers faced by soldiers from one's own country, together with the tasks we require of them and the incident-hungry nature of much media reporting, combine to divert attention from the encompassing political dynamics. A further difficulty is that considerations of coherence fall naturally into mission-specific parameters. To be sure, in politics as in action coherence (at least judged in terms of results) can accommodate a good deal of inconsistency. The argument here, however, is that the political incoherence of peace support operations at the international level is consequential and worsening; that the effective separation of peace support operations from the international political context is not an inconsistency or even a structural paradox but is dysfunctional; and that we are fast approaching the limits of what operational efficiencies can achieve in the absence of a concerted effort to address the encompassing political milieu.

Much as the practical and conceptual inadequacies of traditional peacekeeping after 1988 soon initiated "second generation" operations,[2] so continuing endeavours and incremental improvements, as well as the lessons of our operational failures, may well give rise to a third and succeeding "generations" of humanitarian peace support operations. Then, as now, failures to act will be much more serious than failures in action; however, efforts will doubtless be pursued to improve operational efficiency alongside injunctions that "states should," "governments ought," and "the international community must." But will it suffice? The intention here is not to diminish the moral and practical urgency of furthering the drive to improve national and UN instrumental capacity but to indicate its limitations.

HISTORICAL PERSPECTIVE

For all that is novel about UN humanitarian peace support operations, many of their largest, recurrent difficulties are variations on familiar, historical themes: Divergent national interests within multinational enterprises, the attempt to adapt military means to political ends, varieties of bureaucratic obstruction, patchy policy preparation, and inadequate funding or supply all come readily to mind. The details of our historical triumphs take on a disturbingly familiar hue when glimpsed through the lens of recent peace support operations. Consider, for example, what most experts fairly regard as an operation of unparalleled clarity of purpose and dedication of effort—the Allied campaign against the Axis powers in Europe as it neared its end in Italy.

The occupation and administration of Italy was an Allied nightmare.[3] First, there was uncertainty as to whether to establish an Allied military government or, as General Eisenhower saw the preferable alternative, "to accept and strengthen the legal government under the King and Badoglio; to regard this government and the Italian people as co-belligerents but with their military activity subject to my direction under the terms of the armistice and I, of course, making such military, political and administrative conditions as I find necessary from time to time."[4] When the German occupation of Italy and resistance to Allied pressure proved more tenacious than had been hoped, British and U.S. forces found themselves in the unenviable position of being seen as something between liberators and occupiers, a situation given an ironic twist by the eventual recognition given to an Italian government headed by Badoglio, a man of impeccable Fascist credentials. The Italian monarchy, the Vatican, the Catholic and the Italian-American domestic lobbies in the United States, and ensuing food shortages further complicated the administration (or occupation) of a country in which the military conflict was far from settled. The physical and political rehabilitation of Italy was further hampered by differences between the U.S. and British governments, with the United States intent on establishing a democratic government as a means of reuniting the country and revitalising the economy, whereas the British adopted a pragmatic (if distasteful) approach to the governance of the country and remained determined that the postwar economy of Italy should not be in a position to interfere with their plans for a Mediterranean hegemony.[5] The many failures and inadequacies of the Anglo-American occupation were more a matter of divergent and worsening differences of approach than of lack of coordination:

The American prescription for Italy ran counter to that of Great Britain. Both governments agreed that Italy needed more economic aid, but the British wanted the Americans to pay the bill while they conserved their scarce resources. The British also insisted that increased United States aid to Italy was a concession on their part, for which the Americans must grant them a political *quid pro quo*. Yet the United States and United Kingdom differed most deeply precisely over political matters.[6]

The differences between the occupation and rehabilitation of Italy and recent UN experiences in Somalia, the former Yugoslavia, and elsewhere are obvious, but the many thematic similarities are compelling. Today, for instance, anger and distress is expressed over UN pre-negotiation contacts with individuals suspected of war crimes; fifty years ago, the New York *Herald Tribune* was more sympathetic: "It would be easy for an occupying force, in the interest of 'order,' to freeze Italy's Fascist organization in authority. It is less likely that the Allied authorities would permit the opposite to occur—namely the riotous competition of Anti-fascist groups for power—during the critical period of occupation."[7]

In practical terms the dissimilarities between what the UN now attempts in many parts of the world and what the Allied powers were compelled to undertake in the aftermath of World War II are, in outline at least, less considerable than one might expect: The occupation and administration of a state collapsed politically as well as physically; war crimes trials; reparations; tense and difficult relations with allies over key issues; dealing with the displaced and with refugees; providing basic necessities from food to infrastructure; demilitarisation; balancing in-country needs against the demands of regional security; remaking civil society and the restoration or establishment of democratic politics. Nor are the difficulties of third-party intervention unique to the UN and its institutional machinery.[8] It is no simpler to "unite our strength" than to align interests or synchronise policy-making bureaucracies—even outside the purview of the UN.

However, despite a range of historical precedent in the experiences of occupying armies in the aftermath of war, there are considerable political and practical differences between a situation which befalls an army and one to which that army is assigned—and remarkable, in any event that soldiers should be asked to perform duties in situations that are sometimes little short of battle, but without engaging—that is, while maintaining UN neutrality and impartiality. This is a significant juncture, reflected in the necessity felt by professional militaries for a new, more appropriate doctrine.[9] The concern here, however, is not over the operational differences between war and the hybrids of peacekeeping but over the politics which inform them.

POLITICS AND THE MILITARY: ENDS AND MEANS

The observation of Clausewitz, that "war has its own language but not its own logic," also applies broadly to the deployment of a nation's troops in a UN peace support operation. The tension between the "logic" of political ends and the "language" of military means is common to both. It is hardly surprising that difficulties which beset the deliberations and actions of governments deploying forces for nationally determined purposes will also vex the deployment of the same troops for UN purposes, albeit in sometimes complex configurations. There are four critical junctures of political logic and military language, and while a satisfactory consideration of them does not always precede the deployment of troops (nor guarantee success in the field), they are especially pertinent to the commitment of forces to a UN peace support operation.

Determining Political Ends

The level of commitment required and the importance of identifying and achieving strategic and tactical objectives gives the conduct of war an over-whelmingly operational cast, even in retrospect: war as the suspension of politics, rather than its continuation by other means. Even where the principal objective is of the greatest politico-military clarity—say, unconditional surrender—a larger, encompassing political dynamic continues, as was the case in Germany in 1945, with consequences that are with us yet. The political commitment required of governments to fight and win wars is different in both kind and degree from the political commitment necessary to identify and secure postwar political goals. This is evident in everything from determining Allied postwar goals at the close of World War II to the aftermath of the Gulf War.[10] The Kurdish "safe havens" operation was initiated only after the governments involved were polit-ically embarrassed. (And the continued Turkish repression of the Kurds then and since amply demonstrates the shallowness of the aim.)

The tasks which have come to militaries, often by default, are now the stuff of peace support operations. The missions are "multifunctional," and national militaries, most often working in partnership with many others, will infrequently engage in battle, even in volatile environments, but will find themselves in sup-port roles to the UN political mission or to a humanitarian effort; or they carry out a range of assignments which might include confidence building through ceasefire monitoring and military observation, communications, transport, and infrastructural tasks; or they assist with the organisation of democratic elections.

Before 1990, it was most often the case that a UN military presence was required to implement previously agreed-on political ends between antagonists, a condition for what is now commonly understood to comprise "classic" peace-keeping. Despite the size and complexity of the United Nations Transitional Authority in Cambodia (UNTAC), much the same was envisaged for the im-plementation of the Paris Accords for Cambodia. It might therefore be supposed that, with greatly reduced, sometimes minimal military risk and the common purpose implied in a UN Security Council resolution, the determination of agreed political ends might be the least difficult element in mounting and sus-taining a mission. Although the political objective of a UN peace support op-eration is outlined, if not always detailed, in the sanctioning Security Council resolution, the declaratory nature of many such resolutions, combined with a certain practiced ambiguity, often bespeaks merely a stage in a longer, complex unfolding of ends and means within and between concerned national capitals. Considerations of risk and commitment within governments not only precede Security Council resolutions but are crucially formative—hence recent "lead nation" configurations and "all necessary means" mandates—and remain fully operative throughout.

Aligning Military Means and Political Ends

Between the pride felt by many in the professionalism of their national armed forces and the persistence of misplaced optimism in the utility of military force, the difficulty of matching appropriate military means with political ends might easily be overlooked, as it was, perhaps, during the brief flurry of enthusiasm for what, in 1993, the U.S. ambassador to the UN termed "assertive multilateralism." But the identification of the national interest in a strife-ridden or warring region is not identical with a goal which can be secured by military means (in any event, or at an acceptable cost),[11] nor is national interest synonymous with the use of military forces as a political instrument below the level of intervention.[12] With the demise of superpower domination and an increasing reluctance to risk the lives of soldiers, the utility of military forces as a political instrument through direct or indirect threat may be diminishing, at least in the absence of clarity of purpose and determination to back it. For example, the belated use of force against the Bosnian Serbs in May 1995 proved as effective a probe of NATO political will as the intended, forceful shove in the direction of a political settlement. Furthermore, aligning political ends and military means is but rarely a "threshold" task and often requires a near-continuous balancing of ends, means, priorities and costs—none of which is a guarantee against troop-contributing nations finding themselves committed in a largely negative sense, as in this characterisation of the situation in the former Yugoslavia:

The international approach to the Yugoslav conflict had become like pesticides—each application seemed to strengthen the resistance of those it aimed to defeat, requiring ever heavier doses and tougher formulas for ever less effect. But this approach had not been abandoned in favour of a real alternative by the end of 1994. Instead, each crisis was met with efforts to strengthen the means of leverage over the parties rather than to reconsider the strategy and solution. The instruments chosen—such as economic sanctions against Serbia and Montenegro, safe areas for Muslim cities, and the use of air power against Bosnian and Croatian Serbs aimed, it was said, at bringing the Serbs to the bargaining table—were exhausting their effectiveness, and the world community seemed to be running out of instruments.[13]

With each level of deliberation—national, regional, international, and UN—achieving a balance of consensus, effectiveness, and coherence becomes ever more difficult, as mission-specific issues become inseparable from the larger dynamics of international politics. The commitment of states to such enterprises is likely to be highly conditional, in any event, and most readily takes the form of fixed limits to the size, cost, and duration of their contributions. This may be predictable, prudent behaviour in itself, but for voluntary multinational undertakings sanctioned by the UN, the least common denominator will not always be sufficient to ensure a politically coherent or achievable goal.

Political Control

Civilian political control of national militaries is a key feature of modern democratic states and, while the constitutional particulars are often a matter of debate within states (e.g., over the war powers of the U.S. president), the principle is firmly established. The UN has been without standing military forces since its inception despite the provisions in Chapter VII of the UN Charter, and although the Security Council is empowered to give "strategic direction" (through the Military Staff Committee) to forces made available by member states, the UN Charter does not directly address the question of political control of national militaries and the Military Staff Committee has never been functional.

The issue of the political control of UN-sanctioned military operations remains problematic. In the case of Chapter VII (enforcement) resolutions, the interests of the large military powers are particularly acute; since a UN enforcement operation of any scale or complexity cannot be contemplated without the participation of these powers, or in some cases undertaken wholly by them, the Security Council is placed in the curious position of being supplicant to those whom it empowers, as illustrated by Resolution 678, which authorised the use of force against Iraq in the Gulf War:

[The Security Council] authorises Member States cooperating with the government of Kuwait . . . to use all necessary means to . . . restore international peace and security to the area; Requests all states to provide appropriate support for the actions undertaken in pursuance [of the foregoing]; Requests the States concerned to keep the Security Council regularly informed on the progress of actions undertaken pursuant [to the above].[14]

What is evident here is not a tension between political control and operational autonomy but their bifurcation—hence, the Security Council's need to request "states concerned" to keep it regularly informed of their progress. Nor is this merely a matter of scale: An undertaking of the size of Desert Storm, however anomalous, threw into sharp relief underlying structural and organisational defects that apply with equal force to lesser operations. This was also evident in the attempts in 1993 to shore up the United Nations Protection Force in the former Yugoslavia (UNPROFOR) by employing Chapter VII resolutions. In this instance, the lack of a Security Council mechanism which could provide for the exertion of its political authority beyond a general sanction for the use of force manifested itself in what was effectively an invitation to operational chaos: "[The Security Council] reaffirms its decision . . . on the use of air power, in and around the safe areas, to support UNPROFOR in the performance of its mandate, and encourages Member States, acting nationally or through regional organisations or arrangements, to coordinate closely with the Secretary-General in this regard."[15] Having sanctioned nations and/or regional organisations to act, the Security Council can presently only encourage them to coordinate their actions through the secretary-general. This coordination, though most easily understood in this context as horizontal (i.e., between national commands), is similarly elective vertically (between national commands and the Security Council).

Every variety of proposal to enhance the UN's military capacity—standby forces, a volunteer force, more effective use of regional organisations, to say nothing of the recent practice of granting "lead nation" status in enforcement operations—has the issue of political control hovering over it.[16]

Consolidating a Political Outcome and Disengagement

While the British and American experience after the culmination of World War II in Europe is suggestive of the difficulties inherent in disengagement— neither wanted to be "chained to the corpse of Germany," as Churchill expressed it—the experience of several European states in disengaging from colonialism is probably more instructive with respect to the combination of haste, self-interest, sense of wounded beneficence, and absence of concrete plans for a successful transition of power which so often accompanies such disengagements. Consolidation and disengagement are, of course, separable. Thus the current trend among states supplying troops to UN missions to minimise political risk by tightly constraining military risk works against consolidation, since the continued presence of troops is often essential to the peace process. While the greatest fear of the professional military planner may be what has become known as "mission creep," the strong emphasis recently given to specifying fixed durations and delineating clear "exit strategies" for troops involved in UN operations carries worrying implications for both current and future peace support operations. If the most significant non-mission variable in any peace support operation consists of the domestic political considerations of troop-contributing states, and if these are driven by a fear of "entanglement" and cost, the determination of political ends will be correspondingly narrow; or if military and political risk should suddenly spiral upward, troop-contributing states could declare "mission accomplished" and depart. For instructive examples of this dilemma, consider the two-month French intervention in Rwanda; U.S. participation in the relief effort to that country through Operation Support Hope, which specified providing humanitarian support with the injunction against "get[ting] involved in peacekeeping"[17]; and the failure to secure political stability in Somalia.[18]

RISKS AND INTERESTS

The mechanics of the Security Council together with the range of interests that informs foreign ministry deliberations fairly predict that the common purpose evident in Security Council resolutions will rarely be reflected in the operational particulars and levels of support of the peace support operations authorised thereby. This divergence poses the question whether, in the span of two generations, notions of international peace and security issues which were capable of being addressed by "the four policemen" have given way to a world of human rights calculated on a scale inconceivable to a world then still largely comfortable with colonialism—that is, whether, as universal principles have become increasingly particularised, the level of political and/or military commitment required to secure and/or defend them has correspondingly increased.

The key to understanding the world of Franklin Delano Roosevelt's projected "four policemen" is not that the world was once better ordered but that large swathes of it were once peripheral to the small number of "big players." What were once simply areas or states which could offer little effective opposition to large powers now comprise states or peoples which can, in good measure due to an unabated trade in arms and led by the permanent members of the Security Council, offer determined resistance to once-considerable levels of military force. As Inis Claude foresaw, weak states would come to offer a formidable challenge to international stability.[19] It is neither cynical nor despairing to observe that tea and plantains will always be less important than oil and minerals; that "spheres of influence," though less distinct and more diffuse than formerly, are still intact and operative; and that states will predictably act to protect their perceived interests—under the banner of universal principles if possible, but also in its absence. In any event, the range of national interests, which works as readily as disincentives to action, does not preclude states from responding to humanitarian need. Middle Power internationalism, overseas development assistance, and natural disaster relief programmes are rooted in the same soil, for all that they may sport more attractive foliage. Even the Marshall Plan comprised measures of political calculation, economic self-interest, and humanitarian impulse. Shortly after Marshall's Harvard speech, the head of the U.S. State Department Policy Planning Staff, George Kennan, made these notes:

Marshall "plan." We have no plan. Europeans must be made to take responsibility. We would consider European plan only if it were a good one and promised to do the whole job. Our main object: to render principal European countries able to exist without outside charity. Necessity of this: (a) So that they can buy from us; (b) So they will have enough self-confidence to withstand outside pressures.[20]

But the kinds of UN peace support operations now required to address politically driven humanitarian disasters can entail levels of military and political risk which are not always equal to the variety and degree of perceived interests which more commonly initiate and sustain action on that scale. Beyond the estimation of national interest which generates a calculation of political ends and military means—and finally a Security Council resolution—states no more subjugate their interests to the mission than permit their soldiers to become international civil servants. Geopolitical interests were a formative, though largely passive, element in UN peacekeeping during the Cold War, but these and other complex political dynamics can now be discerned beneath the smooth surface of Security Council resolutions and within the subsequent multinational efforts. In April 1994, for example, the *New York Times* reported that, in the midst of the strenuous efforts being made to secure an end to the fighting in the former Yugoslavia, "on the diplomatic front, the United States is eager to seize upon Russia's deep humiliation over winning Serbian cease-fire pledges only to be double-crossed."[21] Similarly, the forceful military action undertaken in Bosnia by the Rapid Deployment Force (RDF) and NATO in August 1995 undoubtedly also had a complex internal dynamic, reflected in the observation of the London *Times*: "Inaction would have carried its own risks, both of escalation in Bosnia and of terminal disarray in the Western Alliance."[22] It should also be noted that deliberations on this subject are far from a neutral calculus: African diplomats have been quick to point out that "the excuse to reinforce the force in Bosnia was the same as the one used to withdraw troops from Africa: violence continues on the ground unabated, endangering the lives of UN troops."[23]

State interests are also informed and tempered by a changed and changing ratio of political risk to military risk. This, as much as large-scale, Treasury-driven reductions in military establishments, is playing a part in conditioning the military commitments of states, particularly when there is no abiding national interest, as is so often the case with humanitarian emergencies. In 1860 John Ruskin wrote that "the soldier's trade, verily and essentially, is not slaying but being slain. This, without well knowing its own meaning, the world honours it for"—a view that would not have been controversial even half a century later, on the eve of World War I. For the main protagonists of that war and for most of the world beyond, however, soldiers can no longer be regarded as dispensable instruments of the state, perhaps a consequence of the long progress of human rights.

Now, "whatever it takes" only exceptionally means "however many men," but the counterpart to this language in recent Security Council resolutions—"all necessary means"—combines with the absence of any mechanism for the UN to exercise political control over the missions it sanctions. This makes possible forceful, precipitate, or otherwise inappropriate action sanctioned by national authorities. The escalation of force employed by U.S. troops in Somalia and its disastrous consequences may perversely have reinforced a more "stand-off" approach to peace support operations, whether in the form of "logistical support only" or the early and overwhelming demonstration of force. But there can be no guaranteed low-cost or no-cost deployments of military force. The pursuit of this chimera forces policy makers in one of a number of directions: toward "surgical" strikes employing high-tech weaponry; toward missions which are so constrained in terms of objective and duration that they cannot hope to contribute to a politically coherent goal; and, in the case of military operations mandated by the UN, toward a separation of collective political will and national military means.[24] Upon the initiation of a peace support operation, the provision of the necessary equipment, transport, and other logistics, where this is forthcoming, requires its professional counterpart on the ground, and in the difficult and dangerous environments of humanitarian disasters, this means soldiers, the bravery and dedication of nongovernmental organizations (NGOs) such as the International Committee of the Red Cross (ICRC) notwithstanding.

Can risk and commitment be spread? Where the phrase "regional organisation" is not code for NATO, the hope that others can somehow ease the political and practical burden on North Atlantic states and the small number of others with well-equipped, professional militaries is a rather forlorn one[25]; in any event, contending national interests are all the more practiced in a smaller forum, and the response to war in the Balkans by NATO, the EC, and the Conference on Security and Cooperation in Europe (CSCE) is hardly encouraging.[26]

POLITICAL COMMITMENT AND PEACE SUPPORT OPERATIONS

The visibility and drama which naturally attend the dispatch of soldiers abroad easily convey a government's depth of commitment. But while the symbolic meaning has, if anything, increased, government officials are, at the same time, more than ever acutely sensitive to the political risks entailed in the deaths of soldiers in peace support operations. At a time of shrinking resources and a corresponding unwillingness to contract open-ended engagements, states will eschew obligations yet undertake "commitments," with the minimisation of both military and political risk as an organising principle. Paradoxically, then, the dispatch of soldiers can be a substitute for commitment of the character and duration required to address the physical and human problems inherent in the situations which most urgently require peace support operations. This is not to denigrate or discount the contribution made by the soldiers in peace support operations, particularly in volatile environments and in the immediate aftermath of conflict. No one who has witnessed the bravery, dedication, and competence of these individuals could fail to be impressed. The point here centers not on professional militaries but on the national and international politics to which they are bound. Humanitarian peace support operations depend less on military risk per se than on the depth of the political resolution which underwrites the coherence and duration of long-term and sustainable political ends. This remains the case however much the initiation and continuance of humanitarian and political work depend on the assistance or active protection offered by soldiers. Whatever the reasons for constrained and short-duration military deployments for particular UN peace support operations—reduced national military budgets, fleeting public concern engendered by *mediapolitik*, or fear of "entanglement"— the tenuous and highly conditional political commitment extended even to those missions which the UN is able to sanction is truly disheartening.

The considerable attention recently devoted to improving military efficiency and, still more prominently, to UN-military-NGO coordination is of considerable practical import,[27] but it cannot, of itself, broaden or deepen the commitment of states. The impetus behind so many of these improvements is initiated and sustained by field staffs against an established pattern of piecemeal and highly conditional institutional support at national and international levels, evidenced most clearly in the parlous condition of the UN, itself. One might suppose, for example, that, in view of the suffering endured by the people of Angola, and following the lessons learned from the failure of the United Nations Angola Verification Mission (UNAVEM II),[28] that UNAVEM III might attract the kind of concerted effort, or at least support, which a UN return to that country might suggest. The prospects are hardly encouraging. The demobilisation of Union for the Total Liberation of Angola (UNITA), the insurgent movement, the incorporation of its remaining core into an Angolan national army, and the reintegration of soldiers who have never known another life into a society that has been decimated is crucial if Angola is to have any hope of peace and stability. The mission planning section of the United Nations Department of Peacekeeping Operations (DPKO) estimated the military requirement to be fifteen thousand soldiers. When told that more than seven thousand five hundred would probably not be forthcoming, they planned accordingly.[29] Of the 220 UN police officers assigned to the mission, only 16 spoke Portuguese—yet their task, according to a UN official, was "to help national police consolidate the road to peace"; he added helpfully, "without effective liaison it will be difficult to do this."[30] With the demobilisation quartering areas programme already late, the news was that

unfortunately, donor contributions to the 1995 UN Consolidated Appeal for Angola are not materializing as expected. The demobilization and reintegration component of the appeal, requiring a total of US$55,871,739 has received less than 1% of the required resources (0.3%) to date. Lack of basic resources to implement the demobilization and reintegration process in Angola is a matter of great concern, potentially affecting the rhythm of the peace process and even jeopardizing the positive achievements already made in the implementation of the Lusaka Protocol.[31]

The Appeal also signals the need for a further US$50 million for the second phase of demobilisation and reintegration to begin in January 1996. At the same time, UNHCR seeks US$44 million for the voluntary repatriation of some 300,000 Angolan refugees over the next thirty months. Meanwhile outside the immediate compass of the UN but directly pertinent to the prospects for undertaking peace support and humanitarian missions and seeing them through to a satisfactory conclusion, contracting resources and the declining willingness of donor governments have now begun to force hard choices. The ICRC launched an appeal for a considerable increase in funding to stave off limiting aid by choosing among victims in different countries. Whereas triage is based on clinical judgment, "donors tend to shy away from conflicts which have a low media profile and where they have no political interest at stake."[32]

Encompassing these and similar situations is the continuing financial crisis of the UN—a crisis no less real for its familiarity, and worsening. "[The secretary-general] has recently drawn attention to the growing practice of authorising new or expanded UN activities without appropriating the resources to carry them out—the most recent example being the creation of a Rapid Reaction Force to strengthen UNPROFOR."[33]

Were it possible to continue in this way, financially, politically, and morally, it would be necessary to wonder over the motive force that makes possible peace support operations of this character. Quite aside from the waste of human and financial resources and the resultant ineffectual or palliative outcomes, the manner in which we currently initiate and conduct these initiatives does little to address the conditions which cause or support wide-scale human suffering. First, by characterising humanitarian disasters as discrete emergencies, the structural elements and causal relations in which we and our way of life are implicated are partitioned off. De-contextualising human suffering trades seriousness for urgency, making a short-term emergency of a protracted tragedy. Such political commitment and military risk as is required can usually be managed; and if not, it can be retracted. Second, our security paradigms—international as well as national—remain undisturbed. There is little in the conduct of current UN humanitarian peace support operations to challenge the following well-received characterisation of international relations:

The key to understanding the real world order is to separate the world into two parts. One part is zones of peace, wealth and democracy. The other part is zones of turmoil, war and development. There are useful things to say about the zones of peace; and there are useful things to say about the zones of turmoil; but if you try to talk about the world as a whole all you can get is falsehoods and platitudes.[34]

It is not difficult to marshal arguments to counter this view; less simple is to suggest how, in our structural support of the UN or in the political commitment given to specific peace support operations, we are operating from a contrary conceptualisation. If "the problem of world order is, in considerable measure, the problem of inducing and enabling states to shoulder positive responsibilities for supporting the order of the system,"[35] what congruence of national interests and systemic stability—and what concept of international peace and security—do our actions and omissions evince?

A third consequence of the current mode of conducting peace support operations is that the UN remains institutionally underdeveloped. An organisation which is itself in crisis cannot be expected to manage external crises effectively. It is wholly unreasonable to divorce the issue of states' commitment to individual missions from consideration of the UN's effective bankruptcy arising from the failure of members to pay their assessed contributions. The central issue is not UN competence but member states' engagement. Ample evidence suggests that even the more recalcitrant payers would sooner finance the UN than empower it politically, and it is precisely the political and institutional development of the UN which holds the most promise for making peace support operations more coherent and effective.[36] Whatever its demands, humanitarianism requires considerably more than a characterisation of "zones of peace" to suppose that the wealthier and more powerful nations can practice a form of containment against the human forces now being propelled by economic, environmental, sectarian, and technological factors.

CONCLUSION

The dispatch of soldiers in support of a UN peace support operation is the single, most important element common to these initiatives. The difficult government deliberations which precede and attend these operations can be, and to a certain extent have been, streamlined. At the same time, the tensions which arise between Security Council resolutions and the full command exercised by national political authorities will continue to be problematic in some instances, although these, too, can be minimised. At the operational and tactical levels considerable efforts have been expended by UN officials, military officers, and NGO workers to further understanding and cooperation and even some degree of coordination. Any number of further improvements—for instance, in communications, logistics, and planning—are possible and much to be encouraged. Yet because none of these, singly or in combination, will suffice to address more than the worst and most visible consequences of the aftermath of war, strife, or state collapse, the soldiers whom we deploy are on the front line in a double sense. Although the political decision to incur military risk is always profoundly serious, an externally oriented political commitment commensurate with the risks those soldiers must face would better serve the troops and thereby expose them to less danger. The heart of the UN Charter is not law enforcement or even crisis management but development, and the real measure of our commitment to humanitarianism is not what we do *in extremis* but how we structure our lives at the national and international levels to accommodate the needs of humanity.

NOTES

1. The term "humanitarian peace support operation" and its shortened form, "peace support operation," are used here to denote any UN-sanctioned operation, either consensual or enforced, initiated for the purpose of relieving large-scale human suffering and involving the use of national militaries.

2. John Mackinlay and Jarat Chopra, "Second Generation Multinational Operations," *Washington Quarterly* 15, no. 3 (1992): 113–31.

3. For details see David W. Ellwood, *Italy, 1943–45* (Leicester, England: Leicester University Press, 1985), esp. pp. 49–67; also Robert J. Quinlan, "The Italian Armistice,"

in Harold Stein, ed., *American Civil-Military Decisions: A Book of Case Studies* (Birmingham: University of Alabama Press, 1963), pp. 205–310.

4. Cited in Ellwood, *Italy*, p. 41.

5. For an account of the Anglo-American differences over Italy, see James Edward Miller, *The United States and Italy, 1945–50: The Politics and Diplomacy of Stabilisation* (Chapel Hill: University of North Carolina Press, 1986), pp. 67–205; Ellwood, *Italy*, pp. 137–48, 167–223.

6. Miller, *The United States and Italy*, p. 111.

7. The Soviet view at the time was less detached: Soviet author Ilya Ehrenburg asked whether this meant that "London and Washington would deal with Goering when the time came." Quoted in John Lewis Gaddis, *The United States and the Origins of the Cold War, 1941–47* (New York: Columbia University Press, 1972), p. 88.

8. See Alan James, *Peacekeeping in International Politics* (Basingstoke, England: Macmillan, 1990). For a close examination of the difficulties which beset one non-UN peacekeeping mission, see Anthony Mcdermott and Kjell Skjelsbaek, *The Multinational Force in Beirut, 1982–1984* (Miami: Florida International University Press, 1991).

9. See *UK Army Field Manual*, vol. 5, *Operations Other than War*, pt. 2, "Wider Peacekeeping" (D/HQDT/18/34/30); *United States Army Field Manual FW100-23*, "Peace Operations" (Washington, DC: Headquarters, Department of the Army, December 1994).

10. Robert Murphy, appointed political advisor on German affairs to General Eisenhower in September 1944, recalled:

I was aware that an Anglo-American-Russian agency, called the European Advisory Commission, had been at work in London all through 1944 trying to decide how to administer Germany and I assumed at this late date a detailed occupation plan must be in readiness. Paris had been liberated on August 25, Allied armies were advancing from the west, Russian armies were closing in from the east and the surrender of Germany appeared imminent. To my astonishment, I learned in Washington that no American plan was ready yet because President Roosevelt had not made known his own views and the three departments of the government were wrangling among themselves about postwar Germany.

Robert Murphy, *Diplomat Among Warriors* (London: Collins, 1964), p. 279.

11. Of course, supporting the UN may be a legitimate, if uncommon, national interest.

12. A still useful study is Barry M. Blechman and Stephen S. Kaplan, *Force without War: U.S. Armed Forces as a Political Instrument* (Washington, DC: Brookings Institution, 1978), pp. 1–20, 515–34.

13. Susan L. Woodward, *Balkan Tragedy: Chaos and Dissolution after the Cold War* (Washington, DC: Brookings Institution, 1995), p. 377.

14. UN Res. SC 678 (November 29, 1990).

15. UN Res. S/844 (June 18, 1993).

16. See Carl Conetta and Charles Knight, *Vital Force: A Proposal for the Overhaul of the UN Peace Operations System and for the Creation of a UN Legion*, Project on Defence Alternatives Research Monograph no. 4 (Cambridge, MA: Commonwealth Institute, October 1995).

17. U.S. Military Mission update, "Operation Support Hope," August 23, 1994.

18. In a speech to the Chicago Council on Foreign Relations, the executive director of the World Food Programme (WFP) asserted,

Another success story was Somalia—yes, Somalia—Operation Restore Hope. When President Bush sent the Marines into Somalia, the stated goal was one thing alone—to end the starvation that was decimating the families of poor Somalis, especially women and children. We ended that starvation— with the United States, many other nations, UN agencies and NGO's working together. The clan factionalism goes on; no level of intervention other than a complete takeover could have prevented that. But today, no one is starving in Somalia. The recent harvest was 90% of the pre-strife production. Recovery is well under way.

Catherine Bertini, "Feeding the Poor: Are We Facing a Global Crisis?" Statement of the WFP's executive director to the Chicago Council on Foreign Relations, June 7, 1995, p. 10. For a consideration of constructive alternatives to "complete takeover," see Terrence Lyons and Ahmed I. Samatar, *Somalia: State Collapse, Multilateral Intervention, and Strategies for Political Reconstruction* (Washington, DC: Brookings Institution, 1995).

19. Inis L. Claude, "The Central Challenge to the United Nations: Weakening the Strong or Strengthening the Weak?" in Inis L. Claude, *States and the Global System: Politics, Law, and Organisation* (London: Macmillan, 1988), pp. 28–41.

20. See U.S. Department of State, *Foreign Relations of the United States* (Washington, DC: GPO), vol. 3, p. 335.

21. Quoted in Conor Cruise O'Brien, "Dropping Bombs, Winning Votes," *The Independent*, April 22, 1994.

22. "A Tip of the Scales," *Times* (London), August 31, 1995.

23. *Inter Press Service International News*, July 7, 1995.

24. See Jim Whitman and Ian Bartholomew, "Collective Control of UN Peace Support Operations: A Policy Proposal," *Security Dialogue* 25, no. 1 (1994): 77–92.

25. Although leaders of the Organization for African Unity (OAU) "agreed to place their troops on stand-by for peacekeeping missions in Africa under UN auspices . . . Kenyan President Daniel Moi told the OAU Heads of State . . . that Kenya was opposed to the formation of an African peacekeeping force. Moi said that the creation of a peacekeeping force would be in contravention of the OAU Charter . . . [and] that Kenya would give neither moral [n]or financial support to the force" (*Agence France-Presse International News*, June 27 and 28, 1995). However, see Michael Barnett, "Partners in Peace? The UN, Regional Organizations, and Peace-Keeping," *Review of International Studies* 21, no. 4 (1995): 411–33.

26. See James Gow, "Nervous Bunnies: The International Community and the Yugoslav War of Dissolution, The Politics of Military Intervention in a Time of Change," in Lawrence Freedman, ed., *Military Intervention in European Conflicts* (Oxford: Political Quarterly Publishing Co., 1994), pp. 14–33.

27. See Jim Whitman and David Pocock, eds., *After Rwanda: The Coordination of United Nations Humanitarian Assistance* (London: Macmillan, 1996); Jon Bennett, *Meeting Needs: NGO Coordination in Practice* (London: Earthscan, 1995).

28. See Margaret J. Anstee, "The Experience in Angola: February 1992–June 1993," in Whitman and Pocock, *After Rwanda*.

29. Interviews, Mission Planning, United Nations Department of Peacekeeping Operations (DPKO); UNAVEM III.

30. *Reuters News Reports*, June 8, 1995.

31. United Nations, "1995 Consolidated Inter-Agency Appeal for Angola," revised Humanitarian Assistance Programme for Demobilization and Reintegration (Department of Humanitarian Assistance, June 1995).

32. Peter Capella, "Red Cross Warns Donors of Funding Shortfall," *Times* (London), September 7, 1995.

33. *Inter Press Service International News*, June 22, 1995.

34. Max Singer and Aaron Wildavsky, *The Real World Order: Zones of Peace, Zones of Turmoil* (Chatham, NJ: Chatham House, 1993), p. 1.

35. Claude, "Commitments and the Problem of Order," *States*, p. 188.

36. Jarat Chopra has suggested the creation of an operational UN political directorate "that integrates military forces flying the UN flag, civilian administrators, and human rights officers." See Jarat Chopra, "Back to the Drawing Board," *Bulletin of the Atomic Scientists* (March/April 1995).

3

Human Rights and Humanitarian Operations: Theoretical Observations

DAVID P. FORSYTHE

This chapter addresses some general ideas about human rights and humanitarian assistance. It leaves the detailed analysis of concrete situations and agencies to others. It first addresses macro-theory, situating ideas about human rights in broad political context. It then turns to micro-theory, examining more specific ideas about human rights, with special attention to humanitarian assistance. The first section notes the key role played by powerful states in the evolution of human rights norms. The second section notes the probable evolution of a human right to humanitarian assistance, but over considerable time.

IDEAS AND INTERNATIONAL RELATIONS

For some 350 years the world has been undergoing a process of Westernization.[1] Ideas first brought into play in the West, primarily in Western Europe, have slowly but progressively been diffused throughout the world. The clearest example of this is the idea of the territorial state—differentiated in principle from antecedent empires by its sometimes tenuous relationship to a national people. The idea was first articulated, explained, refined, and practiced in Europe. It is now readily accepted around the world as the preferred legal-political organization of persons. Debate rages as to which people should be organized into which state, and who is to say what is a legitimate arrangement. Debate also exists as to whether the state should be superseded by new legal-political organizations such as the European Union. Nevertheless, during some 350 years the basic legal-political organization of the world has evolved to be the state. It is said to be sovereign, which is also a concept that originated among Western intellectuals.

Dominant power centers—states, in modern history—can impose beyond their boundaries not just their power but also their values. Traditionally, hegemonic wars established who the Great Powers were.[2] A fundamental, if open, question is whether hegemonic change can be achieved repeatedly through processes other than war, such as shifting economic resources and technology.[3] However established, Great Powers precisely because of their power are in a position to advance their values. After the Napoleonic Wars the victorious European states were able to impose their preferences at least on Europe and to some extent beyond. Antirevolutionary and antidemocratic values predominated at least until 1848 and in some ways until 1919. Ideas matter in world affairs,[4] and the ideas that matter most are usually those linked to dominant power. Isolationist states may choose not to maximize their potential power—the United States between the two world wars come to mind. But even then, the "soft power" of example at home tends to generate some power abroad.[5]

The power and values of the Organization for Economic Cooperation and Development (OECD) are dominant as we move into the twenty-first century. The Westernized industrialized democracies of the OECD have clearly emerged after the collapse of European communism as the dominant group of states. They control action taken by the UN Security Council, the World Bank, the International Monetary Fund (IMF), and most of the other important intergovernmental organizations (IGOs). They made up the core of the dominant coalition in the Persian Gulf War of 1991. Given sufficient political will, as shown by events in northern Iraq after Desert Storm, the OECD states have superior power to intervene successfully—at least temporarily—almost anywhere in the "zone of turmoil" making up the 85 percent of the world's population outside the OECD zone of peace.[6] The OECD states are not omnipotent. Somalia and, to a degree, the Balkans remind us of limits. But to emphasize a crucial factor, given sufficient political will, the OECD states can do much—and are doing much—to advance certain values.

The core values of the OECD states can be partially summarized as liberal-democratic-state capitalism. The OECD members are all liberal states in the sense of placing emphasis on the worth of the individual. This core value translates into such sociopolitical values as democracy and human rights, and such economic values as private markets and free trade. The mature, stable, or deep democracies of the OECD also value international peace—among themselves, but not necessarily between themselves and either authoritarian states or other types of democracies (immature, unstable, shallow, or "barely participatory").[7]

This OECD agreement on liberalism and democratic-state capitalism is mediated by both limited disagreement on the forms of liberal-democratic-state capitalism and by some illiberal values. Each of the OECD states has adopted a slightly different way of implementing human rights and democracy. The states vary regarding electoral rules, judicial authority, type of executive, use of the death penalty, and so on. Japan seems to retain more of a group orientation than does the highly individualized United States. The OECD states also vary in the economic sphere regarding industrial policy, extent of free trade, scope of taxation and of the welfare state, and so on. The OECD states exhibit a very weak form of cultural relativism, but not to the point of negating core liberal principles.

The OECD states also present differences concerning the blend of liberalism and illiberalism. Being members of the global state system, however much modified by the presence of IGOs, the OECD states are all to some degree realists in addition to being liberals. Realism may be said to be an illiberal view in which national interests or reasons of state can supersede individual worth. When two Americans crossed into Iraq in 1995 and were given prison sentences, the Clinton administration made clear that U.S. foreign policy toward Iraq would not change significantly in an effort to secure their release. The national interest, as subjectively defined, superseded their individual interests. The OECD states also vary regarding the scope given to realist values in competition with liberal ones. British censorship laws, supposedly designed to protect national security, are much broader than those in the United States. An individual right to know what the government is doing is variously restrained by the national interest as defined by state organs.

Illiberalism can stem from reasons other than the anarchic state system and the realist requirements of national security, however defined. Thus, for example, probably all the OECD states have manifested racist elements sometime during their histories. This was certainly true for the United States, in terms of attitudes toward both Native Americans and African-Americans and in terms of various immigration laws designed to exclude southern Europeans, Asians, and others considered undesirable. But these historical facts do not negate the generalization that the OECD states have evolved into basically liberal states politically as well as economically. Nevertheless, persistent tension remains between liberal and illiberal values. Not even the OECD states pursue wholly liberal policies under all circumstances. The core commitment to the equal worth of all autonomous individuals is constantly challenged by various discriminatory views based on nationalism, racism, religion, and so forth.[8]

Especially from 1945 on, the OECD liberal states sought to establish human rights, with democracy as a subset, as part of international relations. The United States, as the most powerful of the OECD states, played an important role in this evolution, positively and not so positively. It played a key role in incorporating human rights language into the UN Charter but was not a consistent leader in establishing or expanding the human rights dimension of the Organization of American States (OAS).[9] From the mid-1970s the United States intermittently interjected human rights standards into its foreign policy to a greater extent than Japan or France or Germany, but not altogether differently from the Netherlands or Denmark. The United States eschewed formal leadership in the human rights activities of the UN between about 1953 and 1977; but after the Cold War, as we shall see, the United States led the Security Council into new human rights developments.

States rarely act consistently or in an entirely principled manner in foreign policy. Concern for human rights may be inconsistently blended with expediential and even brutal and discriminatory policies. British warships helped enforce UN economic sanctions against racist Rhodesia, but Britain also sought to hamper the operation of the UN Tribunal for War Crimes in the Former Yugoslavia.[10] Japan continues to discriminate against Koreans, Vietnamese, and people of African descent, yet Japan suspended trade with and aid to China for a time after the massacre at Tiananmen Square in June 1989. The issue should be defined, not by whether liberal policies are pursued single-mindedly and consistently, but by whether liberal values constitute major goals to which states genuinely aspire over time; it must be understood that states' behavior may fall short of those liberal standards at a given time or on a given issue. That the United States continues to employ the death penalty for common crimes more widely than other OECD states does not negate the fact that the United States is, overall, a liberal state.

Other actors besides the OECD states have had an influence on the evolution of human rights in international relations. Nongovernmental organizations, uninstructed international public agencies, secretariat officials, and a few non-Western states have all played important roles from time to time. But it is primarily the liberal OECD states, through their unilateral and multilateral policies, that have been the formal engine for the incremental but revolutionary addition of human rights to the agenda of international relations. (Many of the important NGOs and independent experts and officials have also been from the West.[11])

The exact interplay of states, NGOs, and IGOs remains an area of important research. It was certain OECD states that pushed the Security Council to act to protect Iraqi Kurds in 1991, even if those states were prodded by Western media coverage and European public opinion. It was the OECD states that kept the human rights pressure on European communist states through the CSCE, even if they were lobbied by Jewish and other Western pressure groups. It was the OECD states that pressed for resolutions against China in the UN Human Rights Commission, even if they sometimes used information from Amnesty International or Human Rights Watch. Although it is surely true that leadership for human rights can vary by issue, time, and place, it remains true that in general as well as in relative terms OECD states have taken most human rights issues most seriously most of the time.[12] Whether they have been mostly pushed into this position by private lobbies is a significant question for ongoing research.

It has been primarily the West that has championed, first the universalization of human rights, and then the internationalization of human rights.[13] At the UN World Congress on Human Rights held in Vienna in 1993, it was the United States and the rest of the OECD that led the effort to reaffirm the validity of universal human rights in the face of challenges based on strong cultural relativism, as articulated by Singapore, Malaysia, China, and others. (As usual, differences of opinion surfaced within the OECD, as at times Japan and Australia differed from the United States concerning how hard to push the Asian states on human rights behavior. Indeed, the United States manifested different views at different times on this subject. The U.S. approach to China on human rights has been inconsistent over time.)

There are other challenges to OECD liberalism beyond the argument of "cultural relativism," which, itself, is a convenient rationale for the continuing authoritarianism of not just a few Asian states but also others like Cuba and Syria. For example, Iran and several other Islamic states have offered up the illiberal model of a fundamentalist Islamic theocracy. The triumph of the OECD in the Cold War does not guarantee perpetual victory over other visions of how to organize domestic and international society. The "end of history" could well prove temporary.[14] For the moment many global trends, but certainly not all, reinforce the values of Western liberalism, however much behavior may sometimes fall short of the liberal standards. (Quite clearly, many ruling and aspiring elites engage in brutal behavior while endorsing liberal standards.)

There is a broad but shallow consensus on standards that actors publicly endorse with respect to democracy and human rights, as well as to capitalism and free trade. More elected governments are extant than at any time in world history (although some backsliding is probable).[15] The Universal Declaration of Human Rights receives almost universal lip service, no matter how hypocritical the homage (only Saudi Arabia officially objects in principle). Formal acceptance of the core UN Human Rights Covenants is at about 140 out of 185 states. All states profess interest in victims of war, as shown by universal formal acceptance of the 1949 Geneva Conventions. Privatization of markets is the reigning norm, with increased attention to free trade as the World Trade Organization (WTO) supersedes the General Agreement on Tariffs and Trade (GATT).

The rules of international governance arise out of and reflect differing values held by nations. The ideas of international relations of the Middle East, for example, reflect views that in the fourteenth century diverged from those held in the West. The difference in rules of governance currently accepted in the Middle East stems not just from disparities in technology and rate of interaction among power centers but, more importantly, from the fact that Islamic power centers continue to hold values different from those maintained by OECD states today. The standards of global governance would be different had Iraq defeated the U.S.-led coalition in Desert Storm or had fundamentalist Iran rather than the United States emerged as the one superpower in the 1990s. Ideas and values do matter, especially when linked to dominant power.

HUMAN RIGHTS AND HUMANITARIAN AID

Global standards of internationally recognized human rights have roots in Western history. (Space does not allow reference to regional human rights norms.) Early international action was manifested in the transnational moralism of mid-nineteenth-century developments concerning the Red Cross movement for victims of war, the antislavery crusade, and even Marxist concern for the brutalized industrial worker.[16] An effort was made to transform these and other moral concerns for the worth of the individual, regardless of nationality, into global personal rights during the League of Nations era. Efforts by some Western NGOs and an occasional Western state to have the league endorse a code of human rights failed.[17] During this period individual rights were developed in international law for laborers and aliens, and for the protection of certain minority peoples in Central and Eastern Europe. A multilateral treaty for humanitarian assistance—framed in terms, not of personal rights, but of the rights and duties of states—was drafted but never went into legal effect. The international law of war, first codified in 1864, was further refined in 1929, but the law of war focused on states rather than individuals as subjects of the law.

The UN era has indeed been the age of human rights, with three major developments: the setting of global human rights standards, the international monitoring of state application of the standards, and, on occasion, the direct international protection of rights by the international community rather than just by the pressing or nudging of states to improve national protection.[18]

Most global human rights standards presume a condition of peace. Thus the UN Covenants on Civil and Political Rights and also on Economic, Social, and Cultural Rights legally obtain in "normal" or peaceful times for consenting states. In situations entailing some departure from full "peace," but of insufficient gravity to merit the label "armed conflict"—situations referred to as "civil strife," "internal troubles," "public emergencies," and the like—it is still the standards of human rights in peacetime that legally govern.[19] The general standards found in the two covenants are supplemented by special conventions designed to protect certain vulnerable persons (e.g., refugees, children, women, targets of genocide or of racial discrimination, and similar victims).[20] Insofar as one focuses on the provision of humanitarian assistance in peace or situations of near peace, this international law establishes rights to adequate nutrition, health care, and shelter, inter alia. The law is silent concerning what entity may provide assistance if public authorities are unable or unwilling to do so. The general presumption is that outside parties operate in-country only with the consent of the established government and under the international principles of sovereign equality, territorial integrity, and nonintervention into the domestic affairs of states.

A law of war, again based in Western developments, has existed for more than a century. Part of this *jus in bello* has concerned itself with victims of war since 1864 and is now the central component in the laws of war. The core of these contemporary legal precepts is still found in the four conventions for victims of war, concluded on August 12, 1949, in Geneva and now supplemented by two protocols from 1977. It is this Geneva or Red Cross part of the law of war that has been called humanitarian law or the law of human rights in armed conflict.[21]

Although the liberal OECD states have played a major role in the development of international humanitarian law, as might be expected from the consideration of macro-theory herein, they have reasons to be less than enthusiastic about some developments put forward to protect war victims. Despite their being liberal states, some OECD countries are definitely prone to war by reason of either power or geography.[22] Thus, some OECD states, such as Britain, France, and the United States, have wanted to protect victims of war in principle but have not wanted international humanitarian law to hamper the effective exercise of military power. The result at times has been a tension in legal developments, with the United States, for example, opposing some extensions of the law.[23]

In the international law of armed conflict, the provisions on humanitarian assistance are complex. Under the Fourth Geneva Convention of 1949, an occupying power in an international armed conflict is obligated to undertake humanitarian assistance to the civilian population under its control and to allow relief provided by impartial third parties subject only to technical controls.[24] Clearly, under 1977 Protocol I, in addition to the 1949 law for international armed conflict, fighting parties are not to use starvation of civilians as an act of war. Goods essential to the civilian population must be protected.[25] Under the 1977 Protocol II for internal war, starvation as a method of war is also forbidden.[26]

Protocol I, unlike the 1949 Geneva Conventions, has yet to achieve universal acceptance. As of December 31, 1994, there were 135 formal adherences, but a number of major states, including most OECD military powers, had not accepted it. Protocol II has slightly fewer adherences (125).

Moreover, considerable complexity remains concerning humanitarian assistance under the modern law of international armed conflict. First, the Fourth Convention speaks of occupied territory, not about civilians who find themselves in harm's way because of ongoing fighting before a victor occupies a territory. The 1949 Geneva Conventions, being intended for situations like World War II, do not impose any legal duties on a belligerent state regarding its own civilian population. Second, Protocol I does not make absolutely clear whether in international armed conflict, apart from its subset of occupied territory, an impartial third party is authorized to deliver assistance without the general consent of a fighting party. Debate continues whether a fighting party can legally withhold general consent for an agency like the ICRC to provide assistance. Protocol I, Article 70, states that if civilians are in need outside situations of occupied territory, humanitarian relief "shall be undertaken, subject to the agreement of the Parties concerned."

Reasoning by analogy to occupied territory, and with special reference to Protocol I, Article 70, the ICRC argues that fighting parties must permit humanitarian assistance to civilians in international armed conflict. In the ICRC view, there is an individual civilian right to impartial humanitarian assistance throughout international armed conflict.[27] Only technical control of logistics is subject to the consent of the fighting parties. But the wording of the 1949 and 1977 laws is not crystal clear on this point, and some scholars as well as states believe that general state consent is still required.[28]

As a practical matter large-scale assistance to civilians in international armed conflict cannot occur without the cooperation of states with effective military power. Large-scale civilian assistance must be overt, based on truck convoys and other obvious methods of delivery; such assistance constitutes an obvious target should one want to disrupt it by military means. The necessity of operational consent is well known to actors like the ICRC with experience in providing assistance. "One cannot see, in effect, how a humanitarian institution such as the International Committee [of the Red Cross] could carry out a relief action on non-occupied territory by a Party to the conflict without its consent."[29] Nevertheless, it remains of some political and psychological importance whether fighting parties in international armed conflict are legally allowed to withhold general consent for humanitarian assistance.

Common Article 3 from 1949 and Protocol II from 1977 pertain to internal or noninternational armed conflict.[30] Neither the "affectionate generalities"[31] of Common Article 3 nor the minitreaty of Protocol II establish clearly an individual or group right to civilian assistance in internal war. Nor is the ICRC or any other impartial third party given the right to act without consent of the fighting parties. Therefore, it was remarkable that the UN Security Council in late 1992, through its Resolution 794, declared the situation in Somalia to constitute a threat to international peace and security and labeled as a war crime the interference with the secure delivery of humanitarian assistance to starving civilians.[32] The pressing issue of that moment was starving civilians *inside* a Somalia torn apart by the violence of competing warlords and local thugs. Somalia in 1992 constituted an internal armed conflict but, according to the Security Council, Somalia had a right to humanitarian assistance. Interference with that assistance was declared a grave breach of international humanitarian law.

If we look beyond the provisions of the 1949 Geneva Conventions and 1977 Additional Protocols, we can see the foundations of an emerging general right to humanitarian assistance in armed conflicts, although some evidence might suggest otherwise. What is more important is the behavior of powerful actors. In the still primitive system of international law, such behavior can have a legislative effect over time. What is less important is the lack of formal treaties or UN resolutions codifying such a right.

United Nations Security Council Resolution 794 pertaining to Somalia can be seen as an important step in the direction of a right to humanitarian assistance in armed conflict. It was preceded by Resolution 688 during the spring of 1991, in which the Council demanded that Iraq cooperate with humanitarian assistance designed for the Kurds in northern Iraq. Eventually OECD power was put at the service of this resolution, albeit without explicit permission from the Security Council. Under military pressure Iraq gave its grudging consent to subsequent assistance operations for the Kurds.[33] Accompanying Resolution 794 for Somalia were repeated Security Council demands that civilians trapped in the fighting in the former Yugoslavia, especially in Bosnia, be assisted. Much UN effort, as well as the efforts of other actors, went into civilian assistance as mandated by the council.[34] In fact, in 1986 the International Court of Justice (ICJ), in its ruling on paramilitary activities in Nicaragua, had held that impartial humanitarian assistance could never be regarded as an illegal intervention in a conflict or otherwise a violation of international law.[35] Moreover, any number of actors have provided humanitarian assistance in armed conflicts without the consent of one or more fighting parties. Even the ICRC, widely known for its cooperation with governments and its preference for action based on consent, has provided assistance without consent in places like Cambodia and Ethiopia.[36] The ICRC also assisted the Iraqi Kurds from Iranian territory in the 1970s without permission from Baghdad. At times the ICRC informs governments as to what it is doing, but it does not necessarily solicit their consent. The ICRC draws a distinction between general consent for assistance, which the ICRC says it no longer needs, and the practical necessity of specific consent to specific operations by specific fighting parties.[37]

Yet some evidence contradicts an emerging right to humanitarian assistance in all armed conflicts. The UN General Assembly failed clearly to endorse such a general right when it debated the issue at the close of the Cold War.[38] Thus during that era a French initiative to formally recognize a humanitarian *droit d'ingérence* failed.[39] At about that time a major study on human rights and humanitarian norms as customary law, while being entirely silent about humanitarian assistance, noted in passing that British quasi-official opinion appeared to hold that there was no customary right of humanitarian intervention to do good abroad.[40] Moreover, in a number of armed conflicts during the 1990s, the UN Security Council took no position on assistance to civilians. This was strikingly the case during 1994 in Rwanda. There even genocide did not compel outside parties either to stop the Hutu massacres of Tutsis or to provide immediate assistance to attacked civilians inside Rwanda, although sizable and commendable effort was expended to assist those Rwandans fleeing into neighboring countries to escape what should have been stopped within the state.

Given such contradictory evidence about an emerging right to humanitarian assistance in armed conflict, given the silence of the law for human rights in peace about assistance in civil strife, and given other theoretical and practical problems about international relief in armed conflict and civil strife, efforts have been made to develop a moral or human rights code affecting humanitarian assistance.[41] The attempt has been to bypass much legal and political wrangling by producing fundamental rules governing humanitarian relief in all—or almost all—situations. Leading the way in these developments, NGOs have and developed several similar codes, all of which advance a right to humanitarian assistance, as might be expected from private agencies whose goal it is to deliver that relief.[42] However, not all central players accept all the norms proffered.[43] Nor have these progressive efforts generated much impact on many conflicts in which the competing parties still "play politics" with the delivery of humanitarian assistance. A case in point is the long-simmering fighting in the Sudan, as is the fighting in the former federal Yugoslavia and the plight of war refugees from Rwanda, some of whom used humanitarian assistance to try to build a Hutu militia capable of contesting the Tutsi-dominated government in Kilgali.

What we see overall concerning human rights and humanitarian assistance is considerable "turbulence" manifested by contradictory trends.[44] Although human rights standards are endorsed by the UN, including those rights relating to adequate nutrition and health care during times of peace, much civil strife continues to imperil human existence. International humanitarian law, or the law for human rights in armed conflict, is further reaffirmed, developed, and codified by the UN, but brutal internal wars affect millions. For every action implying a right to humanitarian assistance in conflict situations, another action suggests the absence of precisely that right.

Yet at the same time we can see the dynamics capable of overcoming this turbulence. Even if many developing states resist endorsing a right to humanitarian assistance, their reaffirmation of traditional concepts of state sovereignty can be bypassed by the UN Security Council and the World Court. Given sufficient political will, the OECD states, acting through the Security Council, can create a new legal regime for assistance, as they did in the case of Somalia. Just as the council broke new legal ground when by council decision it created war crimes tribunals for the former Yugoslavia and Rwanda (international war crimes tribunals in Germany and Japan after World War II were not created by the UN Security Council), so it can bring into being a right to humanitarian assistance. Clear legislation by the council would facilitate the practical operation of assistance. Somalia shows that, where there is genuine need, where the assistance is truly impartial, and where there is OECD leadership, other states will cooperate. (Domestic and international cooperation broke down in Somalia when the primary objective of relief was altered to incorporate a bungled attempt at coercive national reconciliation and nation-building.[45])

CONCLUSION

States, the fundamental building blocks of world order, are increasingly enmeshed in international governing arrangements.[46] Among these governing arrangements are international human rights standards for peace and war. During periods of international peace, including situations of civil strife that threaten the domestic peace, international human rights standards cover nutrition, health care, and shelter, although the law, unfortunately, remains mostly silent regarding agents of action beyond the state. Certainly a need exists also for a new international human rights norm regarding assistance in civil strife. Just as a special legal regime affects civil and political rights in such situations, so a special legal regime must be instituted to deal with assistance. The OECD states need to add this matter to their foreign policy agendas.[47]

Clearly there exists a right to humanitarian assistance in occupied territory during armed conflict. Also emerging, slowly and tortuously, is a general right to humanitarian assistance, primarily through the practical actions of numerous public and private agencies. Future actions by the UN Security Council, as a reflection of OECD leadership, is crucial for the evolution of this right. In the coming decades council action will likely supersede the timid reaffirmations of state sovereignty found in UN General Assembly resolutions about humanitarian assistance a few years earlier. Developing countries are not likely formally to accept treaties or General Assembly resolutions codifying a right to assistance, but the power of the OECD states acting through the Security Council should make a difference over time. There is no denying that inconsistency and lack of political will on the part of OECD states have been problems in the 1990s, with bold language and action in places like Somalia immediately followed by inconsistency in places like the former Yugoslavia and even dereliction of moral and legal duty in places like Rwanda.

A right to humanitarian assistance is not just a matter of UN actions. However much they resisted acting decisively in places like Rwanda in 1994, the OECD states were increasingly troubled by brutal Russian force in Chechnya. They increased their diplomatic pressure on Moscow to implement restraining standards, including those pertaining to humanitarian assistance. They delayed implementing various cooperative arrangements with Russia until the issue of indiscriminate force in Chechnya was resolved. The rules of international governance are as much produced by daily diplomacy as by formal acts of voting in intergovernmental bodies.

In contemporary international relations many political elites are all too prone to disregard the welfare of civilians in their violent quest for victory. Fifty or one hundred years hence the situation is likely to be different. It is important to take a long-term perspective.[48] Some analysts believe that the learning curve about the immorality and dysfunctionality of widespread violence is historical but discernible.[49] For the foreseeable future much depends on the political will of the OECD states and the extent to which they consistently make humanitarian diplomacy part of their foreign policy agenda. However matters evolve in the long run, there is more than enough to do for the short and intermediate future in order to provide humanitarian assistance to those caught up in civil strife and armed conflict.

NOTES

1. Theodore H. von Laue, *The World Revolution of Westernization: The Twentieth Century in Global Perspective* (New York: Oxford University Press, 1987).

2. Robert Gilpin, *War and Change in World Politics* (Cambridge: Cambridge University Press, 1981).

3. John Mueller, *Retreat from Doomsday: The Obsolescence of Major War* (New York: Basic Books, 1989).

4. Judith Goldstein and Robert Keohane, eds., *Ideas and Foreign Policy: Beliefs, Institutions and Political Change* (Ithaca, NY: Cornell University Press, 1993).

5. Joseph Nye, *Bound to Lead: The Changing Nature of American Power* (New York: Basic Books, 1990).

6. Max Singer and Aaron Wildavsky, *The Real World Order: Zones of Peace, Zones of Turmoil* (Chatham, NJ: Chatham House, 1993).

7. The literature on democracies and international peace is a contemporary growth industry. For new views on this subject see, inter alia, Bruce Russett, *Grasping the Democratic Peace: Principles for a Post–Cold War World* (Princeton, NJ: Princeton University Press, 1993); Edward Mansfield and Jack Snyder, "Democratization and War," *Foreign Affairs* 74, no. 3 (1995): 79–97; David P. Forsythe, "Democracy, War, and Covert Action," *Journal of Peace Research* 29, no. 4 (1992): 385–95.

8. A particularly good treatment of racism in the West and the role of power in advancing (or retarding) certain ideas is Paul Gordon Lauren's *Power and Prejudice: The Politics and Diplomacy of Racial Discrimination* (Boulder, CO: Westview Press, 1988), 2d ed. forthcoming.

9. On the United States and human rights in the UN Charter, see the important research by Cathal Nolan in *Principled Diplomacy: Security and Rights in U.S. Foreign Policy* (Westport, CT: Greenwood Press, 1993). On the United States and leadership for rights in the OAS, see David P. Forsythe, "Human Rights, the United States, and the Organization of American States," *Human Rights Quarterly* 13, no. 1 (1991): 66–98.

10. On this point see David P. Forsythe, "Politics and the International Tribunal for the Former Yugoslavia," *Criminal Law Forum* 5, no. 2–3 (1994).

11. This generalization refers to the International Bill of Rights as a whole. If one speaks only of a collective right to national self-determination as a human right, as stipulated in Article 1 of the two basic UN Covenants on Human Rights, then it was the developing countries that championed that one right—understood as an attack on colonialism.

The author is aware of various nuances to the generalization that the OECD states were the principal champions of international human rights. For example, the United States has not accepted the UN Covenant on Social, Economic, and Cultural Rights.

12. In general see Cathal Nolan, "The United States, Moral Norms, and Governing Ideas in World Politics," *Ethics and International Affairs* 7 (1993): 223–39. A number of commentators have observed that many non-Western states formally accept human rights treaties rather quickly but then are derelict in subsequent reporting requirements and other steps for implementation.

13. Louis Henkin, *The Age of Rights* (New York: Columbia University Press, 1990). Universalization refers to establishing human rights standards for all. Internationalization refers to making human rights a proper subject for international action.

14. I refer, of course, to Francis Fukuyama's *The End of History and the Last Man* (New York: Free Press, 1992). Also relevant is the well-known article by Samuel Huntington, "The Clash of Civilizations," *Foreign Affairs* 72, no. 3 (1993): 22–49, in which he posits various civilizational challenges to the West.

15. Singer and Wildavsky, *The Real World Order*; and Samuel Huntington, *The Third Wave* (Norman: University of Oklahoma Press, 1988).

16. See further, Thomas Weiss, David P. Forsythe, and Roger Coate, *The United Nations and Changing World Politics* (Boulder, CO: Westview Press, 1994), 106–11.

17. Jan Burgers, "The Road to San Francisco: The Revival of the Human Rights Idea in the Twentieth Century," *Human Rights Quarterly* 14, no. 4 (1992): 447–77.

18. David P. Forsythe, "Human Rights and the U.N.: An Incremental but Incomplete Revolution," *Global Governance* 1, no. 3 (1995).

19. Treaties on civil and political rights frequently contain a derogation clause permitting modification of the application of some rights during exceptional times of peace—for example, national emergencies. See Jaime Oraa, *Human Rights in States of Emergency in International Law* (New York: Oxford University Press, 1992).

20. Ian Brownlie, ed., *Basic Documents on Human Rights*, 3d. ed. (New York: Oxford University Press, 1993); and especially Oraa, *Human Rights*.

21. Among many sources see Geoffrey Best, *War and Law since 1945* (New York: Oxford University Press, 1994).

22. J. David Singer, *The Correlates of War*, vols. 1 and 2 (New York: Free Press, 1979, 1980).

23. See, for example, W. Hays Parks, "Air War and the Law of War," *Air Force Law Review* 32, no. 1 (1990): 1–226, for the author's opposition to Protocol I of 1977 on grounds that it interferes with effective air power. Parks is a U.S. Army lawyer in the Judge Advocate General's office of the Pentagon.

24. Jean S. Pictet, ed., *Commentary on the Geneva Conventions of 12 August 1949: IV Geneva Convention Relative to the Protection of Civilian Persons in Time of War* (Geneva: ICRC, 1958), Article 59, 319–27.

25. Articles 50–56, and 70, Protocol I, Additional to the Geneva Conventions of August 12, 1949, reprinted in *International Review of the Red Cross*, no. 197–98 (August–September 1977).

26. Article 14.

27. François Bugnion, *Le Comité International de la Croix-Rouge et la Protection des Victimes de la Guerre*, translated by David P. Forsythe (Geneva: ICRC, 1994), 940–42; Cornelio Sommaruga, "Assistance to Victims of War in International Humanitarian Law and Humanitarian Practice," *International Review of the Red Cross*, no. 289 (1992): 376–77.

28. Peter Macalister-Smith, "Protection of the Civilian Population and the Prohibition of Starvation as a Method of Warfare," *International Review of the Red Cross*, no. 284 (1991): 440–57.

29. Bugnion, *Le Comité International*, p. 939.

30. States persist in this complex and not very workable distinction between international and internal armed conflict in an effort to preserve as much autonomy of decision making as possible. Developing countries, in particular, insisted on legal distinctions between internal conflicts and international conflicts during the 1974–77 diplomatic conference that adopted two protocols to the 1949 Geneva Conventions, rather than adopting one legal instrument with simple rules for all armed conflict. They insisted on the traditional distinction so that (1) they could limit or even reject the rules relevant to major violence within states while (2) extending the rules that others might have to apply in dealing with international armed conflict (e.g., Israeli conflict with the Palestinians). Thus this humanitarian conference was fundamentally driven by nonhumanitarian strategy, although some humanitarian advance resulted. Some of this undesirable legal complexity is circumvented by getting fighting parties to agree to apply general humanitarian principles regardless of their view about an internal or international armed conflict. Fighting parties have sometimes made such a pledge. Whether or not they have followed up with practical implementation is another matter.

31. I am indebted to Tom Farer for this wonderful phrase.

32. December 3, 1992.

33. For an overview see Kelly-Kate S. Peace and David P. Forsythe, "Human Rights, Humanitarian Intervention, and World Politics," *Human Rights Quarterly* 15, no. 2 (1993): 290–314.

34. Larry Minear and Thomas G. Weiss, *Humanitarian Action in the Former Yugoslavia: The U.N.'s Role, 1991–1993*, Watson Institute Occasional Paper no. 18 (Providence, RI: Brown University, 1994).

35. Bugnion, *Le Comité International*, p. 949, quoting from *Nicaragua v. the United States, ICJ Reports* (1986).

36. Ibid., 947–48, re Cambodia. William DeMars, "Seeds of Sovereignty: Humanitarian Organizations and War in the Horn of Africa," in Charles Chatfield et al., *Solidarity beyond the State: The Dynamics of Transnational Social Movements* (Syracuse, NY: Syracuse University Press, forthcoming), re Ethiopia.

37. Sommaruga, "Assistance to Victims of War."

38. UN Res. A/43/131 (1988) and UN Res. A/46/143 (1991). These resolutions have been much misquoted. They reaffirm traditional concepts of state sovereignty in the face of claims to action without consent by outside parties. One point of inconsistency remains: Requests for assistance must come from a "country." Since this wording does not refer to requests from a "government" or "state," some insist that various private parties may solicit outside involvement for humanitarian purposes. The remainder of the resolutions is simply inconsistent with this interpretation. Developing countries in the UN General Assembly have never unequivocally accepted a right to humanitarian involvement or interference or intervention, although they did defer to Security Council action in Somalia as an exceptional event, particularly since early forms of UN involvement were agreed to, de facto, by the leading Somali warlords. However, sloppy drafting and ambiguous semantics in the 1988 and 1991 resolutions do not create a workable right of humanitarian assistance.

39. Philippe Guillot, "France, Peacekeeping, and Humanitarian Intervention," *International Peacekeeping* 1, no. 1 (1994): 40. For background see Mario Bettati, "L'ONU et l'action humanitaire," *Politique Etrangère* 58, no. 3 (1993): 641–59.

40. Theodore Meron, *Human Rights and Humanitarian Norms as Customary Law* (Oxford: Clarendon Press, 1989), 216–17, n. 254.

41. It is well known that fighting parties do not always agree on what legal regime should regulate the fighting. Humanitarian agencies are frequently caught between conflicting and unresolved legal claims. At times the ICRC has promoted a bypassing of legal argument, trying to get the fighting parties to agree on humanitarian principles regardless of judgments about type of conflict (e.g., civil strife, internal armed conflict of either the Common Article 3 or Protocol II variety, or international armed conflict). Whether agreed-upon humanitarian principles actually affect behavior is another question.

42. Task Force on Ethical and Legal Issues in Humanitarian Assistance, *The Mohonk Criteria for Humanitarian Assistance in Complex Emergencies* (N.p.: World Conference on Religion and Peace, 1994); *Code of Conduct for the International Red Cross and Red Crescent Movement and Non-Governmental Organizations in Disaster Relief* (no place of publication, publisher, or date listed); Larry Minear and Thomas G. Weiss, *Humanitarian Action in Times of War: A Handbook for Practitioners* (Boulder, CO: Lynne Rienner, 1993); International Institute of Humanitarian Law, "The Evolution of the Right to Assistance," reprinted in the *International Review of the Red Cross*, no. 297 (1993): 519–25.

43. In *The Mohonk Criteria* the code argues for the reporting of human rights violations

by humanitarian agencies acting in-country. The ICRC, in particular, objects to this standard as unwise and unworkable.

44. James N. Rosenau, *Turbulence in World Politics: A Theory of Change and Continuity* (Princeton, NJ: Princeton University Press, 1990).

45. See also Chester A. Crocker, "The Lessons of Somalia: Not Everything Went Wrong," *Foreign Affairs* 74, no. 3 (1995): 2–8.

46. Mark Zacher, "The Decaying Pillars of the Westphalian Temple," in James N. Rosenau and Ernst-Otto Czempiel, eds., *Governance Without Government: Order and Change in World Politics* (Cambridge: Cambridge University Press, 1992).

47. The UN Covenant on Economic, Social, and Cultural Rights is monitored by a UN committee of experts, but this committee is a quasi-legal review panel that tries to influence state parties over time. It is certainly not a committee of operational action with regard to humanitarian assistance in civil strife. Other operational actors for situations of civil strife there do exist, such as the office of the UN High Commissioner for Refugees (UNHCR) and its work with displaced persons. Space precludes treatment of such actors.

48. Singer and Wildavsky, *The Real World Order*.

49. Mueller, *Retreat from Doomsday*.

4

Humanitarian Aid Operations and Peacekeeping

ALAN JAMES

In a very real sense, any operation which helps to maintain peace has a humanitarian aspect. Even when war was a matter of direct battle between formed military units, civilians were liable to suffer both from the actual fighting and from the passage of campaigning armies. With the onset of total war in the twentieth century, noncombatants have been caught up, often deliberately, in its carnage; and with the advent of guerrilla tactics and the increasing frequency in the 1990s of civil conflicts, the distinction between soldiers and non-soldiers, insofar as the degree of suffering is concerned, has been much diminished. Indeed, it often seems as if it is the common people rather than the warriors who are in the front line.

Accordingly, the humanitarian cause is served whenever fighting is held in check, whether just for the time being or, assertedly, on a permanent basis. In this light the activity which has become known as "peacekeeping" has—except where it is totally unsuccessful—an inherent humanitarian quality. Peacekeeping characteristically involves the use of military personnel, with whom civilians may well be operationally associated, in an untypical military role: that of an impartial intermediary exhibiting non-threatening behavior to defuse a crisis, maintain calm, or implement a settlement. Arguably, such enterprises date from the earlier part of the twentieth century and in essence were a specific manifestation of the age-old functions of mediation and conciliation.[1] But the modern variant of this activity was not conceptualised as "peacekeeping" until after the UN had established its first such force—the UN Emergency Force, as it was called—in the wake of the Suez crisis of 1956. Since then peacekeeping has been subject to fluctuating enthusiasms and has experienced mixed fortunes; but it has never disappeared from the scene, nor has it been monopolised by the UN, and latterly, in quantitative terms, it has burgeoned.

Peacekeeping does not make a primary contribution to the maintenance of peace. Instead, it plays a secondary or derivative role, offering disputants help in the implementation of their wish to remain, at least for the time being, in peace. That help will almost certainly be of significant value—otherwise the parties would not seek it—and it may be essential for the achievement of their shared purpose. But they are not being forced to accept it, for peacekeeping, in accord with its nonthreatening nature, depends on the consent and cooperation of those who want to ease or resolve their conflicts. If, however, peacekeeping is so used, it will not just assist in the bolstering of peace. It will, additionally, have a humanitarian spin-off. Some who would otherwise have been injured or killed, whether as fighters or as bystanders, will be spared that fate. The disruption to local routines which armed conflict entails, and the associated psychological stress, will be reduced. The opportunity for men and women to live dignified and fulfilling lives will be enhanced. Truly, peacekeeping and people's well-being are inextricably intertwined.

Over and above this in-built humanitarian contribution, almost all peace-keeping operations tend to become engaged in specifically humanitarian work. This may occur in one of two ways. In the first place, even where the mandate of a mission makes no reference to humanitarian aid either implicitly or explic-itly, it is probable that some such activity will take place. The aid will, as it were, be extended on the side. In the second place, a link between peacekeeping and humanitarian aid may arise out of the assignment to a mission, either directly or by clear implication, of certain humanitarian tasks. The situation may require such tasks as part of a larger mandate, or the mandate of what is supposedly a peacekeeping mission may, in fact, give it a chiefly humanitarian character.

The first of these possibilities—the incidental giving of humanitarian aid—may be accomplished even by very small missions, such as a group of individually seconded military observers. The observers will, of course, be restricted in their ability to do a great deal of humanitarian work because of their limited numbers and lack of organised military units. They may nonetheless facilitate such matters as the repatriation of bodies and the exchange of prisoners of war, the passage of mail from one side to the other, and the holding of family reunions. They may assist in making arrangements for the control of disease or pests in areas between or adjacent to front lines.[2] Members of such missions will also probably personally provide some humanitarian aid from time to time.

By contrast, a peacekeeping force, by its nature comprised of a central staff and formed contingents from the armed services of member states, has a much greater marginal ability to help the regional community in a variety of human-itarian ways and very probably will find itself so doing. Governmental services may well have been disrupted by the conflict which has led to the despatch of the peacekeepers, and their reestablishment may be delayed by political factors. In such circumstances, a peacekeeping force may draw on its administrative, supply, and transport systems to secure and deliver foodstuffs and heating materials. The medical unit of a force may be able to assist in an emergency and perhaps, to a limited degree, offer routine advice and medication. Its engineering component may have the resources to make repairs to out-of-the-way roads and bridges on which certain villages depend, and it may even be able to improve these components of the local infrastructure. Water supplies and sewage arrangements may likewise be restored or extended by the engineers attached to a peacekeeping force. In conjunction with other agencies, a force may assist in providing succour for refugees. And over and above these official contributions, off-duty soldiers may take an interest in the welfare of the folk with whom they come into regular contact, and organise events for their benefit.[3]

Thus, despite the absence of a specific humanitarian commission, the arrival of a peacekeeping force or observer group is likely to be good news for the ordinary people of the area in question—quite apart from the blessings which will accrue from the mission's political work. The peacekeepers are likely to have a beneficial humanitarian impact, though their relevance in that regard may not be immediately apparent. Moreover, in such a context there is little reason to expect that humanitarian aid will induce political complications or obstruct the execution of the peacekeepers' political mandate. Any humanitarian activity likely to have this effect will just not be undertaken, there being no obligation to embark on it. Should a humanitarian initiative have unexpectedly adverse consequences, it can be quietly downgraded or abandoned, leaving the mission to get on with the business with which it has been formally entrusted.

This response is, of course, not available to a peacekeeping body mandated to perform humanitarian functions or faced with performing such functions by the conjunction of the peacekeepers' mandate and their operational context. However, the absence of such an escape route is not necessarily a problem. If, for example, the relevant activity is so minor as not to invite the ascription of political significance, its scrupulous execution should ensure that the peacekeeping mission does not run into trouble on this count.

Cyprus provides a case in point. Part of the mandate of the United Nations Force in Cyprus (UNFICYP), which has been in place since 1964, requires it to do what it can to re-create normal conditions. Since 1974 the outstanding "abnormality" in Cyprus has been the de facto division of the island, which resulted in the movement to the south of virtually all Greek Cypriots, and the movement to the north of virtually all Turkish Cypriots. Throughout the subsequent period UNFICYP has interpreted its mandate as permitting the provision of certain humanitarian services for the relatively few—now about 500—Greek Cypriots who have remained in the north. On this basis it regularly delivers food and other supplies to them and helps to arrange contacts and visits across the ceasefire line.[4] Given the small number of people involved, the fact that they constitute an aging community, and UNFICYP's care in safeguarding the strictly humanitarian nature of the activity, the Turkish Republic of Northern Cyprus does not feel threatened and so allows the aid to continue. Thus it does not imperil the political work of the force.

The other general circumstance in which a humanitarian role for peacekeepers is unlikely to have adverse political repercussions is one wherein it is manifestly, and more or less equally, of benefit to both sides. Cyprus again provides an example, which also relates to that part of UNFICYP's mandate requiring it to promote the resumption of normal conditions. The area between the Greek Cypriot and Turkish Cypriot ceasefire lines is known as the buffer zone. It varies in width between twenty meters and seven kilometers and includes some of the most valuable agricultural land in Cyprus. UNFICYP has gone to considerable trouble to facilitate the resumption of farming in this area by the landowners of both sides, taking conspicuous care to accommodate the security concerns of their governments. Difficulties sometimes arise, but on the whole this humanitarian endeavour has been remarkably successful.[5] The force also encourages a variety of humanitarian contacts between the two communities.[6] Because both sides see the usefulness of these activities and neither is anxious to upset the status quo immediately, these aspects of UNFICYP's humanitarian work also proceed smoothly.

Unhappily, humanitarian aid by peacekeepers is by no means always exempt from political controversy. That it is designed to provide human beings with some of their most basic requirements does not immunise it against political contagion. Such difficulties are by a long distance most likely to occur when the peacekeepers operate within a single jurisdiction rather than at the de facto or de jure interface between two jurisdictions. Of course, internal peacekeeping, as distinct from border peacekeeping, has currently become the norm. A number of reasons explain why the humanitarian work of internal missions is susceptible to entrapment in the local political scene.

The first reason is that those in command of a particular area—whether the legitimate government or simply the group which happens to be in control *ad interim*—are likely to be very sensitive about the activities of peacekeepers. That the latter are engaged in a humanitarian enterprise is, in this respect, neither here nor there. No one likes to put up with an intrusive third party, whatever its brief, and not even if it is the least of the evils on offer. Furthermore, while an authority's ire will undoubtedly be aroused if the peacekeepers are deemed lacking in impartiality, the absence of this aggravation does not assure the peacekeepers of a welcome. What an authority wants is what by definition a peacekeeping body cannot give: partiality, in the authority's favour!

This point may be illustrated by reference to two peacekeeping experiences in the human rights field. The fostering of human rights is by no means coterminous with humanitarian activity; but if the context is one where the rights in question are among the most fundamental, an attempt to establish or bolster them may be seen as having a humanitarian character. Such a context was provided by Cambodia in the early 1990s, the abuse of personal rights in that country having earlier plumbed the depths of inhumanity. As part of the peace process UNTAC was required in 1992–93 to safeguard and promote human rights. However, its work in this regard was one of its least successful activities. For although it did well in fostering an awareness of human rights and investigating allegations of their breach, its record on enforcement was very far from impressive, notwithstanding the wide-ranging authority UNTAC formally enjoyed in Cambodia. The problem was that, even in the area where the UN mission established a strong presence, the indigenous authority refused to bring to trial those arrested and charged by UNTAC.[7] The second context comes from Mozambique, which had also gone through a long civil war. The UN operation to facilitate the Mozambican peace process (ONUMOZ) was in 1992–94 charged, among other things, with the investigation of alleged human rights violations. However, the reports made in that regard to the local police were effectively ignored.[8] It may be anticipated that in other contexts difficulties will likely be encountered much as they were in these two countries.

A second reason for peacekeepers' difficulties in delivering humanitarian aid in an internal conflict stems from the possibility that such aid may undermine, or be seen to undermine, the authority of those who control the area in question, whether this authority is the legitimate government or not. To put it bluntly, peacekeepers may get in the way of what governors wish to do. It is unlikely that the governing authority will refrain from implementing its plan, but embarrassing inconvenience may be entailed, and peacekeepers may suffer in consequence. Thus during the years 1982–85, when the United Nations Interim Force in Lebanon found itself sitting behind the front lines of the occupying Israeli army, the Interim Force's role became overwhelmingly humanitarian. Principally, this involved trying to protect the local people against measures of a "disciplinary" kind, taken by the Israelis and their surrogates. For example, the members of the Interim Force sometimes practised passive resistance in face of perceived violence against people and property.[9] This did nothing to improve the generally poor relationship between Israel and UN peacekeepers.

Another type of event easily seen by a government as undermining its authority is the peacekeepers' assertion of a prerogative traditionally associated with statehood. The United Nations Force in the Congo (1960–64), for example, as part of its effective mandate to assist in the maintenance of order, was authorised by the secretary-general to place under UN protection an area threatened by marauders or armed bands and to defend it. Further, the force was reminded that its law-and-order obligation might necessitate action against lawlessness on the part of the forces of the Congolese state.[10] These are very unwelcome possibilities for any host state, no matter how great the disorder in its domain.

Comparably, in Rwanda—in a matter technically not peacekeeping but closely associated with a peacekeeping operation—it will be interesting to see how the government reacts to the work of the International Tribunal for Rwanda, which the UN established at the end of 1994. This tribunal is meant to try those responsible for the acts of genocide which took place in that state in the early part of 1994. Because the genocide was engineered and carried out by opponents of the present Rwandan government, one might have concluded that the government and the tribunal would happily coexist. Such an outcome should not have been taken for granted, however. The government became very edgy about the work of an alternative jurisdictional body. It may be noted that although it had repeatedly called for the creation of such a tribunal, Rwanda was not satisfied with the details regarding its establishment and voted against the relevant UN Security Council resolution. It was the only council member to do so.[11] Indeed, Rwanda did not wait for the International Criminal Tribunal for Rwanda to take action against alleged war criminals. After the successful invasion of Zaire by Tutsi rebel forces in late 1996 and the evacuation of Hutu-dominated refugee camps there, a large number of Hutu refugees returned to Rwanda, where some eighty-five thousand were held for investigation of genocide-related crimes. The first of almost two thousand Rwandans accused of planning the mass slaughter of one half-million Tutsis in 1994 was put on trial and convicted by the government-appointed court, over the objections of human rights observers who raised concerns regarding the lack of procedural safeguards for the rights of the accused.

A third reason why the humanitarian activity of peacekeepers may run into trouble with the host regime is that they may be seen as protecting or assisting the state's internal enemies. An instance of this occurred in the Congo (now Zaire) in 1960, following the deposition of the prime minister, Patrice Lumumba. He, like some other leading Congolese personalities, was given UN protection in the shape of a ring of UN soldiers around his residence. This was not much appreciated by the Congo's government, which wished to put him under arrest.[12] More generally, in the context of a domestic conflict the provision of food and medicine to civilian members of the side opposing the government is easily seen by the latter as an antigovernment measure. For whatever undertakings may have been given about the final destination of the relief supplies, there can be no assurance that the supplies will not be channelled to the military. Even if supplies are not handed over directly, the same result may be reached through the release to the military of an equivalent amount of material from stores originally earmarked for civilians. In the case of Bosnia-Herzegovina, for example, the UN's protection of relief convoys to the Bosnian Serb community was often viewed with a jaundiced eye by the Bosnian government.

However, the converse of the foregoing proposition is often true in that the humanitarian efforts of a peacekeeping body may also be seen by the government's opponents as helping the central authorities. Thus in respect of Bosnia, for example, it has been said that the UN has been feeding all three armies.[13] But sometimes there may be a clear lack of equivalence in the impact of the peacekeepers' humanitarian enterprise, not least because of the superior formal and substantial position probably held by those who have managed to hang on to, or secure, the seat of government. When, therefore, the United Nations

Assistance Mission for Rwanda (UNAMIR) spoke of the urgency of reintegrating the some 2.5 million Rwandans sitting in refugee camps (most of them in neighbouring countries), the refugees themselves received the declaration less than enthusiastically; only a year earlier they had been terrorising the ethnic group from which the new Rwandan government was drawn, the members of which have plenty of scores to settle with their former oppressors. It may be added that the government suspected, with some reason, that the refugee camps were being used to regroup and revivify its opponents.[14]

What all this, and especially the last two points, reflects is that most internal conflicts which attract humanitarian aid from peacekeepers have to do with the issue of who is to govern the state or area in question. Given the power, perks, and prestige which so often come to those who have secured recognition as the legitimate government, the outcome of the struggle will be of enormous importance to all the competitors. It may even be, literally, a life or death issue. Accordingly, it is not in the least surprising that humanitarian matters are seen through a political prism, just as in modern interstate war sapping the opponent's civilian morale is of prime importance. What is going on domestically in many of the mentioned cases is indeed a war. In that context the contestants always ask first about the politically damaging possibilities of humanitarian aid, rather than about its life-supporting properties. Consequently, they may well subordinate aid to a secondary place.

Especially in situations where a peacekeeping operation is dominated by humanitarian concerns, one possible outside response to the local politicisation of aid is to consider taking over the country. The UN, or those given its authorisation, might envisage pushing the state's politicians out of the way—putting them in their place, so to speak. This could be presented as the triumph of humanitarianism over politics. An equally elevated terminology could be officially adopted to describe the process: "International trusteeship" might well be favoured, partly because of its responsible tone and partly because it is a term that is well represented in the UN Charter. Despite the rhetoric, however, what would really be happening would be the forcible replacement of one political order by another.

However tempting such a scheme might sound to those frustrated by conditions in a particular country and anguished by obstacles to the delivery of aid, implementation of the scheme would be very far from straightforward. For one thing, although we talk about "collapsed" or "failed" states, we must recognise that this process does not result in a political vacuum. The state is not simply there for rebuilding by efficient interveners. Even in the rare event that the state completely loses the loyalty of its people or its bureaucracy disintegrates, lesser political focuses will almost certainly emerge, whether in the shape of families, tribes, clans, ethnicities, warlords, armed gangs, or bandits. Such groups can be relied upon to oppose any intruders vigorously, no matter how impressive their credentials or their armaments. Moreover, in this sort of internal context such interveners may be less than wholly suitable for the suppression of dissent. This leads to the question of which states will have the international interest or the domestic appetite to maintain a presence in the face of the guerrilla tactics which are likely to be used against them. In such circumstances many states tend to be sensitive about casualties, especially when armed opposition is also likely to obstruct the humanitarian objectives which led to the intervention. In turn, this leads to the question of whether the situation will be much improved, or whether any improvement will be maintained, when the intervention is wound up.

All these issues came home to roost in the UN's attempt in the early 1990s to take Somalia firmly in hand. In its second operation there, the United Nations Operation in Somalia (1993–95), or UNOSOM II, set out to establish a secure environment in which humanitarian aid could be delivered and safely distributed. No less than twenty-eight thousand military personnel were gathered for the purpose, with the United States in the van. Annoyed by the opposition of a leading warlord, who enjoyed a firm base in one of the country's clans, the UN Security Council was persuaded to authorise his apprehension. Despite supplementation from American forces lying offshore, the disciplinary effort went disastrously wrong. Casualties were incurred. The United States announced it was pulling out and was quickly followed by half a dozen Western European states and Turkey. The UN abandoned coercion and, before long, the whole operation. The UN claims (and there is no need greatly to discount it) that much valuable humanitarian work was done in Somalia under its auspices—but this was despite, rather than because of, the world organisation's attempt to treat Somalia as an errant ward of the international community.[15] Evidently there is more life in the concept of state sovereignty than many have supposed.[16]

The Somali experience should not have been needed to highlight the hazards of humanitarian intervention. In an earlier UN peacekeeping operation of a somewhat similar kind in the Congo in the early 1960s, the disordered condition of that country led to talk of the possible appropriateness of a UN trusteeship. A tough resolution was passed by the Security Council. Manifestly, it fell far short of placing the Congo under international protection. Nonetheless, the resolution deeply offended the Congolese government, which, despite its weakness, took effective measures to harass the UN force and interrupt its supplies. After a period of serious concern, this particular crisis passed.[17] But apprehension about the apparent direction in which the UN was moving was partly responsible for UN peacekeeping being generally viewed in Africa, for many years, with a markedly suspicious eye.[18] The UN's experience in the late 1970s and the 1980s in southern Lebanon, where the government of that country exercised not a whit of authority, should also have brought home the point that weakness at the center by no means entails the absence of leadership at the periphery.[19]

There is thus no obvious external means for bypassing internal political obstacles to the receipt of humanitarian aid. If such obstacles present themselves, as they so commonly do, and the humanitarian operation is not to be abandoned, some form of coexistence has to be struck with those on whose goodwill the operation depends. This draws attention to what may be seen as a by no means untypical humanitarian predicament. On the one hand, impartiality is essential to any humanitarian mission because only on that basis will the mission be made welcome by those who have the ability to obstruct it.[20] On the other hand, the highly charged political context within which many humanitarian operations take place means that it is easy for an operation to be perceived by one of the parties as favouring the other. In this manner, the credibility of the operation as an impartial activity is threatened, raising the possibility of impediments being placed in its path. If, further, the humanitarian effort is backed by force, the party on the receiving end of the force will almost inevitably view the operation as fundamentally biased. The mission's members will henceforth be distrusted, and the aid they proffer may well be rejected. The whole purpose of the mission will very possibly have been undermined. It may be added that traditional peace-keeping missions can be undermined for the same reasons.

This suggests a strong argument for avoiding the use of force in support of humanitarian missions. The argument is espoused by a number of practitioners.[21] Beyond that, however, the political complications that may attend humanitarian tasks simply have to be coped with as they arise. The guiding principle must surely be a resolute attachment to the principle of impartiality; in the hope that even if an operation is criticised for leaning in the other side's direction, critics may consider this the result of contextual factors rather than of planned parti-ality. In other words, the aim must be to convince the parties of the good faith of the executants of humanitarian aid. If this belief is achieved, it will by no means result in an acceptance of all the humanitarian mission does, but it may mean that an operation is able to survive a fair amount of criticism.

One further matter about the relation between humanitarian aid and peace-keeping calls for consideration: It concerns the advisability of the frequent or-ganisational link between the two, evidenced by the operations individually cited in the present chapter. Sometimes this link is wholly unavoidable, inasmuch as humanitarian work takes place only as an unmandated spin-off from the peace-keeping agenda. Where the mandate calls for humanitarian activity as a minor facet, relatively and absolutely, of the peacekeeping operation, the link is a prac-tical necessity; but where the humanitarian aspect of a peacekeeping operation is sufficiently big to stand on its own feet, or at least to enjoy a measure of autonomy, there is a viable question as to whether it should be so established. Further, where a peacekeeping operation is primarily humanitarian in character, the appropriateness of its being treated as an instance of peacekeeping demands examination.

To the greatest extent possible a clear line of demarcation should be estab-lished between peacekeeping and humanitarian aid. This course will not some-how insulate the humanitarian work of a peacekeeping operation from the political interpretations and hazards which have been discussed above. There is no way in which humanitarian aid can be sealed off from the political context in which it is being given. But it remains that the directly political activity of a peacekeeping mission is one thing, and its humanitarian activity another. It follows that it is at least a possibility that one of these elements will run into more trouble with the host state or some lesser internal authority than does the other. In which case the separation of the two may diminish the spillover effect of such unpopularity—in both directions. Administrative separation might also make it easier to withdraw the one but not the other, should that be desired. Furthermore, inasmuch as a general class of occurrences tends to acquire a reputation, good or bad, which may affect attitudes to its subsequent use, isolating humanitarian aid from peacekeeping to the extent possible would be a good idea; this would minimise any adverse spillover at that level.

In the case of a mixed operation administratively susceptible to subdivision, bureaucratic considerations will in any event probably point in the direction being urged. Thus in the Congo in the early 1960s, the UN operation was divided into military and civilian elements, the chief of each element being subordinate to the secretary-general's special representative (whose exact title varied somewhat). In Cambodia thirty years later the operation was subdivided into seven components: one military and six civilian, all under the authority of the special representative. It remains worth saying that this approach should be pursued to its maximum extent.

An operation heavily weighted in the humanitarian direction provides good ground for its being so described and for its being put into a separate category from peacekeeping. There is here a semantic issue in which academics can be expected to take a close interest, yet there is surely more than academic myopia to justify the observation that the concept of peace has in recent decades been stretched far beyond its plausible ambit. Of course, one thing is connected with another, that other with a third, and so on, so that there is not much which is totally unrelated to peace. It is also the case, though, that distinctions can be drawn between various areas of activity, and that drawing them assists communication and understanding.

Humanitarian aid and peacekeeping provide a case in point. The UN's operation in Rwanda, for example, was overwhelmingly humanitarian in character and offered virtually no direct contribution to the maintenance of international peace. Giving the operation a more appropriate designation would be sensible and helpful. Likewise, the activities of the United Nations Protection Force in Bosnia-Herzegovina (UNPROFOR II) were chiefly devoted to saving civilian lives. Had the activities succeeded, the effort could well have been termed a humanitarian operation, with the UN's attempts to establish and maintain cease-fires. The UN ultimately failed because it had insufficient means to become a distinctively peacekeeping enterprise.

There is more to this point than a concern with semantics and their immediate implications. Neither of the two just-mentioned operations was conspicuously successful, and this is contributing to a growing disenchantment with peacekeeping. This could possibly have a negative impact on future discussion about mounting and participating in a peacekeeping force. General impressions do influence politics and the media. It would, therefore, be highly desirable for peacekeeping, as a category, to be confined to situations where there is indeed some kind of peace to be kept, rather than also encompassing situations of civil conflict and domestic chaos. Additionally, at least in respect of Bosnia, the ultimate replacement of the current military regime might require the inclusion of nongovernmental humanitarian agencies to dissociate humanitarian aid from the military apparatus established as part of a supposedly peacekeeping force. Were the UN's main presence redefined as humanitarian rather than peacekeeping, further consideration could more easily be given to the extent of its military requirements—at minimal levels.

Of course, formal and bureaucratic repercussions at the UN's headquarters in New York would result were this approach to be implemented, and hence there might be resistance to it. The Security Council, having a competence which is confined to matters bearing on international peace and security, could hardly be the agency through which an avowedly humanitarian operation could be established, nor could it be administered by the Department of Peacekeeping Operations. The latter has to work within the categories established by the UN's principal organs, and in that regard the UN General Assembly might welcome the opportunity to play a bigger role in respect of the organisation's work in the field. That could be no bad thing for the UN's general health, given the dominant position the Security Council has established of late and the resentment which that development has elicited.

One issue needs to be noted, however. The chapter of the UN Charter under which enforcement measures may be taken, Chapter VII, refers just to the Security Council and threats to or breaches of the peace and acts of aggression. Therefore any wish to engage in humanitarian enforcement, such as was attempted in Somalia and with which the UN experimented in Bosnia, would have to be authorised by the Council. In form it would also have to be justified as a response to some peace-threatening circumstance. It is most unlikely that the Council—notoriously lax about legal matters and much enamoured of the concept of peace—would choke over this last requirement. By the same token there is no reason why a humanitarian matter should not be passed by the General Assembly to the Security Council if tough measures should be imposed. Such action would be positively beneficial and categorised as in the cause of humanity rather than of peace. In most circumstances, however, it is likely to be far from clear that humanitarian aid can successfully be thrust on a reluctant host state or a turbulent political scene.

People in many parts of the world are much in need of humanitarian assistance. Quite a few states could also do with peacekeeping help. One of the most encouraging features of the last decade of the twentieth century is that the UN seems to be coming into its own as the provider of an extended range of peacekeeping operations, and it is heartening that these operations often include valuable humanitarian contributions. It must be recognised, however, that the latter are not free from politicisation, and it would be highly desirable if it were accepted that the interests of both humanity and peace are served by distinguishing between these two concepts and, where practical, between the administrative vehicles for their implementation. Each of them is far too important to be put in needless jeopardy through an unnecessarily close association with the other.

NOTES

1. Alan James, *Peacekeeping in International Politics* (Basingstoke, England: Macmillan, in association with the International Institute of Strategic Studies, 1990), pp. 18–42.

2. F. T. Liu, "Peacekeeping and Humanitarian Assistance," in Leon Gordenker and Thomas G. Weiss, eds., *Soldiers, Peacekeepers, and Disasters* (Basingstoke, England: Macmillan, in association with the International Peace Academy, 1991), pp. 34–35.

3. Ibid., pp. 35–38.

4. UN Doc. S/1994/1407 (December 12, 1994), *Report of the Secretary-General on the United Nations Operation in Cyprus* (June 1–December 12, 1994), UN 1994–2: para. 22.

5. UN Doc. S/20310 (November 30, 1988), *Report by the Secretary-General on the United Nations Operation in Cyprus* (June–November 1988), UN 1988: para. 21.

6. UN Doc. S/1994/680 (June 7, 1994), *Report of the Secretary-General on the United Nations Operation in Cyprus* (November 23, 1993–May 31, 1994), UN 1994: para. 33.

7. Trevor Findlay, *Cambodia: The Legacy and Lessons of UNTAC*, SIPRI Research Report no. 9 (Oxford: Oxford University Press, 1995), pp. 63–68.

8. UN Doc. S/1994/1449 (December 23, 1994), *Final Report of the Secretary-General on the United Nations Operation in Mozambique*, UN 1994–3: para. 20.

9. Alan James, *Interminable Interim: The UN Force in Lebanon* (London: Centre for Security and Conflict Studies, Institute for the Study of Conflict, 1988), pp. 6–8.

10. UN Archives, *UN Operation in the Congo Papers* (New York, 1960), Outgoing Cable nos. 2923, 2924, and 2925, October 26, 1960.

11. UN Information Centre, London, News Summary NS/35/94 (1994).

12. Brian Urquhart, *Hammarskjöld* (London: The Bodley Head, 1972), pp. 478–79.

13. Larry Minear and Thomas G. Weiss, *Humanitarian Action in the Former Yugoslavia: The UN's Role, 1991–1993*, Watson Institute Occasional Paper no. 18 (Providence, RI: Brown University, 1994), p. 121.

14. UN Doc. S/1995/107 (February 6, 1995), *Progress Report of the Secretary-General on the United Nations Assistance Mission for Rwanda*, UN 1995: paras. 37–38.

15. UN Doc. S/1995/231 (March 28, 1995), *Report of the Secretary-General on the Situation in Somalia*, UN 1995–2: paras. 26–40.

16. Alan James, "Peacekeeping, Peace-Enforcement, and National Sovereignty," in Ramesh Thakur and C. A. Thayer, eds., *UN Peacekeeping in the 1990s* (Boulder, CO: Westview Press, 1995).

17. Alan James, *Britain and the Congo Crisis, 1960–1963* (Basingstoke, England: Macmillan, 1996), chap. 8.

18. Victor Eno-obong Archibong, "The Organization of American States and the Organization of African Unity on Issues of Peace and Security: A Comparative Analysis of Selected Disputes" (Ph.D. diss., University of Kansas, 1987), p. 203.

19. David Gilmour, *Lebanon: The Fractured Country* (London: Sphere Books, 1983).

20. *A UNHCR Handbook for the Military on Humanitarian Operations* (Geneva: UNHCR, 1995), chap. 3.

21. Richard Latter, *Coordinating U.N. Peace Support Operations*, Global Security Programme report based on a conference organised by the Global Security Programme in association with the Royal College of Defence Studies, the Royal Institute of International Affairs, and the United Kingdom United Nations Association (Cambridge: University of Cambridge, 1994), p. 11.

PART II

Humanitarian Aid Operations: Case Studies

5

The Case of UNRWA: Five Decades of Humanitarian Aid

NITZA NACHMIAS

Mounting criticism of international humanitarian and peacekeeping operations rightfully remarks on their blundering growth in number, intensity, and complexity and the fact that too many of them have become entangled in hopeless violent situations. This study examines UNRWA, the oldest, most-established and perhaps most successful international humanitarian operation. The United Nations Work and Relief Agency offers an unparalleled fifty-year experience in humanitarian aid, and its successes and failures could help in adapting strategies and tactics developed by the agency in other precarious situations.

INSTITUTIONAL BACKGROUND

UNRWA was created by the UN General Assembly on December 8, 1949, as a temporary humanitarian agency in response to the urgent problem of the Palestinian refugees.[1] It replaced the short-lived, stopgap agency, United Nations Relief for Palestinian Refugees (UNRPR), created by the General Assembly in November 1948, but lacked the means and the authority to deal with the complex political problem.

The first issue on the new agency's agenda was the definition of a Palestinian refugee. The UN General Assembly Resolution 194 (III) of December 11, 1948, granted refugee status to any "person whose normal residence was Palestine for a minimum of two years before the 1948 Arab-Israeli war and who lost both home and livelihood as a result of the conflict and took refuge in one of the areas which today comprise Jordan, Lebanon, the Syrian Arab Republic and the West Bank and Gaza Strip."[2] Direct descendants of registered refugees were also eligible for UNRWA's assistance. Clearly, this definition is far different from the common definition of a "refugee," namely, a person uprooted from a land where he and his ancestors had lived from time immemorial.

A two-year residency provision made transients eligible for resettlement, repatriation, or financial compensation. Claimants were not required to provide any proof of having suffered all of the above disabilities. Instead, UNRWA accepted a personal declaration as the sole necessary condition for granting refugee status. In 1949 UN officials estimated the refugee population to be between 330,000 and 500,000.[3] Not surprisingly, by 1993 that count had grown to 2.8 million people receiving UNRWA's assistance. In 1994 almost 400,000 pupils attended UNRWA's elementary and preparatory school. As the largest humanitarian operation, by 1995 UNRWA employed over twenty thousand local Palestinians and was managed by about 135 international civil servants. The agency remains far larger than UNICEF and UNHCR.[4] Inevitably, the refugee population has come to include large numbers of second- and third-generation refugees. Only about one third of the refugee population, about one million people, live in fifty-nine refugee camps in Israel (West Bank and Gaza), Lebanon, Syria, and Jordan.[5] The relief agency also provides services to about 600,000 (exact number not available) "displaced people" added to UNRWA's mandate after the 1967 Six Day War. Among these refugees who fled mainly to Jordan and Lebanon were some 200,000 refugees from 1948, who were displaced for the second time.[6] The civil war in Lebanon during the 1970s and 1980s added more refugees to the already overburdened UNRWA's care.

The agency's impressive 1994–95 budget carried over $300 million per year. The budget request for 1995–96 asked for an increase of 55 percent (i.e., $138 million) for new support programs for the interim period of the Palestinian autonomy. The agency did not plan a transfer of responsibilities to the Palestinians, which is perhaps in direct foil of its mandate to operate "with a view to the termination of international assistance for relief."[7]

Whereas most UN humanitarian operations are carried out by the UNHCR, which operates on a level parallel to UNRWA, the Palestinian refugees were singled out by the UN General Assembly, which took direct responsibility for them. Because UNRWA was created as an autonomous UN agency, directly accountable to the General Assembly and not incorporated as a convention or an international treaty, its accountability system has been flawed. (This will be discussed later.)

The W in UNRWA reflects the original intent to launch major public works programs to create permanent employment and build essential infrastructures in the camps. The agency's modus operandi has been unlike that of UNICEF or UNHCR, the two welfare agencies which focus on formulating and coordinating programs while leaving the execution of programs to governments and various private agencies. In contrast, UNRWA executes its programs and, in fact, has been the second largest employer in its field of operation. Consequently, a conflict of interest developed between UNRWA the international humanitarian agency and UNRWA the nonelected, nonaccountable bureaucracy, executing duties usually rendered by elected local governments. The agency's argument that there exists no local authority capable of carrying out these functions raises questions about UNRWA's efforts to develop self-reliance. The agency's very existence may have discouraged local residents from initiating programs that could have promoted their self-reliance. The lack of local autonomy argument was also used by the Arab countries and Israel to shift responsibility from them to the international agency.

Actually, UNRWA may have been created because of a misperception that the United Nations was responsible for the flight of the refugees from Palestine. Hence, the General Assembly accepted the Palestinian refugees as its wards until the umbrella of its protective agencies was no longer needed. In this, the UN was influenced by its first mediator in Palestine, Count Folke Bernadotte. He argued that "both in origin and disposition the refugee problem entailed a United Nations responsibility."[8] His was primarily a legal, not humanitarian, argument. He argued that, since the Palestinians were without citizenship and were residents of a former League of Nations–mandated territory, the international community was responsible for them until a final settlement was achieved. United Nations General Assembly Resolution 194 (III) of December 11, 1948, reflected this view, proclaiming that the refugees had a right of repatriation or compensation. UNRWA was an unprecedented follow-up. "No other [such] intergovernmental international organization exists."[9] Only after the failure of numerous efforts to settle the Israeli-Arab conflict did the UN replace its initial legalistic approach with a humanitarian one; and in the 1960s, after the public works plan failed, it shifted its focus to education, with health care and relief as second and third priorities.

While UNRWA's mandate and duties changed over time, its raison d'être remained the same: to promote a settlement of the refugees problem. In fact, even the Declaration of Principles (DOP) of September 13, 1993, did not change UNRWA's position. Ilter Turkmen, the commissioner-general of UNRWA, stated that "in the Gaza Strip and the West Bank, the situation in principle will be no different."[10] Possibly UNRWA, like most bureaucracies, seems reluctant to yield any part of its authority.

STRUCTURAL DILEMMAS

The agency's operation created unpredicted political and administrative dilemmas. First, UNRWA virtually became a nonterritorial administration, taking on national governmental responsibilities. However, UNRWA does not have any legal jurisdiction over either the territory or its inhabitants. The agency cannot be subordinated to any sovereign government; conversely, no sovereign government would submit to the authority of UNRWA. On the issue of the powers, authority, and accountability of international "non-territorial administrations," UNRWA is worthy of particular attention.[11]

Second, UNRWA might expect to enjoy corporate and personnel immunity from territorial authorities. Often, though, this has not been the case. Israel Defense Forces (IDF), believing that UNRWA's camps were used for training and harboring terrorists, regularly raided and searched UNRWA's compounds and detained its staff. No authorization by UNRWA was requested or granted.[12]

Third, it has been argued that UNRWA's operation prompted adverse results. It actually enhanced the refugees' living situation and thus reduced their motivation for a settlement. It "reifies, for Palestinians, their refugee status. . . . The camps . . . have been breeding grounds for national violence and . . . their facilities have been used for military purposes."[13]

Fourth, UNRWA has succumbed to major bureaucratic pathologies. The agency has become an inefficient and ineffective self-serving, work-creating agency, suffused with favoritism and patronage. However, UNRWA has argued that the refugees are better housed, better fed, healthier, and better educated, yet its personnel accounts for only 2 percent of the total number of posts (i.e., 20,592 total posts for 1992).[14]

Moreover, UNRWA's activities probably played a quite minor political role in the peace process. The continued and ever-growing discontent among the refugees, culminating in the 1987 outbreak of the Intifada in the Gaza Strip, indicates that UNRWA's humanitarian and social operations have been irrelevant to the refugees' political and social situation.

Critics have further argued that UNRWA's duty has been purely humanitarian, not political. The agency has insisted, though, that it indeed has a political goal: Providing humanitarian assistance to the refugees is intended to influence the peace process.[15] The agency's structure allows it broad freedom of action, making it "capable of engaging in commercial transactions and establishing legally defined relations with governments, other international organizations, and employees."[16] The agency has mostly been left to fend for itself both in policy-making and in collecting its own voluntary contributions. The agency is headed by a commissioner-general (originally titled a director) who is appointed by the UN secretary-general for a term of five years. No process of confirmation is required. The commissioner-general reports directly to the General Assembly by way of the Fifth Committee (Political and Decolonization). The report is discussed and is forwarded to the General Assembly for a resolution and a vote.

In 1991 the authority of the commissioner-general was broadened. The General Assembly eliminated the provision requiring the commissioner-general to reach decisions in consultation with the secretary-general. The commissioner-general has to consult only with UNRWA's Advisory Commission, founded by France, Britain, the United States, and Turkey but later enlarged to ten members, adding Syria, Jordan, Egypt, Lebanon, Belgium, and Japan.[17] Contrary to expectations, the addition of the host Arab governments did not improve relations with the contributing governments, especially the United States, UNRWA's major contributor ($68 million for fiscal year 1993). The frequent disagreements within the commission impeded the development of a minimum consensus necessary for constructive policy making.

In fact, UNRWA functions as a self-contained agency, its staff appointed or removed by the commissioner-general, who promulgates his own policies. A case in point is UNRWA's extensive educational system, established with little or no guidance from appropriate General Assembly resolutions. The agency's structure and procedures have led to questionable budgetary practices. Its expenditures, unlike those of UNICEF and UNHCR, "are not subject to formal approval either by its Advisory Commission or by the Special Political Committee of the General Assembly."[18] The agency's founding resolution does not include provisions for formal consideration and approval of its budget. Indeed, UNRWA's "fund-raising techniques and budgetary methods developed idiosyncratically within the UN family."[19] In recent years the Advisory Commission, without providing justification, declined even to review UNRWA's budget, not withstanding a possibly negative effect on contributors. "Consequently, a contributor is well positioned to use the pledging conference—final stage of UNRWA's annual appearance at the General Assembly—as an occasion for attaching conditions to its contribution."[20] The formal review of the budget is done by the General Assembly following UNRWA's annual report. However, this forum cannot and should not serve as a policy review forum. Unlike the annual reports of UNICEF and UNHCR, which are first considered by the Economic and Social Council, UNRWA's annual report is submitted directly to the General Assembly with the assumption that the Advisory Commission has scrutinized it first. This, unfortunately, has not been the case. The General Assembly's and the Advisory Commission's abdication of supervisory authority have left UNRWA virtually autonomous in its policy-making process. Until the mid-1980s UNRWA used to submit artificially inflated budgets in order to increase its funding. Consequently, UNRWA lost the trust of its donors. By the end of the 1980s, UNRWA found itself in a severe financial crisis. Whereas the number of its dependents increased, the voluntary contributions shrank. The agency reduced its workforce, overhauled its budgetary and fund-raising processes, and developed some degree of financial accountability. In 1986 the first informal meeting of the donor states was held at the Vienna headquarters and for the first time, budget proposals, long-term plans, and new financial controls were introduced. Since 1986 a closer working relationship has developed between UNRWA and its donors, especially with the United States, UNRWA's largest contributor.

It is difficult to reconcile the complex political context in which UNRWA operates with the lack of guidance, accountability, and control from either the Advisory Commission or the General Assembly. The lack of a governing or an overseeing body is equally disturbing. It had been wrongly assumed that UNRWA would be a short-lived operation; thus, the creation of an oversight apparatus would not be necessary. Why the General Assembly has since left in place this administrative and policy-making void is unclear. Agency officials, however, openly enjoy their autonomous status and argue that headquarters bu-reaucratic controls are unnecessary.[21]

Thus, UNRWA autonomously determines "who gets what, when, and how" but is not accountable to its constituency or the institutions responsible for its creation, its finances, and its continued operation. This freedom of action, how-ever, bears a price tag. The agency has been solely responsible for its every failure. Whereas "UNHCR has been remarkably successful in healing political rupture (the reference is mainly to Europe after [World War] II) . . . UNRWA has not."[22] The relief agency was charged with lack of accountability, inefficiency, and even corruption.

Indeed, for almost five decades UNRWA has been operating without proper financial accountability and control standards. Evidently, (1) UN agencies can become extremely autonomous, (2) a head of a UN agency can exert vast in-dependent power and authority, and (3) the UN system lacks administrative and regulatory mechanisms.[23]

UNRWA'S MANDATE: THEORY AND PRACTICE

Because UNRWA's original mandate was neither clear nor specific, the agency set its own two-pronged policy: (1) to provide humanitarian and relief assistance; (2) to promote economic development through educational, health, and social networks. In addition, the agency maintained its political agenda: "UNRWA itself became a channel for efforts to solve the refugee problem as well as a channel for technical assistance such as educational and vocational training."[24] Its mission could be defined as "peace-servicing," a strategy different from either "peace-making" or "peacekeeping," the two most common forms of peace-servicing, which implies mainly humanitarian, economic, and social services. However, UNRWA seemed to assume that its responsibilities ranged far beyond the purely humanitarian. The agency sought to achieve a political objective, namely, a settlement of the refugee problem, for which it had neither the means nor the proper qualifications. It argued that the "basic goal of the UN is to help avoid or ameliorate conflict through socioeconomic programs."[25] Yet only on the humanitarian level did the agency enjoy any successes. Olaf Rydbeck, UNRWA's commissioner-general between 1979 and 1985, stated: "Either dissolving UNRWA or making it permanent would be an admission by the United Nations that there was no solution to the Middle East struggle. That leaves us with a permanently jerry-built structure to keep the fiction alive."[26]

The pursuit of political goals led UNRWA to conflicts with the Conciliation Commission on Palestine (CCP), on "which of the two subsidiary organs was primarily responsible for action on the question of repatriation and or/resettle-ment of the refugees."[27] "CCP-UNRWA meetings during 1950 [were] charac-terized by friction. . . . The origin of the conflict was basically a matter of institutional jealousy."[28] Consequently, "The two UN organs . . . were under-cutting each other's efforts."[29]

The agency, it seems, has not changed its tactics. Since 1994 UNRWA has been competing for development contracts with the newly created Palestinian Economic Council for Development and Reconstruction (PECDAR). Today, as fifty years ago, it "appears clear from the records that [UNRWA's] personnel were concerned primarily with protecting the status of their organ."[30] The agency seems to take advantage of the fact that (1) its mandate lacks clarity, (2) the Advisory Commission lacks interest in UNRWA's operations, and (3) UN headquarters fails to guide, regulate, and control its agencies.[31] Indeed, in policy making the field anticipated headquarters: Agendas, policies, and executive action were initiated in the field and only later legitimized by UN resolutions. For UNRWA, the "General Assembly is a sounding board for policy initiatives that have occurred elsewhere."[32] This practice explains why the "the Commissioner-General receives little guidance from either the Advisory Commission or the General Assembly."[33]

The "right of return" was another political issue that received UNRWA's attention, although it was never mentioned in its original mandate. The agency pursued the approach presented by Bernadotte, arguing that Israel had to provide the refugees with the right to return. He suggested it "for humanitarian reasons and because I consider the danger to Jewish security slight," but Israel rejected the idea because it "is still beset by enemy armies . . . and [this] would relieve the aggressor states of a large part of the pressure exerted on them by the refugee problem."[34] Israel, however, did not preclude repatriation linked to a lasting peace.

In the 1950s UNRWA initiated a resettlement plan through a UN grant of $250 million to participating Arab governments. As expected, their response was utterly negative.[35] Failing to achieve its political goals, UNRWA had to tend the most pressing needs of the refugees. During the early years (1950–52) it provided direct relief, anticipating that this would soon be replaced by public works. However, UNRWA's first director, Major-General Howard Kennedy, soon reported to the General Assembly that public works provided "no enduring benefit for refugees nor financial relief for the Agency." The public works plan was abandoned in mid-1951.[36] Since the late 1950s UNRWA's operations moved away from self-support and retraining programs to more expanded relief and rehabilitation programs. This was in effect a reversal of UNRWA's original mission as a temporary emergency agency. The agency's early hopes to get most of the refugees off the relief rolls by 1952 had to be reconsidered. That a political solution could not be achieved so quickly required the planning of long-term operations such as education and health care.

In 1959 UNRWA abandoned its plans for resettlement and/or repatriation and focused on long-term programs, namely, health care and education. Shortly after this shift in direction, UNRWA decided to take on additional duties. In the 1960s it began to provide civil and social services and became a de facto local administration. It argued that no alternatives were available to refugees. Thus, the dependence syndrome was established.

The Six Day War of 1967 marked a turning point in the history of UNRWA. In addition to an unexpected increase in the number of refugees, thousands of displaced people were added to the long list of UNRWA. Moreover, a new issue, human rights, became the focus of attention. As the refugees' position changed from subjects of Egypt and Jordan to subjects of Israel's occupied territories, in an exchange of letters UNRWA and Israel agreed to recognize their status as it had existed under Egyptian and Jordanian rule. Israel, however, insisted on reserving a free hand in matters of military security (i.e., when and if it perceived a security threat, it would not honor the UN Privileges and Immunities Protocol).[37] Indeed, Israel did not hesitate to use harsh measures against UNRWA's employees.[38] Although UNRWA and Israel tried to maintain appropriate relations, UNRWA found it difficult to act as a simple bystander when confronted with alleged human rights abuses by Israel. Conversely, UNRWA has been perceived in Israel as an agent of the Palestinians. "It would be disingenuous to claim that UNRWA can perform its tasks without reference to politics," said Giorgio Giacomelli, the agency's commissioner-general between 1985 and 1991. "It could treat its humanitarian responsibilities as if nothing had changed from earlier days of 'benign' occupation, or reinterpret its mandate to intercede between the occupying army and the refugee community in whatever measure possible."[39] The agency's staff witnessed the people of Gaza "surrounded and occupied, with a real sense of helplessness and isolation,"[40] and they believed it their responsibility to address the urgent needs of the Palestinian population.

Based on UNRWA's Commissioner-General Annual Reports, the secretary-general attested in the annual reports (1969, 1970, 1971, 1972, and onward) that although economic conditions of the refugees had improved, the state of their human and legal rights had worsened. Consequently, on October 11, 1978, the General Assembly adopted a resolution, later repeated annually, condemning Israel's denial "of the inalienable rights of the Palestinian people under the United Nations Charter and the Universal Declaration of Human Rights and [declaring] that the full respect for those rights was indispensable for the establishment of a just and lasting peace in the Middle East."[41]

The issue of human rights created friction between Israel and UNRWA in the early 1980s. Israel's decision to relocate camp dwellers in Gaza from their shanty dwellings to government-supported housing projects outside the camps and to demolish their camp dwellings following the relocation became a major human rights issue. Following UNRWA's reports the General Assembly adopted a resolution urging Israel to desist from further removal of refugees and destruction of their shelters.[42] The project, Israel argued, advanced the refugees' health and safety. Moreover, it declared in 1988 that "the waiting list of applicants wishing to join this Israeli housing project is full for the coming three years."[43]

Until the mid-1980s neither Israel nor the Arab states wished UNRWA to become involved in human rights. Only following the outbreak of the Intifada were these claims put forward in a serious manner. Until then the Arab states' ultimate interest was to maintain the status quo and to block refugee resettlement in Arab countries. To that end they expected UNRWA to "extend relief, education, and other essential services . . . to carry out major economic development projects, and to expand and accelerate the existing refugee training program."[44] Moreover, the Committee on the Exercise of the Inalienable Rights of the Palestinian People created by the General Assembly on November 10, 1975, maintained complete silence regarding UNRWA's operation.[45] In its annual reports submitted to the secretary-general, who later submitted them to the Security Council for consideration, the committee made no mention of UNRWA's services. Israel, for its reasons, chose not to attribute great importance to UNRWA either. Consequently, UNRWA complained that "the agency's mandate does not extend to all the ramifications of the problem."[46]

Only after the outbreak of the Intifada in 1988 did the then-secretary-general Perez de Cuellar urge the General Assembly to extend UNRWA's services to Palestinians with or without refugee status to help them "cope with day-to-day difficulties of life under occupation, such as security restrictions, curfews, harassment, etc."[47] Indeed, the secretary-general's proposals were more of what UNRWA had already found itself doing. The proposals were vetoed in the Security Council by the United States, but after much debate the General Assembly adopted resolution A/43/57, I (1988)—which was again rejected by the United States and Israel—thereby creating a new function within UNRWA: the "Refugee Affairs Officer" (RAO), or an observer, whose duty was to "uphold the safety and security and the legal and human rights of the Palestine refugees . . . under Israeli occupation in 1967 and thereafter."[48] The RAOs, who reported on trouble spots to UNRWA's local legal advisors were assumed to fulfill a dual mission, namely, to provide early warning of possible abuses and to deter possible abusers by their presence. Later the RAOs also assumed mediation and third-party negotiation tasks. In 1995 UNRWA employed twelve RAOs in the West Bank; the nineteen RAOs who had served in Gaza departed following the DOP agreement. These RAOs came mainly from the United States, Europe, Australia, and Canada. But Israel refused to cooperate with the RAOs, having rejected UN Resolutions A/43/57, I (1988) and A/47/69, I (1992).

POLICIES AND OPERATIONS

Of the three main operations education has been the most important, aiming to produce "socially useful human beings who contribute to society rather than impose a burden on it."[49] Health and relief have been second and third. Twenty percent of the refugees have attended UNRWA's 641 schools. About ten thousand teachers have been employed by UNRWA in its eight vocational and technical training centers, attended by over five thousand students.[50] In 1994 UNRWA reported on the population density of refugees, citing areas of residence:

Refugees

Lebanon	338, 290
Jordan	1, 193, 563
Gaza Strip	643, 600
Syria	327, 288
West Bank	405, 070

These statistics have been questioned, however, and lower numbers have been assumed because of fraud, lack of information, and UNRWA's refusal to conduct a census of its clients.[51]

The educational program, UNRWA's prime project, has been greatly criticized for using the politicized and biased curriculums of Arab countries and their abrasive, inflammatory, anti-Israeli texts. It has also been accused of providing inadequate supervision, although UNRWA has argued that it worked in cooperation with the United Nations Educational, Scientific, and Cultural Organization (UNESCO). Additional criticism has cited poor student performance, resulting from programs aimed at promoting political goals rather than education, and lack of cohesion in the whole educational system.

Indeed, standardized tests in science and mathematics showed that "the results of UNRWA's schools in both Jordan and the West Bank were disappointing . . . and the results among West Bank students were far below those of their counterparts in Jordan."[52] UNRWA admitted the poor scholastic achievements but blamed it on Israel security measures.[53]

The Palestinians, too, seemed unhappy with UNRWA's education system. In 1984, for example, following Israeli demands, UNRWA constructed fences around the schools to "prevent Palestinian students from stoning Israeli vehicles on roads near West Bank UNRWA schools."[54] This move was viewed as cooperation with Israel and thus attracted Palestinian criticism. In the early 1990s UNRWA executed major reforms in its education system. In 1993 all divisions were integrated into the "UNRWA Institute of Education" in Amman, Jordan, and the number of students was cut in half. The DOP agreement and cooperation between the Palestine Liberation Organization (PLO) and Israel was expected to end Israel's practices of school closedowns, searches, and seizures and thereby help the education system to thrive.

Although UNRWA's health care and relief operations have been less extensive than its educational operations, they have nonetheless been impressive. In 1993–94 UNRWA operated about 500 health and dental clinics, employed about 3,203 professional and auxiliary health workers, including 207 doctors and dentists, 683 nurses, hygienists, and midwives, and 230 paramedical staff members. Highest in proportion of clinics to patients was Gaza because of the dire conditions in its nine refugee camps.[55]

Relief, however, has also been the subject of much controversy. The agency disbursed little cash and provided mostly food rations donated by the EC. In 1982 to make up for the lack of cash, recipients developed a barter system. When UNRWA experienced severe financial crisis, it chose not to cut the education budget but, rather, to reduce relief operations. Since the mid-1980s, direct relief and food rations have been given only to the most vulnerable groups, namely, to children six to thirty-six months and to the sick and handicapped. The relief program for 1994–95 was further reduced to include only babies, pregnant women, nursing mothers, and several hundred chronically sick people. The agency's 1994–95 expenditures for relief were estimated to be $71,791 million.[56]

ADMINISTRATIVE AND SUPPORT SYSTEMS

To carry out its mission UNRWA needed the support of the host governments (i.e., the Arab countries and Israel), the international community (i.e., the UN), and the affluent donor countries. First, the Arab governments' support of UNRWA was not unambiguous. On the one hand, they welcomed the agency's operation because it helped keep the refugees issue on the international agenda, thereby maintaining constant pressure on Israel and turning their problem into an international crisis. On the other hand, they wished to limit the scope and intensity of UNRWA's operations in order to keep the refugees dependent until their contemplated repatriation. They thus shared UNRWA's interest in inflating the rolls of registered refugees, resulting in UNRWA's clientele growing exponentially.

Second, the international support system was greatly flawed. The resolution creating UNRWA included several contradictions, which generated many problems. One was that the agency was granted responsibilities and means for a temporary, humanitarian mission, but it soon became long-term, immense intervention. It proved utterly wrong to assume that within "two or three years relatively few refugees would still be dependent and [UNRWA's] own services would no longer be necessary."[57] Moreover, in 1949 the General Assembly carelessly entrusted the responsibility for the refugees to two agencies, the CCP and UNRWA, resulting in fierce, destructive competition. The international community failed to establish either a system of accountability or responsible governing institutions, allowing questionable operational tactics to develop. Finally, the failed pursuit of unrealistic objectives, such as UNRWA's $110 million project for irrigating the Sinai desert for the resettlement of 150,000 to 200,000 refugees,[58] led to a legacy of frustration and bitter failure.

In 1954 the General Assembly passed Resolution 818 (IX), establishing a $200 million rehabilitation fund, but UNRWA was never able to execute any large-scale development plan. In 1956 UNRWA reported that "it had received only $37 million of the amount authorized. Approximately $19 million were actually spent, and the balance was kept as essential working capital; the dream was abandoned."[59]

Third, the donors, especially the United States, were continuously frustrated by the lack of political progress. The Eisenhower administration even threatened to withhold all further financial support for UNRWA,[60] and by 1958 UNRWA was forced to restrict expenditures on education and use money allocated to rehabilitation for essential relief. The agency's finances improved somewhat in the 1960s, but only enough to expand educational and health services. The Soviet Union generously provided the Arab countries with vast quantities of arms but made no direct or indirect contributions to UNRWA and often even opposed UN plans for a settlement.

In short, the international community was not committed to a compelling humanitarian operation. The growing hostility between Israel and the Arab states was inimical to a settlement. And the arms race further reduced incentives for a political settlement. In addition, Israel's offense at UNRWA's pressure for repatriation or financial compensation created a barrier to settlement.

HUMANITARIAN AID AND HUMAN RIGHTS

The 1967 war added refugees and displaced people to UNRWA's list and heightened the problem of human rights for the 1,350,000 refugees then living under Israeli rule in the occupied territories. As Israel was settling into the uneasy responsibility of controlling a large and hostile Palestinian community living in dire conditions, the Palestinians were experiencing their worst nightmare: life under Israeli occupation. The international community swiftly charged Israel with the responsibility for the safety, welfare, and security of the inhabitants of the occupied territories and requested that Israel allow the new refugees to return to their homes.[61]

Soon Israel, UNRWA, and the PLO became entangled in a political quandary. In 1964 the PLO had instituted in Gaza a form of conscription. Recruits received military and political training, often at the refugee camps, and UNRWA's local staff was not exempt from the conscription. Although it was UNRWA's policy to terminate employment of people recruited by the PLO or any other state military force, Israel claimed that in reality UNRWA chose to ignore the PLO's operations in the camps. Consequently, Israel accused UNRWA of harboring, protecting, and employing PLO members, and Israel often raided and searched UNRWA's compounds. The international agency strongly protested these measures, demanding immunity within its areas of operation. A major obstacle in Israel-UNRWA's relations for many decades, the issue has yet to be resolved.

It is possible that Israel has misperceived the issue of the refugees and UNRWA's role. Initially the refugees and UNRWA were considered only temporary problems. Israel had hoped that the refugees would voluntarily leave the camps and move to Jordan, Egypt, and the other Arab states. That this did not happen was blamed, in part, on UNRWA, whose extensive operations seemed to have reduced the refugees' incentives for a permanent resettlement.

Indeed, in December 1967 the then-commissioner-general, Laurence Michelmore, reported to the General Assembly that the refugees were not leaving the newly occupied territories. On the contrary, an additional "110,000 refugees joined the 332,000 refugees living on the West Bank."[62] Moreover, UNRWA's first five-year report after 1967 noted that "the GNP of the Gaza District rose at an annual average of 18 percent in real terms, . . . [the] growth rate later slackened somewhat to a still impressive average of 8 to 9 percent."[63] Private building starts rose from 17,000 square meters in 1969 to 250,000 meters in 1976. In 1972 only 6 percent of the families possessed refrigerators, and only 2 percent owned television sets. In 1977 29 percent had refrigerators and 42 percent owned television sets. Both Israel and UNRWA claimed credit for the refugees' improved conditions.

However, these impressive improvements were not exhibited in the area of human rights, and until 1988 the issue was very much on the back burner. Only after former Under-Secretary-General for Special Political Affairs Marrack Goulding visited the occupied territories and submitted a critical report[64] did the secretary-general initiate a resolution (A/43/57) placing UNRWA in charge of the safety and human rights of the Palestine refugees.[65] The agency eagerly espoused its new role. "UNRWA leadership had to decide whether the agency would be a simple bystander to these conditions . . . or reinterpret its mandate to intercede between the occupying army and the refugee community in whatever measure possible."[66] Giorgio Giacomelli, then commissioner-general of UNRWA, said promptly: "Our mission must take political reality into account . . . [and] of course we sympathize with the Palestinians. It is our mission to help them. Our relations with the Israelis are naturally strained."[67]

The 1987 outbreak of the Intifada created new, unforseen problems. Because UNRWA's employees were mainly local Palestinians, many sympathized and even actively participated in the uprising. The agency also became involved in the controversy over the Jewish settlements, expressing strong opposition to them. "There was no way in which Israeli occupation could be made acceptable to the Palestinian people," UNRWA argued.[68] Predictably, Israel reacted with harsh measures against UNRWA's Palestinian staff. The situation was soon aggravated by the Gulf War. Severe security measures combined with the loss of remittances devastated the already weak Palestinian economy in the West Bank and Gaza.[69] The agency could hardly be of help. The mission of the RAOs proved futile; they could neither prevent nor halt clashes between the Palestinians and the Israeli forces. Indeed, they could not affect any actions taken by Israel's defense forces.

LIMITATIONS TO HUMANITARIAN OPERATIONS

The experience of UNRWA highlights the administrative and political limitations to international humanitarian aid operations. First, on the conceptual level humanitarian assistance needs to be redefined in both general terms and specific terms. Included in the redefinition should be long- and short-term objectives, the timeframe, possible risks, and potential resources. Hardly any relevant precedents existed when UNRWA was established; however, in the five decades of its existence, UNRWA has not been successful in creating any.

Second, the international community, namely, the UN, seemingly lacks the administrative and management resources necessary to lead and oversee large-scale, long-term assistance operations. The General Assembly has provided neither an accountability framework nor operational regulations, allowing UNRWA to enjoy complete operational autonomy. Consequently, UNRWA has grown from its beginnings as a trivial, ephemeral agency to become a permanent, vast bureaucracy troubled with partisanship, inefficiency, and mismanagement. For example, "a lucrative racket long flourished in Jordan, in which 'ration merchants' paid fees to refugees for use of their UNRWA identity cards, which they presented at distribution centers to obtain food to sell later on the black market."[70] Although the ration program in Jordan was terminated, many other forms of swindle and fraud seem to exist under the umbrella of UNRWA's services.

Third, lack of basic cooperation from the host countries and UNRWA's advisory commission probably affected the agency's fund raising and eroded much-needed political support. This was most disturbing when UNRWA conflicted with its own constituency and when the political environment became extremely hostile.

Fourth, international assistance agencies such as UNRWA face complex and controversial legal status. They have autonomous responsibilities in providing an array of public services while lacking formal territorial authority. "Especially difficult has been the conduct of programs of relief and education without a basic understanding with the territorial authority as to the prerogatives of international organization."[71] Also the legal status of UNRWA's local staff presents an unresolved problem, probably because the General Assembly never planned to create such a vast bureaucracy of civil servants employed by a UN agency.

Fifth, on the political level there persists the question should the primary responsibility for the refugees be borne by the UN and not by the host governments, and if so, should this responsibility be unlimited in time? The existence of UNRWA clearly allowed both Israel and the Arab states to dodge their responsibilities for half a century. Israel argued that "after they created a refugee problem, the leaders of the Arab states and the Palestinians blocked any attempt of making these refugees proud members of their societies and economies."[72] The Arab states, meanwhile, claimed to be the victims.

Sixth, UNRWA's operation has not been consistent with its mandate. Instead of enabling the refugees to become self-reliant, it intensified their dependence. With vast resources, thousands of employees, and a responsibility without parallel in the UN experience, UNRWA bears the ultimate stigma of failure: It has failed to accomplish its main mission. The agency's longevity should not be a shield against critical questions concerning the agency's right to continue operations, especially given its steadily expanding modus operandi. Clearly, after the DOP was signed, UNRWA should have considered phasing out its operation as swiftly as possible. However, UNRWA's Horizon Plan of January 1995 suggests the agency thought otherwise. "The UN should concentrate its resources . . . [and] should emphasize the direct and indirect creation of 15,000 or more job opportunities through direct employment in UN activities."[73] The agency seems to have ignored the fact that the members of its constituency have reached maturity.

FUTURE ROLE OF UNRWA

In its *Horizon Report* of 1995, UNRWA suggested that it should continue operating for "practical as well as political reasons."[74] The report advised the international community that a reduced UNRWA could have "potential political consequences . . . for the Palestinian Authority, the host countries and the peace process itself."[75] The agency's request for a budget increase for fiscal year 1995–96 to carry out its new Peace Implementation Program has been approved, and the agency received an additional $138,250 million for 1996. This replaces UNRWA's Expanded Program Assistance of 1988.[76]

Although the future of UNRWA's operation is open-ended and difficult to predict, it is possible to assume the future of UNRWA in the individual countries of operation. First, if the political status quo is maintained in Lebanon, UNRWA's headquarters until the late 1970s, UNRWA's operations there can be expected to continue without major changes. In Syria UNRWA's operation will probably not change in any meaningful way either, since the issue of refugee repatriation will be decided only at the last stage of Israeli-Palestinian negotiations. In Jordan, the West Bank, and the Gaza Strip, however, substantial changes can be expected. The high reproductive rate of the Palestinian refugees living in Jordan and in Gaza (3.7 percent per year) multiplies the number of refugees by almost 50 percent every decade. According to UNRWA, one third of the three million residents of Jordan are registered Palestinian refugees.[77] If the current trend is maintained and if the nature of UNRWA's operation does not change, UNRWA could become a government within a government in Jordan!

However, UNRWA's past record makes doubtful the Palestinian Authority's willingness to continue to relinquish its authority to the international agency. Since the future of UNRWA has not been determined by the individual Israeli-Egyptian, Israeli-PLO, and Israeli-Jordanian peace agreements, UNRWA's best policy would be to transfer its duties to the Arab and Palestinian authorities gradually. What mechanisms will replace UNRWA's services is difficult to predict, since the donor states are apprehensive about transferring funds to the Palestinians. Following the January 1996 elections in the West Bank and Gaza, and under provisions of the DOP, the newly elected Palestinian Interim Authority (the "Council") assumed overall responsibility for the Palestinian community for a transitional period not exceeding five years. Although the creation of an independent Palestinian state might be several years away, the DOP clearly said, "Immediately after entry into force of this DOP . . . authority will be transferred to the Palestinians on the following spheres: education and culture, health, social welfare, direct taxation, and tourism."[78] That UNRWA was left out of all the Israeli-Arab agreements by coincidence is highly unlikely. The DOP further provided that "the Council . . . promote economic growth . . . [and] establish a Palestinian Electricity Authority, [a] Gaza Sea Port Authority, [and] a Palestinian Development Bank."[79] Both Israel and the Palestinians chose not to include UNRWA in the agreement.

At issue are $2.4 billion pledged in October 1993 in an economic summit in Washington by the industrialized countries for the projects mentioned. Expecting to receive a large share of the attractive pie, UNRWA had offered to serve as an intermediary agent between the Palestinians and the contributors "to ensure a smooth transition to subsequent phases at which time programs run by organizations such as the World Bank, other organizations of the United Nations system and bilateral aid agencies will have become operational."[80]

Interestingly, for various reasons Israel has revised its policy and begun to support UNRWA. Indeed, Israel has preferred that the vast reconstruction and development funds be transferred to an international agency and not directly to the Palestinians. Additionally, Israel has desired to keep the issue of the refugees dormant as long as possible. The Palestinians, in contrast, have wished to assert their independence and take control over the pledged projects and funds. This has led to conflicts between UNRWA and PECDAR.[81]

The unexpected Israeli-Palestinian dialogue has caused UNRWA's bureaucracy to fight for its continued existence, in clear contradiction to its mandate. The agency has desperately tried to preserve a status quo that no longer exists, arguing that "the United Nations assistance should address the needs of the health and education sectors, through upgrading existing facilities and constructing new ones where needed."[82] The agency has overlooked the fact that for many years the PLO has been providing its own education, health, and welfare services.

CONCLUSION

Perhaps the most important lesson derived from UNRWA's experience concerns the issue of dependence. During its five decades of operation, UNRWA has made half of the refugee population dependent on its services for their livelihood. The agency has failed to encourage the growth of private industry and business, and its graduates now roam the region looking for jobs.

Yet, since donor institutions will not likely agree to transfer the pledged funds to the Palestinians, UNRWA will doubtless continue to play a meaningful role for the next five years. The Palestinian Council would, if asked, have probably preferred it otherwise.

However, if UNRWA is to avoid conflict of interest with its clients and to fulfill its mission, it must terminate its services and transfer its operation to the proper sovereign authorities. Israel has acknowledged that the time has come to transfer authority to the Palestinians. Now UNRWA should acknowledge the same.

NOTES

1. General Assembly Res. 302, IV (1992), authorized UNRWA's operation through 1996.

2. The validity of the two-year residency standard may well be questioned, given the migratory patterns of population in the Middle East. For documented massive migrations from Syria, Lebanon, and Jordan to Palestine before 1948, see Joan Peters, *From Time Immemorial* (New York: Harper & Row, 1984), p. 4.

3. Milton Viorst, *Reaching for the Olive Branch, UNRWA and Peace in the Middle East* (Washington, DC: Middle East Institute, 1989), p. 5.

4. UN Doc. A/49/13 (1994), *Report of the Commissioner-General of UNRWA* (July 1, 1993–June 30, 1994).

5. Over one million refugees live in Jordan, the largest refugee concentration in any Middle Eastern country. Jordan's population is normally about 3.5 million.

6. General Assembly Res. A/32/90 B endorsed UNRWA's humanitarian assistance to those persons. This was reiterated by the secretary-general's report (UN Doc. A/32/263). Later the General Assembly adopted Res. 32/90 E, equating "displaced people" with Palestinian refugees eligible for UNRWA assistance.

7. General Assembly Res. 302, IV, para. 5.

8. Edward H. Buehrig, *The UN and the Palestinian Refugees* (Bloomington: Indiana University Press, 1971), p. 11.

9. Benjamin Schiff, "Assisting the Palestinian Refugees," in Emanuel Adler and Beverly Crawford, eds., *Progress in Postwar International Relations* (New York: Columbia University Press, 1991), p. 363.

10. Commissioner-General Ilter Turkmen's statement of November 15, 1993, to the Special Political and Decolonization Committee.

11. The term was used by Buehrig, *The UN and the Palestinian Refugees*, p. 7.

12. In June 1982 Israel announced that it had discovered in Lebanon documents proving that UNRWA's school of Siblin was used by the PLO to train terrorists. *Ha'aretz* daily, June 27–30, 1982.

13. Schiff, "Assisting the Palestinian Refugees," p. 364.

14. The cost of the international posts for 1992–95 has been about $10,605 million per year. This is paid by the UN regular budget. The relief agency pays its international staff $6,108 million out of its budget.

15. General Assembly Res. 302, IV (December 8, 1949), said, "Continued assistance for the relief of the Palestinian refugees is necessary . . . to further conditions of peace and stability."

16. Ibid.

17. Original resolution establishing the Advisory Commission, General Assembly Res. 302, IV, para. 8.

18. Buehrig, *The UN and the Palestinian Refugees*, p. 53.

19. Schiff, "Assisting the Palestinian Refugees," p. 370.

20. Buehrig, *The UN and the Palestinian Refugees*, p. 53.

21. Interview with William Lee, UNRWA's liaison in New York, November 30, 1993.

22. Buehrig, *The UN and the Palestinian Refugees*, p. 58.

23. "[A] question does arise about the ability of the United Nations secretariat to handle this amount of business—and, hence, whether some of the problems in the field

are perhaps attributed to the shortcomings in New York." Alan James, "Peacekeeping in the Post–Cold War Era," *International Journal* 1 (spring 1995): 244.

24. David Forsythe, *United Nations Peacemaking* (Baltimore: Johns Hopkins University Press, 1972), p. 32.

25. Ibid., p. 2.

26. Viorst, *UNRWA and Peace in the Middle East*, p. 6.

27. Forsythe, *United Nations Peacemaking*, p. 73.

28. Ibid., p. 79.

29. Milton Viorst, *Reaching for the Olive Branch: UNRWA and Peace in the Middle East* (Washington, DC: Middle East Institute, 1989), p. 36.

30. Forsythe, *United Nations Peacemaking*, p. 79.

31. UN headquarters have been equated with "a corner grocery shop undertaking." Alan James, "Peacekeeping in the Post–Cold War Era," p. 245.

32. Buehrig, *The UN and the Palestinian Refugees*, p. 54.

33. Ibid., p. 57.

34. Bernadotte's letter to Foreign Minister Moshe Sharett, and Sharett's reply to Bernadotte. Quoted in Buehrig, *The UN and the Palestinian Refugees*, pp. 11–12.

35. The Arab states rejected economic development plans designed to resettle Palestinian refugees in the Sinai, insisting instead on their repatriation within Israel. *U.N. Yearbook*, 1950.

36. Viorst, *Reaching for the Olive Branch*, p. 114.

37. These provisions were included in the Michelmore-Komayi Agreement signed in 1967 between the government of Israel and the commissioner-general of UNRWA.

38. See lists of staff members arrested and detained in *Report of the Commissioner-General* (various).

39. Viorst, *Reaching for the Olive Branch*, p. 9.

40. Paul Cossali and Clive Robson, *Stateless in Gaza* (London: Zed Books, 1986), p. 28.

41. Secretary-general's report regarding Palestinian refugees in the Gaza Strip, October 11, 1978 (UN Doc. A/33/285); General Assembly Res. A/32/90.

42. Ibid.

43. Statement by Israel's Ambassador Uri M. Gordon to the UN, Special Political Committee, General Assembly 43d regular session, November 15, 1988.

44. Fred J. Khouri, *The Arab-Israeli Dilemma* (Syracuse, NY: Syracuse University Press, 1968), p. 179.

45. General Assembly Res. 31/318 (1975).

46. UN Doc. A/33/13, *Report of the Commissioner-General* (September 15, 1978), pp. 1–9.

47. Secretary-General's report regarding refugees in Gaza, October 11, 1988 (UN Doc. A/43/285).

48. General Assembly Res. A/43/903 (I); UN Doc. A/43/PV. 7 (December 2, 1988).

49. UN Doc. A/33/13, *Report of the Commissioner-General* (July 1, 1977), p. 2.

50. *UNRWA Update*, April 1994.

51. Among the reasons for the inaccuracy are "the listing of non-existing persons and widespread duplication of registration." *Demographic Report*, 1995 (Canada: York University, Center for Refugee Studies, 1995).

52. UN Doc. A/48/13, *Report of the Commissioner-General* (July 1, 1992).

53. Between July 1992 and June 1994 Israel arrested sixty-two UNRWA employees;

they were later released without being charged or tried. Six other employees were charged, tried, and sentenced, and thirty-eight were in detention in 1994. Five staff members were detained and later deported to Lebanon. Because UNRWA's schools were considered centers for anti-Israeli activities, Israel often ordered schools closed. UN Doc. A/49/13, *Report of the Commissioner-General* (1993–94).

54. Schiff, "Assisting the Palestinian Refugees," p. 391.

55. UN Docs. A/48/13 (1993) and A/49/13 (1994), *Reports of the Commissioner-General*, 1993–94.

56. Ibid.

57. Viorst, *Reaching for the Olive Branch*, p. 37.

58. Forsythe, *United Nations Peacemaking*, p. 89.

59. Khouri, *The Arab-Israeli Dilemma*, p. 141.

60. Ibid., p. 141.

61. Security Council Res. 237 of June 14, 1967, and General Assembly Res. 2252 (ES-V).

62. UN Doc. A/SPC/121.

63. UN Doc. A/33/285, *Report of the Secretary-General* (October 11, 1978).

64. UN Doc. S/19443 (January 21, 1988).

65. UN Doc. A/43/PV.71 (December 9, 1988).

66. Viorst, *Reaching for the Olive Branch*. p. 9.

67. Ibid., p. 10.

68. Marrack Goulding's report submitted to the Security Council by the secretary-general, January 21, 1988 (UN Doc. S/19442), p. 7.

69. UN Doc. A/47/13, *Report of the Commissioner-General* (July 1, 1991 June 30, 1992), p. 2.

70. Viorst, *Reaching for the Olive Branch*, p. 85.

71. Buehrig, *The UN and the Palestinian Refugees*, pp. 67–68.

72. Statement by Ambassador Uri Gordon, p. 9.

73. *UN Task Force Report on UNRWA*, September 1993, p. 3.

74. "UNRWA and the Transitional Period: A Five-Year Perspective on the Role of the Agency," *UNRWA Horizon Report*, Vienna, January 31, 1995.

75. Ibid., p. 3.

76. *Commissioner-General's Report to the General Assembly Fourth Committee*, November 15, 1993.

77. Viorst, *Reaching for the Olive Branch*, p. 83.

78. DOP, Article 4, no. 2.

79. Ibid., Article 7, no. 4.

80. Chairman of the Advisory Committee to the Commissioner-General: "In order to ensure the further progress of the peace process, it is imperative that a significant improvement in the social and welfare services and the daily life of the Palestinians be achieved. . . . UNRWA had unique competence in these fields . . . [and] it is therefore essential to build a firm financial base for the Agency." UN Doc. A/48/13 (October 6, 1993).

81. For example, in 1995 the World Bank had to cancel a sewage project in a refugee camp in Gaza because of bickering between the two agencies. Interview with World Bank officials, Jerusalem, June 1995.

82. UN Doc. A/48/13 (October 6, 1993).

6

The Case of Rwanda and Burundi: Two Perspectives

The political, economic, and logistical problems of mounting humanitarian assistance programs in underdeveloped areas of the world that are torn asunder by ethnic conflicts are dramatically demonstrated in the recent interventions in Rwanda. The further difficulties of providing assistance that can assure long-term remedial effects were demonstrated in the following two case studies.

RWANDA AND BURUNDI: A FUTURE PATH FOR RECONCILIATION IN CENTRAL AFRICA

Kenneth F. Hackett

Rwanda is no longer a front-page story in the print media or on the nightly television news. The grisly images of dead and dismembered bodies and of human suffering of unimaginable dimensions have apparently begun to recede from our consciousness. Under the seemingly placid surface, the ethnic conflicts that have fractured the societies of Rwanda and Burundi continue to teeter on the edge of eruption. Perhaps, as events are removed from the glare of the limelight, one can reflect upon their ramifications with greater objectivity.

The author has been visiting Rwanda and Burundi off and on for twenty years. These years have witnessed the slow economic growth, the onset of HIV/AIDS, the coups, the massacres, and also the very positive steps toward democracy taking hold in Burundi. Then in late 1993 a monstrous conflagration flared up and began—seemingly unstoppably—to ravage both countries. A brief review of the intertwined histories of these developments in both countries is prerequisite to formulating a more promising approach to dealing with these problems.

HISTORICAL BACKGROUND

According to one school of thought, the problems in Central Africa may be traced to the Berlin Conference of 1884, when most of Africa was carved up by European colonial powers. Proponents of this view contend that the arbitrary determination of borders imposed by the Europeans left permanent scars in the social psyche of the inhabitants of the Ruanda-Urundi area, as it was then called.

Another school of thought reaches farther back in history for an explanation of the recent upheavals. Advocates of this view take as the starting point of analysis the migration of a group of Hametic people into the lakes region of Central Africa in the sixteenth century. Over the next one hundred years or so, this Hametic group absorbed the local language and developed a monarchical form of government. Society in Burundi, and to a similar extent in Rwanda, became stratified into classes: A group called the Ganwa represented the monarchy and the politicians; farther down the social strata were the Tutsi, who were cattle herders; the Hutu, who were the cultivators; and the Twa, who were the hunters, potters, and entertainers.

However, whatever occurred in the sixteenth and seventeenth centuries, there was clearly a defining period during the 1920s and 1930s. It was at this time that the Belgians saw fit to classify all the peoples in Burundi into three distinct races: the Ganwa-Tutsi, the Hutu, and the Twa. Furthermore, in 1934 the Belgians undertook a census in Burundi, for purposes of which they classified people into groups by the number of cows they owned: If a person had more than ten cows, he was a Tutsi. Thus, a richer Hutu became Tutsi; a poorer Tutsi became Hutu. Caterine Watson, a consultant for the U.S. Committee for Refugees, in a 1993 study of the Burundi situation states: "At this point in time 'Hutuness' became even more associated with poverty and powerlessness. . . . In Rwanda, there were no Ganwa, and Hutu regarded the monarchy, more centralized and demanding than Burundi's rather lax kingship, as a purer tool of Tutsi rule."[1]

There seems to be some debate in the literature as to whether any genetic distinction exists between Tutsi and Hutu. Even if genetic, racial, or ethnic differences existed, at this point they are blurred into class distinctions. As late as 1993 a Hutu could still buy an identity card that would change his or her identity to Tutsi.

Those who present the immediate crisis—which has meant the murders of close to 500,000 in Rwanda and another 200,000 in Burundi from 1993 through 1994—as simply an ethnic clash between Hutu and Tutsi are incomplete in their analysis. There is nothing simple about what happened in Rwanda and Burundi during that twelve-month period. The catastrophe that engulfed these countries arose out of a long history of tension fueled by class struggle, aggravated, however unintentionally, by acts of colonial convenience, and fermented by the desire of one class or group to hold onto power out of an insidious fear that, without power and control of the government, that group or class would be annihilated by another group or class. The more proximate causes arise out of the events of the last three decades.

THE LAST THREE DECADES

In 1959 independence came to Rwanda after a violent uprising of the Hutu against the Tutsi. Some contend that the uprising was abetted by the Belgians. In any event the monarchy was overthrown, thousands of Tutsi were slaughtered, and tens of thousands fled to Uganda, Burundi, Tanzania, and Zaire.

There was no violent uprising in Burundi that year, but the Ganwa-Tutsi monarchy split into two groups. One was led by Prince Rwagasore bearing the title "President" of the UPRONA Party. The opposition Christian Democratic Party was dominated by another Tutsi faction.

The UPRONA party controlled things at independence. The prince effectively balanced the Hutu and Tutsi tensions, even relinquishing his position in the party and installing a Hutu as the party president. However, in 1961, the prince, who was seen as a moderate, was assassinated and tensions in Burundi between Hutu and Tutsi soon began to surface. A period of violence and vying for power ensued in Burundi. In 1966 President Micombero, a southern Tutsi and army captain from Bururi, took over power. Nevertheless, tension persisted between northern and southern Tutsi, as well as between Hutu and Tutsi. Periodically throughout the period of the 1960s there were localized massacres of Tutsi and Hutu.

In May 1972 things came to a head: Burundi experienced the infamous "Events." Identifying the origins of the Events depends largely upon whether one is listening to a Hutu or a Tutsi. Most observers, including Catholic Relief Services (CRS) workers who were in Burundi at the time, estimate that over fifty thousand people were slaughtered in the first week. Some claim that the Tutsi planned to exterminate the "Hutu Peril." Others claim that everything was sparked by an infiltration into the southern part of the country by Hutu refugees living in Tanzania. It was alleged, in a report published in the London *Daily Telegraph*, that the Hutu had distributed pamphlets exhorting their people to "kill every man, woman and child. Do not take prisoners. Kill every Tutsi." However, this infiltration and slaughter lasted but a few days as the Hutu infiltrators were ill-equipped and not very well organized.

Radio Burundi incited a retaliatory spirit among the Tutsi: Reports are that the radio called upon the citizenry to "hunt down the enemy" and to "be united . . . to exterminate for once and for all the enemy."

Tutsi set about massacring Hutu with wanton abandon. The first victims were Hutu with any education. The killing continued for a month at a fever pitch.

Tens of thousands of Hutu fled the country to Rwanda; hundreds of thousands were slaughtered. By 1973 only scant vestiges of a Hutu educated class were visible in Burundi.

The economy deteriorated, and Burundi remained mired in a state of virtually complete paralysis until 1976, when President Micombero was overthrown in a bloodless coup. His deputy chief of staff, Colonel Jean-Baptiste Bagaza, took over the presidency. Bagaza remained in power from 1976 until 1987 without major ethnic violence. However, like many of his counterparts in other African nations at the time, he managed the economy in statist fashion. He placed Tutsi back into the economy in force, expropriating the businesses of Greek, French, and Belgian businesspeople. He nationalized and often closed church schools. He expelled missionaries, portraying them as pro-Hutu because most of their activities were carried on in rural areas. After many such dislocations of the social and economic fabric of the country, Bagaza was deposed by a group of army officers in a bloodless coup in September 1987.

Major Pierre Buyoya was next installed as president in Burundi. Generally, his administration was both more benign and more enlightened than those of his predecessors. However, local Tutsi government officials could not lay claim to the same reputation. In 1988 a violent massacre took place in an area close to the Rwandan border in which an estimated twenty thousand Hutu and Tutsi were murdered. Tens of thousands of Hutu again fled to Rwanda and Tanzania. Local skirmishes, with consequent reprisals, punctuated the period from 1987 until 1992.

On June 1, 1993, Burundi held what was considered to be a classic African democratic election. Power passed from UPRONA's president, Major Pierre Buyoya, to FRODEBU, a Hutu-dominated party headed by Melchior Ndadaye. There was a 97 percent voter turnout. Election monitors, provided by the National Democratic Institute and financed by the United States Agency for International Development (USAID), filled every hotel room for weeks. To all, including the author working in Nairobi at the time, a new day seemed to have dawned.

But that new day was short-lived. The last Event on the Burundi side of the border was a sad sequel to the promising election of June 1993. In October of that year, a small group of Tutsi military officers, discontent with what they saw as the overly rapid and all too pervasive appointment of Hutu officials to key posts within the new government, shot and killed the new president and many of his close associates. This unleashed another period of violence, massacre, and reprisal in Burundi, in which over 200,000 people were killed.

In fall 1994 a government was formed in Burundi. Like its immediate predecessor, it set about yet again to pursue the goal of ethnic balance.

It would only needlessly belabor the issue to go into the same amount of detail concerning the history of more recent events in Rwanda. The 1990 invasion of the Rwanda Patriotic Front (RPF), the Tutsi refugee–dominated party and fighters that had been based in Uganda, has been widely reported. Equally well publicized has been the second invasion of the RPF in February 1993, and the impact that had on bringing the former Rwandan government to the Arusha peace talks. Suffice it to say that the magnitude of the human losses and dislocations resulting from these developments has been staggering: some 1.5 million refugees outside the country; over three million people displaced within the country; and up to half a million killed—all this in a year's time, following the downing of the plane carrying the president of Rwanda and the president of Burundi.

THE SEARCH FOR NEW SOLUTIONS

Rwanda and Burundi present, in starkest form, an insidious pattern of violence and power struggle—a struggle that has played itself out in massacre and genocide; a struggle that has demonstrable ethnic, social, class, and power elements. This conflict dominates the history of both countries. Every child, be he Hutu or Tutsi, whether in Rwanda or in Burundi, can readily recite a catalog of past atrocities. This is the challenge with which the relief agencies (including the one with which the author is affiliated, CRS, a major relief and development agency operating in Rwanda and Burundi) are wrestling. How can such a long-entrenched pattern of violence be brought to an end? How do the people in Rwanda and Burundi live together and heal their wounds? Who can lead this healing process? How can their efforts be assisted? In the author's view, it is imperative to address these issues before effective consideration can be given to how these countries can rebuild their economies and refashion their nations.

No doubt, when scholars and historians have researched the recent genocide in Rwanda, they will document a long history of events fed by a conscious and well-planned program to cultivate ethnic hatred. They may well be able to document the use of governmental resources to support this campaign of terror. At the very least, they may be able to show that the Rwandan governmental apparatus, which U.S. tax dollars supported in its economic development effort and which the UN attempted to coax into taking steps toward a more pluralistic and democratic society, was used as an instrument for spreading the violence. It seems safe to predict that the world development community will be seen to have failed to halt—in any effective way—a manifest pattern of hatred and violence.

The author's thesis is that unless and until Rwanda and Burundi can reconcile their peoples—unless and until they can diminish the mutual fears that have been created and nurtured over decades—they will not be able to establish any cognizable form of democratic society. It should be noted, however, that recent reports from Rwanda indicate that the Tutsi-led government has taken the position that "once the organizers of the genocide have been convicted and executed, it will be easier to show leniency for those who followed their orders."[2] With some two thousand prisoners in the category of primary organizers of the massacres and some eighty five thousand prisoners in the category of lesser war criminals, the policy followed currently in Rwanda seems one not of reconciliation but of settling scores.

A recent book by the Center for Strategic and International Studies[3] appears to place some of the onus for situations such as those in Rwanda and Burundi upon the diplomatic community. The editors contend, as have many others, that many of the armed conflicts presently afflicting the world—for example, the Bosnian crisis, the conflict in southern Sudan, the continuing Cambodian problems, and the Central Africa conflagration—do not spring from the familiar clash of Cold War ideologies, but from different roots. At a recent luncheon Douglas Johnston, one of the editors, articulated the premise of the book by stating: "What is required is not a shrewd understanding of the interests of both parties, which can be explained to diplomats by other Ivy League trained diplomats from the countries in conflict, but rather an understanding of the *emotional* stakes. These are best understood through a deeper appreciation of the history, the cultures, the issues of justice, social divisions and perceived injustices."[4]

The crux of this view is that it is often individuals outside the traditional domain of diplomacy—individuals such as religious or spiritual leaders—who not only can best apprehend and explain the nature of the conflict but also, and perhaps more importantly, can and have played a pivotal role in mediating similar conflicts in analogous situations. A corollary proposition posits that conflicts of the future will tend to be increasingly less amenable to traditional diplomatic compromise because they will likely be more highly charged by ethnic, religious, and nationalistic motives than the conflicts of the past, which centered principally upon considerations of power politics and tangible material interests.

The world of the author's agency, CRS, is one deeply intertwined with conflicts of an ethnic, national, or religious nature. On the weekend of September 17–18, 1994, the author and three CRS deputies clutched cellular phones tightly, standing prepared for possible evacuations of CRS staff from Sarajevo, Huambo, Bujumbura, Kigali, Monrovia, and Port au Prince. Never, in two decades of experience with CRS, had there been such a wide array of conflictive situations, all ready to explode. Happily, CRS was evacuated from only one locale— Huambo, Angola—and has since returned. But for CRS this array of conflictive situations has added a completely new dimension to its work. The agency now sees that the traditional working paradigm of moving assistance through a continuum from *relief* to *rehabilitation* to *development*, as has been attempted in Rwanda and in Burundi so many times in the past, is patently inadequate. Stated otherwise, CRS responded to multiple crises in Rwanda and Burundi over the thirty years of its history there, but it continually failed to add to its efforts a process of reconciliation: Lip service was given to reconciliation, but it was never made an integral part of CRS's response. Now, however, the realization has dawned that, unless *reconciliation* is consciously integrated into all aspects of the work, nothing lasting will be accomplished.

Accompanying this realization, moreover, must be the frank acknowledgment that, as external agents, neither CRS nor USAID nor the World Bank nor various UN agencies can bring about reconciliation. Reconciliation is a very personal process. Only certain people have the moral authority legitimately to issue a call for reconciliation. Reconciliation, as Robert Schreiter identifies it in his study of processes in many Latin American and other countries, "involves a fundamental repair to human lives, especially the lives of those who have suffered."[5]

President Bizimungu of Rwanda told the author in early September 1994 that the call for reconciliation had to come from the Church. But the bishops of the Catholic Church and most other church leaders cannot yet, as institutional representatives, issue that call because, for the most part, church leaders, Catholic and Protestant, were so close to the problem that they were traumatized and institutionally paralyzed by it.

As an active external assistance actor, CRS is undertaking a deep process of self-examination and reflection. At the very least it is essential to look hard at the manner in which CRS undertakes its relief activities to ensure that it is not creating blockages to reconciliation. The agency now accepts that the injustice and trauma caused by the pattern of violence is not healed by simply putting the structures of government efficiently back into the same molds they occupied before the conflict. It is vitally important to engage and support the actions of a range of people who heretofore may not have been factored into the process of conflict resolution.

More particularly, as regards Rwanda, CRS is convinced that, along with continuing provision of food assistance to the displaced, it must begin to deal with the more vexing issues of how communities can live together and next to each other: There cannot be blind reinforcement of the status quo. Clearly, problems of land, fear of reprisals, and personal hatred are not eliminated by a few human rights monitors or by any of the immediate measures proposed as short-term package solutions. Resolving such issues will take years and patience and a variety of large and small efforts at all levels.

Recently a group of nine African Catholic bishops, all of whom were somehow engaged in conflict resolution, came together at Duquesne University to reflect on the issues of reconciliation and peace. They came from Angola, Benin, Burundi, Liberia, Mozambique, Nigeria, South Africa, and Zimbabwe. They discussed their individual experiences, their hopes, and their methods of solving problems. It is through such nontraditional measures and searches that the leaders of future reconciliation processes will emerge.

CONCLUSION

The recent turmoil in Rwanda and Burundi, inter alia, compels the conclusion that Marshall Plan–type packages for the nations of Central Africa, or the Bosnias, Cambodias, Haitis, or any other of the seemingly intractable conflicts of our day, will prove unavailing. The state-based diplomatic or foreign aid solutions applied in the past are simply not going to work. A new diplomatic paradigm for peace must be sought, just as new paradigms for humanitarian and economic assistance are sought during and after situations of ethnic and social conflict.

Diplomats and foreign assistance bureaucrats must be taught to look outside the halls of the departments of foreign affairs or the national banks for solutions to problems that carry such emotional baggage. For it is not in the language of statecraft or economic models, nor in the transplanted models of Jeffersonian democracy, that lasting solutions will be found. Such lasting solutions may well be found in concepts and techniques that flow from dialogue with mullahs, with bishops, or with individuals who live deeply in the passion and the emotion that often fuel the problems. If the search is diligent, the right individuals will surface, and if good sense prevails, they can be helped to reach for peace.

TO SAVE ONE LIFE IS TO SAVE THE WORLD: THE ISRAELI OPERATION IN RWANDA

Michael Wiener with Nitza Nachmias

THE INTERNATIONAL AID CONTEXT

When the international community embarked on its emergency assistance operation in Rwanda, it had already accumulated a half century of experience in humanitarian assistance. Nevertheless, the relief effort in Rwanda suffered from many of the same misconceptions and shortcomings that had marred earlier relief efforts.

First, the Rwanda operation incorporated three overly ambitious and, in some respects, conflicting, functions: (1) a political function, to be carried out by the United Nations Observer Mission Uganda-Rwanda (UNOMUR), created by the Security Council with the objective of facilitating implementation of the Arusha peace agreement between the Rwanda government and the Rwanda Patriotic Front (RPF)[6]; (2) a strategic function, to be carried out by the United Nations Assistance Mission for Rwanda (UNAMIR),[7] consisting of a military force of a few thousand personnel charged with the duty of containing the escalating violence and imposing a ceasefire; and (3) a humanitarian function, also to be carried out by UNAMIR, of providing assistance to about one million sick, hungry, and defenseless refugees. In the execution of these three functions the UN system was hobbled by duplication, conflicting objectives, and lack of coordination and administrative support. This stands in sharp contrast to the Israeli operation of a field hospital for Rwandan refugees in the Zaire refugee camp. The Israelis sought and received no institutional UN support; they relied solely on their own resources. In carrying out their humanitarian mission the Israelis established regular contacts with the other missions in the field and participated in the creation of a network of administrative support among the various missions operating in Goma.

Second, at the outset the UN missions either failed to appreciate or ignored the deeply rooted and intense rivalry, if not hatred, between the two major ethnic groups in Rwanda. The secretary-general acted on the optimistic assumption that the UN could induce these bitter rivals to forge a democratic, pluralistic, and tolerant political environment in Rwanda.

Third, at the request of the secretary-general the Security Council appealed to the member states to provide assistance to Rwanda; however, it failed to equip the dispatched teams with the bureaucratic and logistical infrastructure necessary to execute such a large-scale and complex operation. The participants received no guidelines, no operational procedures, no specific objectives, no bureaucratic support mechanisms, no security arrangements, no accountability system, no chain of command, no authoritative leadership, and no adequate resources. Consequently, each mission had to fend for itself, take care of its own security, create its own agenda, follow its own objectives, and, in a word, decide who got what, when, and how. These inadequacies are reflected in the poignant plea for help contained in a letter from Dr. C. Bourgeois, medical coordinator of UNHCR, to the head of the Israeli mission, saying: "I would be grateful if you could advise me whether it might be possible to get some of the above material (tents, stretchers, perfusion holders, hand cleaning tanks, field tables and chairs, resuscitators (ambu[latory] pediatric and adult) from your present stock?"[8] Manifestly, the UNHCR was unprepared to address such large-scale human tragedy.

The Israeli mission airlifted all its medical supplies and other necessities, such as food and water, from Israel. It also provided for its own security using Israel Defense Forces personnel and weapons. The mission provided for its resupply, arranging flights on the basis of bilateral agreements negotiated with the Zaire government. Further, the Israeli mission made all operative decisions, such as determining the choice of location of the hospital, the scope and character of its services, the client population, and the timetable for offering its services. The UNHCR did not have a supportive infrastructure in place on which either the Israeli, or, for that matter, any other relief mission, could rely. Neither the UNHCR nor the Security Council had provided for the requisite legal or diplomatic clearances to facilitate the operation of the relief effort on Zaire territory.

THE UN AND THE INTERVENTION IN RWANDA

The evident lack of administrative leadership bespoke a structural flaw in the UN's ability to mobilize effectively so as to meet emergency requirements for humanitarian aid: It was never sufficiently anticipated that the UN headquarters or its agencies might be called upon to carry out such vast and complex humanitarian operations in combat zones and across national boundaries. In the case of Rwanda, most of the writing was on the wall long before the firestorm that erupted in April 1994, since various UN missions had been on the ground for some time but had failed to appreciate the dimensions of the problem of chronic interethnic fighting.

Fighting in Rwanda did not begin when a plane carrying President Juvenal Habyarimana (Rwanda) and President Cyprien Ntaryamira (Burundi) was shot down on April 6, 1994. Fighting actually began in 1993, long before the world became aware of the enormity of the developing human tragedy. On February 24, 1993, the cruel civil war having erupted, the UN secretary-general dispatched to Rwanda a "good will mission." Negotiations between the OAU and the governments of Tanzania, Uganda, and Rwanda took place in March of that year; these led to a very short-lived ceasefire. On June 22, 1993, the Security Council authorized the establishment of UNOMUR, while the OAU expanded its Neutral Military Observer Group (NMOG) to Rwanda. By September 1993 UNOMUR included eighty-one military observers, ten international staff, and six local support staff.

Several weeks later came UNOMUR's report, leading to the establishment of UNAMIR, which would contribute to the establishment and maintenance of a climate conducive to the secure installation and subsequent operation of the transitional government in Rwanda. The tasks of UNAMIR were to include monitoring the ceasefire, establishing demilitarized zones, demobilizing the militia, providing security for democratic elections, assisting in mine clearing, and investigating and reporting noncompliance with the peace agreement. The fact that the small and unqualified UN force could not adequately perform these complex and difficult duties was soon revealed.

When UNAMIR was established initially on October 5, 1993, planners at UN headquarters optimistically envisioned the following phased schedule for its work: (1) a first phase providing for installation of a transitional government; (2) a second phase of ninety days, involving 2,548 military personnel, during which there would be disengagement of the parties, demobilization, and integration of the armed forces and the gendarmerie; (3) a third phase of nine months, involving 1,240 military personnel, during which demilitarized zones were to be established and secured, Kigali (the capital) made safe, and the disengagement, demobilization and integration of all indigenous armed forces brought to a conclusion; and (4) a fourth phase of four months, involving 930 military personnel, during which the transition of Rwanda to a democracy would take place.

The UN had two missions in Rwanda: UNOMUR, with headquarters in Kabale, Uganda, and UNAMIR, a military force headed by Brigadier-General Romeo A. Dallaire (Canada), in Kigali.[9] The secretary-general announced to the Security Council on December 15, 1993, that "UNOMUR had been a factor of stability in the area and that it was playing a useful role as a confidence-building mechanism."[10] Subsequently, on December 20, the Security Council extended UNOMUR's mandate by six months.[11] Meanwhile, NMOG was integrated into UNAMIR, and the first Belgian battalion arrived in Kigali. The secretary-general appointed Jacques-Roger Booh-Booh of Cameroon as his special representative to Rwanda, and so far as the UN headquarters was concerned, all seemed to be going well.

In his report of December 30, 1993, to the Security Council, the secretary-general announced that most tasks of the first phase (pertaining to installation of a provisional government) had been successfully accomplished. He underlined the fact that the parties "had continued to show good will and cooperation in their contacts with each other and with the United Nations."[12] No cognizance whatever was taken of the virulent, open animosity and extreme expressions of ethnic hatred reported by field personnel.

On January 5, 1994, Major-General Juvenal Habyarimana was sworn in as president of Rwanda for a transitional period. However, the requirements of the Arusha peace agreement for the establishment of a transitional government and a transitional National Assembly could not be fulfilled because of ethnic conflict. This bad omen was entirely ignored by UN headquarters, whose policies appeared to be based upon misperceptions and wishful thinking.

In point of fact the UN should have been aware by April 1993, if not earlier, that the situation in Rwanda was unraveling. At that time the president of Rwanda had informed the UN that about one million people, totaling about 13 percent of the population, had already been displaced, and he had requested urgent international assistance to meet their basic needs.[13] Soon the number of refugees had increased threefold, and an appeal was made for an assistance program of $78 million. By the end of 1993, while the secretary-general was talking about the "good will" of the fighting parties, over thirty refugee camps had been created, camps whose inhabitants were suffering from widespread diseases and starvation. Consequently, it became necessary for an additional UN agency to begin operating in Rwanda: the DHA, which prepared an emergency relief program focusing on food, health, water, sanitation, and shelter for the refugees. Notwithstanding continuing deterioration of the situation in Rwanda, the secretary-general reported to the Security Council that he was "encouraged by the fact that, in spite of increasing tensions, the parties had maintained the process of dialogue."[14] Just one day before the event that served as the catalyst for the carnage and human misery that would engulf Rwanda, namely, the downing of the airplane carrying the presidents of Rwanda and Burundi, the mandate of UNAMIR was again extended.[15] The Security Council expressed its concern that the transitional democratic institutions had not yet been established, but it otherwise refrained from commenting on the situation in writing.

Following the death of the two presidents, widespread ethnic massacres erupted all over Rwanda. Among the victims were Prime Minister Agathe Uwilingiyimana and ten Belgian members of UNAMIR. In reaction the Belgian government ordered the withdrawal of its forces, and UNAMIR abandoned its four-phase plan, focusing instead on negotiating a truce (failed), reaching a ceasefire (failed), rescuing refugees (failed), providing humanitarian assistance (hardly fulfilled), and providing protection to displaced persons under UNAMIR shelter. Ironically, on April 19 UNAMIR headquarters was directly hit. On 20 April the secretary-general announced to the Security Council that "UNAMIR personnel cannot be left at risk indefinitely when there is no possibility of their performing the tasks for which they were dispatched."[16] UNAMIR was already down to 1,515 from a total of 2,165 personnel when the number of military observers was reduced to 190 from 321.[17] The secretary-general presented to the Security Council three alternatives: a massive build-up of UNAMIR to enable it to enforce a ceasefire; a reduction of the force to about 270, just to perform mediation tasks; or a complete withdrawal of UNAMIR.

On April 21 the Security Council adopted the second option and reduced UNAMIR to the number of personnel suggested by the secretary-general.[18] For all practical purposes this ended the UN's peacekeeping mission in Rwanda and shifted the effort to the humanitarian level. Within days a newly created organization, the United Nations Rwanda Emergency Office (UNREO), was established. It was given an impressive title but little capacity to function. Its duties were limited to cross-border humanitarian assistance from Uganda, Burundi, and Zaire.

The humanitarian scene soon included a plethora of organizations attempting to provide assistance—the WFP, the UN interagency Advance Humanitarian Team (AHT), the Department of Humanitarian Affairs, the UNDP, the UNHCR, UNICEF, the WHO, and various NGOs.[19] However, the scale of the tragedy and the number of refugees crossing the borders exceeded their aggregate capabilities, and especially those of the UNHCR. On April 30 the Security Council called upon the member states to assist the UNHCR and the other relief agencies in meeting the urgent needs of the refugees in the bordering states.[20] In May UNAMIR, UNREO, and the NGOs operating in the field agreed to a division of labor and tried to establish a set of operating principles. These included provisions for security of the relief workers; joint identification of distribution sites by UN agencies; clear identification of representatives of the authorities; accepted procedures for reporting to the respective UN agencies on all the humanitarian operations; and adherence to the principle that aid was to be provided according to need, regardless of political affiliation, ethnic group, or race.[21]

Upon the recommendation of the secretary-general, the Security Council authorized the expansion of UNAMIR to 5,500 troops and imposed an arms embargo on Rwanda.[22] The other agency, UNOMUR, was terminated, its function having become manifestly irrelevant to the conflict. Meanwhile, UNAMIR was charged with securing the strategic objectives and, in addition, was asked to provide humanitarian assistance to refugees in Rwanda, Zaire, and other neighboring countries.[23]

A ceasefire was arranged in July 1994, and a broad-based government controlled by the victorious Tutsi was formed on July 19. However, the UN was confronted with a new problem of daunting proportions: providing relief and security for many thousands of Hutu refugees gathered in camps in Zaire. This massive influx presented logistics, security, and relief problems. By the end of 1994, the secretary-general had managed to mobilize the international community to raise almost $500 million for the Rwanda operation. It was in response to the pleas of assistance from the international community that the Israeli government made available the field hospital that is the subject of the following case study.

THE ISRAELI FIELD HOSPITAL IN GOMA: A CASE STUDY

During the spring of 1994 television brought graphic accounts of massacres in Rwanda into living rooms around the world on almost a daily basis. The details were harrowing, the pictures nightmarish: children, women, and men hacked to pieces by machetes or cut down by bullets in an orgy of ethnic violence between Hutu and Tutsi. As the carnage spread, the world was stunned to learn that over one million people had been killed and that many thousands had fled to refugee camps in neighboring countries. The revelations spurred a concerted effort by the UN and other relief organizations to aid the refugees. France began dispatching troops to Rwanda and neighboring Zaire. The killing continued unabated, however, even as some emergency food relief and medical staff began to arrive at the refugee camps.

In mid-July the Tutsi seized power in Rwanda. Almost immediately hordes of Hutu, fearing revenge for their massacre of Tutsi, became refugees and fled to the town of Goma in Zaire. Goma, lying along the banks of Lake Kivu some sixty miles from Kigali at the Rwanda-Zaire border, was originally a city of some 150,000 people; within weeks the city was engulfed by the arrival of more than 1,200,000 refugees. As a consequence the city's infrastructure collapsed. The refugees suffered from severe shortages of food and drinking water and a lack of sanitation and medical supplies. Cholera broke out and soon reached epidemic proportions, claiming the lives of thousands daily. The plight of the refugees, made particularly vivid by media reports and pictures of cholera victims, engendered a wave of compassion that galvanized governments and relief organizations to mount a rescue effort.

Following an appeal to member states by the UN secretary-general, the Israeli minister of the environment, Yossi Sarid, took the initiative and recommended to Prime Minister Yitzhak Rabin that Israel take part in the international aid effort. On July 15, a Friday evening, the head of the IDF Medical Corps received a direct order from the prime minister to prepare a contingency medical assistance plan for the refugees in Goma. Minister Sarid offered to head the overall mission, and Brigadier General Dr. Michael Wiener, one of the coauthors and then IDF Surgeon General (SG), was asked to make the necessary arrangements and to head the medical team. An initial planning meeting was set for Saturday morning at IDF headquarters.

Preparations for the operation actually began on Friday evening, when the order was received. Dr. Wiener began by inviting his deputy and several other assistants to join him at the planning session. He also made calls to high-ranking military medical staff asking them to prepare draft plans for the operation for the Saturday meeting. The proposal had to include a personnel chart; lists of physicians and medical staff needed; and estimates of medical supplies requirements and logistical requirements, such as transportation, power supply, fuel, and the like. It was also necessary to compile a list of prospective volunteers, including commanding field officers, particularly military physicians with extensive experience in field hospitals. By Saturday morning a draft proposal was ready for review.

The Saturday meeting, which was held at the IDF headquarters, was attended by Minister Sarid and representatives from all units mentioned in the draft proposal, which, when presented, provoked animated discussion, including controversy with respect to the size of the mission, the nature and scope of its security arrangements, its liaison with the UN and other international organizations, and its communications and press personnel. Invaluable insights were provided by veterans of Israel's assistance program to Zaire, who had maintained consistent contacts with officials of Zaire and were familiar with the territory.

The draft proposal was approved at the Saturday meeting, although additional fine tuning and special attention to details were deemed necessary. Assignments were distributed among the officers attending the meeting. They were asked to continue fleshing out the plan and to add details to the overall concept. It was decided that the final plan would be ready the next day.

The general plan of operation for a field hospital was based on the following principles:

1. the hospital would serve as the major medical unit and the headquarters for all the medical units and teams operating in the field;

2. hospital teams would be available to reach out and support the field teams (i.e., operate outpatient day clinics) while the hospital served as the home base; and

3. the mission would draw on the experience and expertise of other international organizations inasmuch as Israel had very limited experience in operating a hospital in a refugee environment. The Israeli team could, however, contribute to the other agencies its extensive experience and expertise in operating mobile medical field teams.[24]

The first step in preparing the mission for departure was to divide the staff into different task forces, each specializing in a particular regimen. The second step was to organize the necessary medical supplies and equipment, which were collected from various military depots. Medical supplies and equipment for children, however, had to be purchased ad hoc. A special task force was put in charge of assembling tents, electric generators, food, water, and similar necessities. Since the plan called for self-sufficiency in transportation, provisions were made to airlift two trucks, one jeep, one command car, a radio station, and a small unit of infantry for security.

A retired Israeli military officer, Colonel Gonen, who lived and worked in Kinshasa, was contacted. He was asked to provide essential information and help in establishing contacts with government officials in Zaire. Through his efforts the mission members were granted permission to work as a military group, to wear IDF uniforms, and to carry their personal weapon systems. Colonel Gonen agreed to take a leave of absence from his work in Kinshasa to join the mission in Goma.

The first task was to prepare treatment protocols for the rampant outbreak of cholera, which was deemed to be the most urgent medical need. Second, an immunization program and antibacterial regime for mission personnel was prepared. On Saturday night another meeting was held to compile reports and review the final preparations. Also that evening, the volunteers were vaccinated and received other immunization injections and were issued their personal equipment. All other materials were sent to the airforce base, where eight C-130 military transport planes were ready to take off for Zaire at 21:00 hours on Sunday; estimated arrival time would be nine hours later, on Monday morning. The group got no more than two to three hours' sleep on Saturday night, because the teams continued to work to complete all the necessary arrangements.

Sunday morning about ninety volunteers gathered for a penultimate briefing; boarding began at noon, and by 18:00 hours the head of IDF operations and the commander of the airforce held a final briefing. A news conference was held, also, to outline the plan of operation and to answer questions. Most often asked was, Could the mission make a difference? Wasn't the aid just a drop in the ocean? Dr. Wiener's response was to quote the Sages: "To save the life of one person is to save the whole world."

On Sunday at 21:00 hours, less than thirty-six hours after the mission team had first been recruited by the SG, the first of eight C-130 airplanes took off. He and Minister Sarid were aboard the first airplane, and the staff was dispersed among the other airplanes, which took off an hour apart. The planes were loaded with pharmaceutical supplies, but space was insufficient to load all other supplies. Clearly, another sortie would be necessary within a few days. Finally, however, the mission was on its way, ready to cope with problems that might arise and to deal with whatever difficulties it might encounter. The group could not foresee the conditions it would meet in Goma, but when it landed in Zaire at 05:00 hours on Monday, it was ready for all eventualities.

While the airplanes were being unloaded, an official welcoming committee arrived: the district governor, the mayor of Goma, and a colonel who was the military commander in Goma. Colonel Gonen, the retired Israeli airforce officer working for the Zaire airline, accompanied the group. After a short but warm welcome, the group was briefed on the situation. About 1.2 million refugees were living in the city and in three camps around it. The only government hospital was overcrowded and could not cope with the number of local and refugee patients. Cholera was spreading and killing people by the thousands. The epidemic had apparently spread from Rwanda. The hosts, in turn, were briefed on the mission's capabilities. All agreed that the prerequisite task was to locate a proper site for the hospital, close to Goma. It was contemplated that the hospital would treat patients from the city as well as from the refugee camps, alleviating the pressure on the overburdened local medical facilities.

The staff's initial sortie was to review the medical situation in the Mogunga refugee camp. The sights shocked even experienced military physicians. There were piles and piles of corpses of all ages rolled in blankets or straw mats along the roads. One could not avoid the appalling sight of the dead and the dying everywhere. The living were moving endlessly to and from Lake Kivu to fetch water, which, the mission was informed, was contaminated with cholera. The town itself looked as if it had been stricken by locusts: Not a tree survived. All shops were closed, and the town was overrun with refugees.

An estimated 250,000 refugees lived in the Mogunga camp, which seemed to stretch for miles on end. The refugees who made it to the camp were trying to survive in any way they could. The lucky ones found refuge under a tree or under some plastic sheets provided by the UNHCR. The less fortunate had to suffer the blazing heat of the merciless sun.

Amidst this human ocean of misery could be spotted some uniformed people, who looked well fed, well dressed, and somewhat organized. They were defeated Hutu soldiers who had fled Rwanda when the victorious Tutsi seized power. In various places in the camp, international aid organizations maintained an established presence, trying to provide help in an obviously desperate situation. Clearly, it was impossible to situate the hospital in the refugee camp, since the influx of people would be impossible to control. The Israeli mission concluded that it was essential to station the hospital in a more private and isolated area. They found a suitable place, about five kilometers west of the city, which, as it happened, was the private estate of the Zaire minister of finance. It was a perfect choice because it was close enough to the city to provide treatment to local people as well as refugees. The mayor of Goma was briefed on the location and gave his approval, but the mission still needed official permission. Luckily, the prime minister of Zaire visited the area that day, was impressed by the operation, and approved the location of the hospital.

The Israeli team established contact and coordinated activities with the UNHCR, whose headquarters were in Goma. The chief coordinator, Dr. Claire Bourgeois, was in charge of medical care. The UNHCR was briefed on the nature and site of the Israeli mission and expressed satisfaction as to both. Neither the UNHCR nor the Israeli mission felt it necessary to coordinate activities with UN headquarters.

The Israeli team then returned to the airport, where its planes were still being unloaded. Soon the whole group had arrived, ready to begin its work. The Israeli mission had envisaged the establishment of a unique field hospital capable of providing medical care beyond the primary care usually provided in such circumstances. The other medical teams worked in the refugee camps but resided in the city. They could not treat inpatients or perform surgery, since staff was not available during the night. The French military was operating a small field hospital, but it could not accommodate all the patients or even a majority of them. However, because the Israelis had obtained permission to construct the hospital on the private grounds of the finance minister's estate, they expected to enjoy optimal conditions for operating a full-fledged hospital. The area was ideal: It was close enough to Goma, but not far from the refugee camp at Mogunga, and just about 100 yards from the beautiful house on the lake shore belonging to the head of the local airline, SCIBE, who generously allowed the members of the mission to use the grounds as their base.

To everybody's surprise the group was ready to begin treating patients the morning following its arrival—after having worked throughout the night erecting tents and organizing the hospital beds and supplies. By daylight the pharmacy was in place; the laboratories ready with teams; the x-ray facility, kitchen, communication room, and other facilities operational. In short, by Tuesday morning the idea that had begun to take shape the previous Friday night in Tel Aviv had become a reality in Zaire.

The first patients arrived and were treated on Tuesday by staff members who worked as a coherent and well-orchestrated team. On that morning Dr. Wiener and his staff met with Dr. Bourgeois at the headquarters of Médecins Sans Frontières and the UNHCR to discuss cooperation and coordination of their activities. A delicate situation arose when it was suggested that the Israeli mission should take over the treatment of the Rwandan soldiers interspersed among the civilian refugees in the camp; the mission should do so, the argument went, because the Israelis were themselves soldiers. The situation was sensitive for the Israelis because cooperation with the UNHCR and the other NGOs in the field was essential. Accordingly, the SG took pains to explain that the Israeli mission was a purely humanitarian one and that the team consisted of medical personnel, not soldiers. Indeed, most of the physicians on the team were pediatricians because the mission's highest priority was to treat the children. The plan of operations did not contemplate treatment of soldiers. After some discussion it was decided that the Israeli mission could proceed with its operation as planned, with the modification that the mission would serve as a referral hospital for all.

The issue of who should be treated and who should receive priority was never fully resolved. It was known that the refugees in the Mogunga camp were of the Hutu tribe, and that the Hutus were blamed for the genocidal murders of Tutsi. Clearly, these massacres could not have been committed solely by soldiers, without help from the Hutu civilian population. This meant that the Israelis might be treating and perhaps saving the lives of mass murderers. The issue was raised in the team's nightly briefings and debated in the group's discussions. On the one hand, the members of the team were professional physicians and paramedics, performing a humanitarian mission. On the other hand, was the past of their own people not relevant to the issue of the possibly genocidal conduct of their patients? Could they suppress the feeling that they were perhaps saving the lives of monsters? For the Israelis this posed a peculiarly painful dilemma. Dr. Wiener emphasized, however, that as members of the medical profession, they were obliged to treat all people in need of medical attention; he pointed out that in Israel medical care was provided even to terrorists and to enemy personnel, without discrimination. The issue was resolved in favor of treatment, although the feelings of ambivalence never fully disappeared.

Maintenance of team morale was a constant imperative. Cholera was the number one enemy. The fierce struggle to save lives resulted in deep frustration, since it was clear to the team members that while hundreds were being treated, thousands were dying from lack of care. Moreover, the members of the team had to struggle against the feeling that their hard and dedicated work would prove futile. They knew that the operation was only temporary, and they feared that when they departed, they might be leaving their patients, and especially the children, who had been successfully treated, to become victims again of starvation, misery, disease, and perhaps even renewed violence. The Israelis were not alone in these concerns. The subject was earnestly debated within the aid community. The UNHCR argued that it was best to use all possible resources to turn the refugee camps into semipermanent dwellings. Dr. Wiener, in contrast, believed that, in the long run, it would be more beneficial to help the refugees return to their homeland in Rwanda. He contended that working to keep the refugees in the camps was an ineffective and, in the end, counterproductive policy; that repatriation, supported by the UNHCR and the other international organizations, could provide the only permanent and constructive solution—in a word, that lack of institutional leadership in this regard could only contribute to the pursuit of short-term solutions at long-term expense.

Despite the policy debates, the deprivation, and the crushing scale of the human misery all around, the Israeli hospital managed to develop an effective operating routine. The workday extended fourteen hours, during which time the medical teams treated an average of two hundred patients. A small team was on duty during the night, and emergency cases were admitted twenty-four hours a day. In case of an emergency, the night team was reinforced. However, as the work accumulated, the SG realized that the team needed help in cleaning, cooking, and other housekeeping duties. Consequently, following regulations established by the UNHCR for hiring local personnel, he hired local workers as well as a local truck owner, who was in charge of disposal of garbage and waste.

The hospital soon achieved its goal of self-sufficiency, providing for all its needs except for the supply of water. The mission had to borrow some water pumps and two water containers from the Médecins Sans Frontières. These were filled every two hours. The water went through a process of chlorination and could be used for all hospital needs, including staff showers and laundry. Patients were usually brought to the hospital by the various medical teams operating inside the camps. The Israeli team also quickly concluded an agreement with the Irish organization, CARE, to use CARE's trucks and buses as a regular means of transportation to and from the hospital and as a means of transporting recovered patients back to the camps.

Cooperation with the other organizations was the key to success. Each organization operated independently, mobilizing its resources, airlifting supplies and equipment, and controlling its unique operation. But each organization counted on the others for help in covering shortages of necessary equipment and supplies. For example, the Israeli mission operated two regular supply flights per week from Israel to Goma. On occasion, however, the Israelis lacked rehydration solutions or blankets, which they could always receive from UNICEF. In a reciprocal act the Israeli mission flew eighty thousand doses of measles vaccine from Israel to help UNICEF immunize all the children. Representatives of all the organizations participated in the daily meetings organized by the UNHCR, during which important epidemiological information was exchanged and delegates of all the missions were briefed.

Every two weeks the whole hospital team was replaced. During these two weeks the replacement team was being organized in Israel. The overlapping time was four days, during which the new team was briefed on procedures, regulations, routines, and protocols. In mid-August, during the second team's tour of duty, a Dutch military medical team arrived and asked to join the Israeli mission. Their request was warmly accepted: The mission added a recovery department and increased its capacity by about 20 percent. Special medical cooperation and warm personal relationships developed between the Israeli mission and the French field hospital. When there was a need, Israeli and French physicians alternately used each other's operating rooms. The Israelis' laboratories and x-ray facility provided services to all the medical teams, while the hospital also served as a main trauma center. This shows graphically how effortlessly and naturally cooperation in international operations is achieved in the field, where political objectives and principles alien to the humanitarian cause are absent.

The Israeli operation lasted six weeks. Three teams rotated in Goma, treating a total of about three thousand people. Of these, fewer than one hundred patients died in the hospital, usually because they had arrived at the hospital too late for treatment to be effective. For about ten days the mission operated a camp clinic in Katindo, a small refugee camp on the outskirts of Goma. An Israeli team of two physicians and four medics assisted the local medical teams, consisting of two Rwandan physicians and several local nurses. The patients did not require hospitalization, but the treatment, which was conducted under field conditions, required great aptitude for improvization.

Approximately four weeks after the Israeli hospital had begun treating patients, the cholera outbreak subsided, but meanwhile new medical problems surfaced. Dysentery and meningitis attacked the children, who also suffered from malnutrition, malaria, and other diseases. After much delay the UNHCR managed to establish regular water and food supplies to the camps with the generous help of the U.S. military and other government agencies. The camps became better organized, and the refugees who had settled in Goma were transferred to one of the two camps north of town, either to Kibumba or to Katale.

The Israeli government decided to end the mission before the Jewish high holidays in September. August 30 was chosen to be the last day of operation. The closing down of the hospital was a complex act, requiring coordination and organizational skills. All the patients had to be transferred to other facilities that provided only ambulatory care. Two days before leaving coordination meetings were held with the other missions operating in the camps, over twenty in all. The Israeli mission decided to contribute all its equipment and supplies to the remaining missions, and lists of requests were received from all the other teams.

Blankets, food, stretchers, and water were distributed among the teams, while the operating room equipment was donated to the French field hospital. As expected, the French hospital doubled its operating capacity after receiving the Israeli operating room equipment.

For the Israeli team the most important consideration was the treatment of the patients left behind. The mission did its utmost to ensure that its departure would not hurt them. The returning team members felt that their humanitarian mission, notwithstanding all its limitations, had nonetheless been important and rewarding. The Israeli operation was not expected to radically change the situation in Rwanda, or even in Goma; nor could it have. But as part of a larger effort by the international community, it was in some measure instrumental in helping the distressed people of Rwanda, regardless of their ethnic background, and developing in the field a spirit of cooperation that might be a basis for a better future.

NOTES

1. *Africa Report* 38, no. 5 (1993): 58–61.
2. Associated Press Report in *The* [Baltimore] *Sun*, January 4, 1997.
3. Center for Strategic Studies, Douglas Johnston and Cynthia Sampson, eds., *Religion: The Missing Dimension of Statecraft* (New York: Oxford University Press, 1994).
4. Speech delivered at luncheon, October 1994 (unknown location).
5. Ana Maria Pineda and Robert Schreiter, eds., *Dialogue Rejoined: Theology and Ministry in the United States Hispanic Reality* (Collegeville, MN: Liturgical Press, 1995).
6. Security Council Res. S/846 (June 22, 1993).
7. Based on *Report of the Secretary-General* (September 24, 1993), the Security Council recommended the establishment of UNAMIR. Security Council Res. S/872 (October 5, 1993).
8. Letter sent to Dr. Michael Wiener by Dr. C. Bourgeois, August 3, 1994.
9. General Dallaire assumed his position on October 22, 1993.
10. *Report of the Secretary-General*, December 5, 1993.
11. Security Council Res. S/891 (December 20, 1993).
12. "The United Nations and the Situation in Rwanda" (UN DPI publication, April 1995), p. 4.
13. "The UN and the Situation in Rwanda" (Reference paper, UN Department of Public Information, New York, April 1995), p. 5.
14. *Report of the Secretary-General*, October 6, 1994.
15. Security Council Res. S/909 (April 5, 1994).
16. Security Council Res. S/1994/470, *Report of the Secretary-General* (April 20, 1994).
17. "The UN and the Situation in Rwanda," p. 15.
18. Security Council Res. S/192 (April 21, 1994).
19. *Report of the Secretary-General*, October 6, 1994; see also *Statement of the UNHCR*, October 21, 1994.
20. Security Council Meeting 3371, April 30, 1994 (S/PRST/1994/21).
21. "The UN and the Situation in Rwanda," pp. 14–15.

22. Security Council Res. S/918 (May 17, 1994).

23. Security Council Res. S/928 (1994).

24. This experience was gained in Thailand in 1979, in Cameroon in 1986, and in Armenia in 1988. Dr. Wiener personally headed the last two of these operations.

7

Cambodia: Relief, Repatriation, and Rehabilitation

JANET E. HEININGER

The international effort in Cambodia illuminates the three major stages of a humanitarian aid operation: the initial crisis intervention with massive food aid principally in 1979 and 1980, which then evolved into a long-term maintenance operation for hundreds of thousands of refugees on the Thai-Cambodian border; and finally, resolution of the political conflict, in which the long-term aid recipients on the Thai-Cambodian border were repatriated as part of a multifaceted UN peacekeeping and peace-building operation.

This chapter is not intended, however, to be a comprehensive examination of the UN mission in Cambodia from 1991 to 1993. For that see Janet E. Heininger's *Peacekeeping in Transition: The United Nations in Cambodia.*[1] Rather, this is an assessment of the international effort to cope with the specifically humanitarian aspect of the Cambodian conflict from 1979 to 1993. It focuses in particular on the initial relief effort for Cambodians inside the country and those who fled across the border, and on the repatriation process in 1992 and 1993. It also examines the UN mission's coordination of the effort to rehabilitate and reconstruct the country. As a case study it is unique. Whereas other humanitarian interventions tend to illustrate a particular phase, Cambodia encompasses them all from start to finish.

Especially in its first phase, the Cambodian endeavor also illustrates how humanitarian aid operations can have unintended consequences. Designed to relieve human suffering, particularly involving large refugee flows and hunger, they are neither intended nor are they able to resolve political crises that governments have created or at least failed to address. But neither are they supposed to be an engine that perpetuates the underlying political conflict. In the case of Cambodia, that is precisely what happened with the initial relief operation. Repatriation of refugees and rehabilitation of the country were not able to take place for another thirteen years until Cambodia had ceased to be a pawn in its neighbors' power struggle.

Vietnam's invasion of Cambodia in December 1978 caused hundreds of thousands of refugees to flee into Thailand. Weakened from flight and four years of Khmer Rouge rule, they refused to return home. Reports began to circulate that spring and summer of the toll wreaked on Cambodia by the Khmer Rouge. As predictions of widespread famine reached the West, governments, nongovernmental organizations, and just plain people opened their hearts and wallets to stave off what they believed was impending famine. The West (and to a lesser extent, the Soviet bloc) rapidly undertook an aid effort that was massive in scope and multinational in dimension. Subsequently it was found to be based on inaccurate assumptions and assessments. Even worse, the aid program was used by nearly all parties involved—intentionally or unintentionally—to reinforce the political stalemate.

While many ordinary Cambodians received aid from the international community, the program became a political football used by all sides for their own purposes. Vietnam used it as the wherewithal to build up what the international community saw as an illegal administration in Phnom Penh. The Thais and the Chinese used the aid to shore up a resistance based on the Khmer Rouge. The donors used it to help both sides. The net effect—the unintended consequence—was to make both the infant regime in Phnom Penh and the defeated Khmer Rouge viable. Instead of being used to resolve the humanitarian crisis, the aid was used by all to perpetuate a festering sore that remained unresolved for nearly fifteen years until UNTAC repatriated 365,000 refugees from Thailand to Cambodia between March 1992 and April 1993.

Return of the refugees was viewed as necessary for preparing to rebuild Cambodia. As long as a substantial number of Cambodians remained dispersed—and many had fled overseas or had sought political asylum outside the region—it would be difficult to bring about national reconciliation. The first step was to repatriate the refugees from the border. It was hoped that the changes Cambodia would undergo during UNTAC's tenure would lure back expatriate Cambodians whose skills were desperately needed for the country's long-term reconstruction.

If return of the refugees was the first step toward rebuilding Cambodia, rehabilitation of the country's human and physical infrastructure would be the final step, although UNTAC's mandate on reconstruction was not to complete the task but to jump-start it. The Paris Accords gave UNTAC the task of planning and coordinating an international effort to rebuild Cambodia. The process thus began during UNTAC's tenure with projects that were designed to meet Cambodia's immediate and medium-term needs and was funded by international donors. UNTAC laid the groundwork for long-term reconstruction by mobilizing and positioning donors, defining what was necessary and setting priorities.

The Cambodian endeavor from 1979 to 1993 illuminates the inextricable link between politics and humanitarian operations. All too often such operations get caught in political cross-fires. The international community's experience in Cambodia suggests that it is far easier for all parties to be in accord—and to remain so—to meet an operation's objectives if the political problems are resolved in advance. For that reason, this chapter focuses on just the relief, repatriation, and reconstruction parts of the Cambodian effort; it does not examine UNTAC's broader peace-building aspects for which Khmer Rouge opposition created obstacles. By 1991 all parties to the conflict, including those external to Cambodia, were unified in their desire to return the refugees and rehabilitate the country. That unity was absent during the earlier relief phase.

THE RELIEF OPERATION

Exodus from Cambodia: The Impetus for Intervention

When Vietnam invaded Cambodia in late 1978, it set in motion a series of events that led to a political stalemate lasting nearly fifteen years. Vietnam installed a client regime in Phnom Penh that was headed by Khmer Rouge defectors Heng Samrin and Hun Sen. The regime received no international recognition. In fact, its very existence caused international support to coalesce around its avowed enemy—the Khmer Rouge. Vietnam paid for the invasion with a decade of supporting 200,000 occupation troops, international ostracism, and a drain on its economy exacerbated by the end of East bloc aid in the late 1980s.

Although the Vietnamese invasion achieved its basic objective—ejecting the Khmer Rouge from rule over Cambodia—it failed to eliminate it as a guerrilla force. As Vietnamese forces marched westward across Cambodia, hundreds of thousands of Cambodians fled before them. Fearful of Vietnamese troops and brutalized by four years under the Khmer Rouge, they fled to what they believed was a safe refuge in Thailand. Few found a true safe haven. Many were forcibly repatriated by Thailand. Others languished for years in abject conditions, denied the right to emigrate and settle in a third country yet unwilling to return home. They became psychologically as well as physically dependent on international handouts. Those who remained in the camps were often caught in the cross-fires as fighting continued between the resistance, Vietnam, and the Phnom Penh regime. Never accorded the official status of refugees, the Cambodians became pawns of all other players. The resistance factions–the Khmer Rouge, the non-Communist FUNCINPEC party of Prince Sihanouk, and the non-Communist KPNLF party of the former prime minister, Son Sann—recruited from their midst. The West supplied the aid but also politically and militarily assisted the resistance. Vietnam's continued occupation of Cambodia and support for the Phnom Penh regime perpetuated the stalemate. China's material aid kept the

Khmer Rouge viable. Thailand exerted its influence by controlling the keys to the camps' gates.

From its inception competing political objectives contaminated the aid effort. Much of what happened to the aid effort can be linked to "Vietnam's instinct to dominate its neighbors . . . and its neighbors' instinct to resist."[2] Historically, Cambodia resides on the "fault line" between Indochina's so-called Indianized and Sinicized states. Although more heavily influenced by India than by China, Cambodia has served as the buffer zone between the two regions, particularly between Thailand and Vietnam. Each has sought in turn to dominate Cambodia, or at least ensure its neutrality against the perceived aggressive intentions of the other. At the same time Vietnam, a one-time province of China, exists in China's shadow. Its "history has been a confusing mosaic of its lust to dominate the weaker Indianized peoples to its south and west and its own obsessive resistance to China's repeated efforts to impose its imperial will on a tributary state."[3]

The relief effort reflected these historical tensions. As William Shawcross noted, "Nearly all the players used humanitarianism as a fig leaf for either the poverty or the ruthlessness of their politics. The humanitarian instincts of people around the world, and the mandates of the organizations that are supposed to protect and to implement our collective conscience, were exploited by almost all sides to serve political ends."[4]

From the first recognition by the international community that a problem was building on the Cambodian border, Thailand became an obstacle to be overcome. Driven by its fear of Vietnam's intentions, Thailand covertly allowed the Khmer Rouge to operate out of its territory and permitted transshipment of military assistance to it. In early 1979 the UNHCR offered Thailand help in dealing with Cambodian refugees fleeing from the fighting between Vietnamese and Khmer Rouge troops. The offer was ignored. Instead, Thailand labeled the more recent flood of Cambodians as "illegal immigrants" and confined them in camps separated from those who had fled to Thailand prior to the invasion. International aid officials, journalists, and relatives were barred from the camps. The "illegal immigrants" soon became pawns in the struggle. By April 1979, as the Vietnamese offensive pushed thousands of Cambodians across the border, Thailand retaliated with successive forced repatriations of thousands of refugees, despite international pleas to desist.

The international relief agencies, at this time chiefly the UNHCR and the ICRC, hesitated to press Thailand too hard. They wanted to stop the forcible repatriation, but they also wanted Thailand to establish a proper program of refugee assistance. To have pressed too hard on one issue could have adversely affected the other. In May UN Secretary-General Kurt Waldheim asked the Thai prime minister, General Chamanand Kriangsak, to halt forcible repatriation. Kriangsak proposed that the UN provide Thailand with food and money for the refugees on condition that the food be distributed by the Thais, not by foreign relief officials. Despite the UN's eventual reluctant acceptance of this proposal, Thailand's forced repatriation did not stop. Between forty-three thousand and forty-five thousand Cambodians were shoved back over the border by mid-June 1979.

Initiation of Relief

Rumors of impending famine in Cambodia caused the relief organizations' attention to begin to focus on Cambodia. The ICRC and the United Nations International Children's Emergency Fund (UNICEF) had unsuccessfully petitioned Vietnam since January to allow relief workers to survey Cambodia to determine the needs of the population. Vietnam had referred all queries to the Phnom Penh regime, from which there had been no response. That spring alarming reports that the lack of planting in Cambodia for the major monsoon rice crop "could lead to . . . catastrophic famine . . . of unexpected dimensions" began to galvanize international attention toward efforts to avert disaster.[5]

However, neither Vietnam nor the Phnom Penh regime was seeking massive food aid. Although it was not known at the time, bilateral aid had been arriving quietly in Cambodia during the spring of 1979 from Vietnam and its allies, particularly the Soviet Union, Cuba, and some Eastern European countries. The first written request from Phnom Penh for international aid arrived in the West, in a letter, dated July 3, 1979, addressed to the World Food Program (WFP) and other UN organizations. It claimed that about three million of Cambodia's 7.5 million people had died under the Khmer Rouge and that the four million surviving Cambodians were suffering from malnutrition with 2.25 million of them threatened by famine.

A two-person joint UNICEF-ICRC survey mission arrived in Phnom Penh on July 17, 1979. They returned from their short visit convinced of Cambodia's vast needs, but their draft relief program was based on far less than complete or accurate information.

Obstacles inside Cambodia

The subsequent aid program was burdened by numerous problems. First, there were two populations in need of assistance: those refugees on the Thai-Cambodian border and those inside Cambodia. Different problems impeded the delivery of aid to each.

Inside Cambodia, Phnom Penh and Hanoi officials placed restrictions on the international agencies' ability to do their jobs. Initially, they hindered relief officials' freedom to travel around the country to prepare an accurate survey of Cambodia's needs. As the restrictions were eased, relief officials changed their minds several times about the nature of the crisis Cambodia was facing. Nonetheless, the hue and cry of imminent famine was useful for fund-raising purposes. By the end of 1979, after more extensive trips around the country, aid officials began to revise their assessments. The needs remained vast yet did not amount to impending famine. However, as an Oxfam official noted later, "the fundraising

machinery was unstoppable."[6] It was too late for the international or nongovernmental agencies to explain that the appeal for aid to Cambodia had been
based on inaccurate assumptions.

The second daunting obstacle was the country's abysmal infrastructure that
made the logistics of getting food to hungry Cambodians exceptionally difficult.
Woefully insufficient port facilities rapidly became clogged with ships loaded with
supplies. There was no one to unload them and too little dock space on which
to do so. Roads into Cambodia's interior were dreadful. Trucks were in short
supply. Worse, Vietnam placed limits on relief flights and required costly and
time-consuming detours around Cambodia instead of direct routes from Bangkok.

Third, the Phnom Penh regime insisted that all aid be handed over to it for
distribution, promising only to give reports to the ICRC and UNICEF. Ultimately, this meant that the regime's bureaucrats got fed, as did some of the
townspeople. Few ordinary peasants—who were supposedly facing famine—did.
Although what had been distributed was far less than the estimated need, the
international organizations' wrenching problem was that it had no choice but to
provide unintended aid to the Phnom Penh regime in the hope of reaching the
intended beneficiaries.

Obstacles on the Thai-Cambodian Border

If anything, the situation on the border was even more complicated. Like the
Phnom Penh regime, the Thai government insisted on controlling the distribution of aid, which minimized the international organizations' ability to monitor
disbursement of their aid. Thailand also insisted that most relief supplies, including food, be procured inside Thailand—"for convenience and economy."[7]

The refugees had been clustered into three sectors on the border, partly by
geography, but also to suit Thailand's political and military needs. By the end of
1979, an estimated 600,000 to 700,000 Cambodians had fled across the border.
The refugees were organized into camps run by the three resistance factions.
International aid agencies were permitted access to some and denied access to
others. A parallel system of each faction's military camps was located near the
civilian camps. The international agencies were barred from feeding fighting
forces, yet the close proximity meant it was easy for civilians to divert food aid
to the fighting forces. Along the border UNICEF and the ICRC jointly delivered
food to camps, mostly in the central sector (confusingly known as the "north-
west" sector), where massive diversion took place but civilians were fed. The
WFP handed food over to the Thai army for it to distribute in the northern and
southern sectors.

The Human Land Bridge

In December 1979, after the Phnom Penh regime refused to open the road or
railroad from Aranyaprathet in western Cambodia, an informal system began to

funnel food into the country. At the instigation of ICRC official, Robert Ashe, UNICEF agreed to supply food for distribution at Nong Chan camp for Cambodians to take home to the interior. By early 1980 over 100,000 people were coming each week from the interior to pick up rice. Nearly all were peasants. By year's end about 148,500 tons of rice had been distributed via the land bridge; although some of this supply was lost or stolen, most of it, it is believed, went into Cambodia to feed ordinary civilians.

The land bridge was even more valuable as a conduit for getting rice seed and farm tools into the country. Impetus for this program came from the U.S. embassy, headed by Ambassador Morton I. Abramowitz, and CARE, one of the larger American organizations on the border. The embassy was looking for a way to ensure as large a harvest for 1980 as possible and knew that the country's infrastructure was insufficient to handle import of seed as well as food. The United States believed that the Phnom Penh airlift was wasteful and that far more seed could be gotten into Cambodia quickly and more cheaply via the land bridge. That route also had the attractive side benefit of circumventing the Vietnamese overlords and their client regime.

Expansion was controversial, however, because it would make the border effort disproportionate to the Phnom Penh operation and could act as a magnet attracting people away from their fields. The ICRC, which largely controlled the land bridge, was opposed to its expansion for fear that its neutrality would be compromised but reluctantly acquiesced to U.S. pressure. By the end of 1980, the United States had provided $5 million to voluntary agencies for purchase of rice seed that went across the land bridge. In 1981 it provided another $4 million for the program. When the seed land bridge ended on June 20, 1980, 23,521 tons had been distributed at the border. By comparison only little more than half of the thirty thousand tons the Food and Agriculture Organization (FAO) planned to ship to Phnom Penh had arrived.

Coordination of the Relief Effort

The initial relief effort suffered from a lack of coordination among the many UN and nongovernmental organizations that were involved in various aspects of the operation. Although the secretary-general designated UNICEF as lead agency, an unusual move for an agency not accustomed to directing such a large operation, he never fully defined that role. Furthermore, Waldheim's tardy appointment of a special representative—Under-Secretary-General Sir Robert Jackson did not assume that position until January 1980, nine months after UN efforts had started—meant that it was virtually impossible to coordinate the agencies' activities, which, like the enormous number of private voluntary organizations, had quickly become deeply entrenched.

The agencies most deeply involved in the early years were UNICEF, ICRC, and the WFP. Both UNICEF and ICRC were poised for early involvement in Cambodia because they had ties to the region and had maintained representatives in Hanoi after Phnom Penh fell to the Khmer Rouge in 1975. In addition, the ICRC's Hanoi representative had been in Phnom Penh prior to that. In 1973 UNICEF had opened an office in Hanoi over the Nixon administration's opposition. As in other areas in crisis, the WFP distributed surplus food.

One of the most curious elements of the Cambodian relief program's early stages, particularly on the border, was the low-profile role of UNHCR, the logical agency whose mandate was to protect the rights of refugees. Thailand had ignored UNHCR's January 1979 offer to help with new Cambodian refugees. Not only had Thailand labeled the refugees illegal immigrants; it had refused to allow them to go deeper inside Thailand to UNHCR holding centers for pre-invasion arrivals. The agency's leverage was also limited because Thailand had never ratified either of the UN documents relating to treatment of refugees.

By contrast, UNICEF's ability, unique among UN agencies, to operate in any country without other governments' approval gave it greater latitude in dealing with Thailand. As the operation accelerated, however, UNICEF became increasingly uncomfortable with what was turning out to be a longer-term role than it believed was consonant with the agency's mandate. Because disasters usually affect women and children first, UNICEF is often one of the first agencies to undertake emergency relief. Once beyond the initial phase of determining the needs of Cambodians inside the country and those of the border refugees, UNICEF wanted UNHCR to take over the border operation. UNHCR was reluctant to do so, particularly with many donor pledges unmet. By the end of 1979, philosophical differences between the agencies had emerged: The UNHCR did not want to create long-term exiles and argued that the feeding programs acted as a magnet holding people there who would be better off if they returned home. Thailand opposed UNHCR's taking over the border operation; it preferred an enlargement of the UN role there, not just the substitution of one agency for another. Between 1981 and 1992 the relief effort drifted into exactly what UNHCR had opposed: long-term maintenance of exiles in UN-run border camps.

STALEMATE: THE MAINTENANCE PHASE, 1981–92

In the early 1980s thousands of refugees drifted back into Cambodia, leaving over 200,000 people on the border by 1983. The border population fluctuated between 200,000 and 400,000 over the next decade depending on the level of fighting between Vietnamese and Phnom Penh forces and the resistance. As fighting escalated, so, too, did the border population. In times of relative calm, families would drift back to their homes in Cambodia.

Gradually the difficulties mounted for the aid program inside Cambodia. International attention drifted from Cambodia to the world's next crisis and then the next one. By early 1980, as the Phnom Penh regime consolidated itself with the assistance being delivered by the agencies, it placed greater rather than fewer barriers in their way. Relief officials were denied permission to set up headquarters in Phnom Penh and were confined to the Samaki hotel. Trips to the countryside became more difficult to arrange. Contacts with Phnom Penh officials became rarer as government propaganda began to target aid officials as imperialist spies.

Increasingly, it became clear that, if Cambodia were to be rehabilitated, the agencies would have to shift from relief to development; but the regime's increasing hostility, likely a product of its failure to win international recognition and the deeper involvement of Vietnamese cadres in Cambodia's administration, made it virtually impossible to undertake development projects. Intent on minimizing non-Communist involvement in Cambodia, Vietnam welcomed Western material aid, but not advice or technical involvement. The United States also adopted a rigid policy of refusing to provide anything "beyond the subsistence level which contributes toward consolidation of the Heng Samrin regime's control over Kampuchea."[8] In 1980 the U.S. government began to interpret rigidly the U.S. Trading with the Enemy Act and the Export Administration Act of 1979, which distinguished between emergency and development aid. As a result, private voluntary organizations had to obtain federal export permits to ship virtually anything, except seed and rice, to Cambodia. This serious hindrance to their work lasted throughout much of the decade.

Moreover, donor funds overall had largely dried up. In 1982, recognizing that the relief effort was turning into a long-term maintenance operation, the UN created a new organization, the United Nations Border Relief Operation (UN-BRO), to care for the Cambodian refugees.[9]

At the same time the aid program inside Cambodia dwindled away in the face of Vietnamese hostility and as it became clear that famine—if it had ever been a real threat—had been averted. The logical progression to rehabilitation development projects never took place as the international community maintained its implacable hostility toward the Vietnamese-installed regime. Opposing the Vietnamese occupation—and Vietnam's Soviet backers—became more important than opposing the reviled Khmer Rouge. To ensure a resistance sufficiently strong to bleed the Vietnamese occupiers, the Western governments, China, and the Association of South East Asian Nations (ASEAN) (Thailand, Malaysia, Singapore, Indonesia, the Philippines, and Brunei) overtly and covertly funded the resistance forces. International support largely coalesced around the Coalition Government of Democratic Kampuchea (CGDK), a paper coalition of the non-Communist factions and the Khmer Rouge. The CGDK was formed at Western insistence in 1982 to prevent Cambodia's UN seat from falling into Soviet hands via the Vietnamese client regime in Phnom Penh. While the outside players perpetuated the civil war, the refugees continued to squat on the border, confined to camps, waiting for the political climate to change so they could return home. As Jean Pierre Hocke, the ICRC's director of operations, concluded, "In Cambodia, humanitarianism was used to prolong an agonising political deadlock."[10]

REPATRIATION AND RECONSTRUCTION, 1991–93

Return to Cambodia: UNTAC's Repatriation Mandate

Setting the stage so that Cambodian refugees could return home was not easy. It required independent decisions by the outside powers to end their use of Cambodia as a pawn in their own struggles and entailed finding a way to resolve the underlying conflict over who would govern Cambodia. This took political will by the four Cambodian factions backed by international commitments to terminate the civil war. It also necessitated the negotiation of a comprehensive peace agreement, known as the Paris Accords, shaped largely in 1990 but not finalized until October 1991. Finally, it entailed a nearly two-year-long process of UNTAC's implementation of the Paris Accords.[11]

The Accords were not a solution to Cambodia's problems per se but, rather, a face-saving framework that allowed the parties most immediately involved— the Phnom Penh regime, now known as the State of Cambodia (SOC), and the three armies arrayed against it, those of Prince Sihanouk, Son Sann, and the Khmer Rouge—to jockey for control in a manner that met the needs of the international community in a changed political environment. The Paris Accords became the stage on which the Chinese—supporting the three rebel factions, particularly the Khmer Rouge—and the Vietnamese could do their Kabuki act and slowly back off, matching each other step by step. Neither side could say it had won or lost. The decisions to withdraw established new ground rules for the Cambodian factions struggling for power: Neither China nor Vietnam would get back in the game. These decisions made the framework for a peace agreement possible and allowed each foreign patron to end its military supply relationship with its surrogate.

What the Paris Accords attempted to provide was a means to attain a government that could resolve the debate over power sharing and be recognized internationally as legitimate. Such a government, the international community hoped, would be able to attract the assistance needed to rebuild the country, which had been devastated by Khmer Rouge rule and fifteen subsequent years of warfare and stalemate.

One essential element on which all parties agreed was the need to return the refugees from the Thai-Cambodian border. Consensus on a written document for refugee repatriation was reached early in the negotiations and never wavered. This remarkable unanimity of opinion is noteworthy, not only by comparison with the other tasks entrusted to UNTAC, which were subject to repeated reconsideration, but because it signaled the necessity of depoliticizing humanitarian issues after nearly two decades of conflict. That consensus presaged cooperation from the competing factions that was not seen to the same degree in any of UNTAC's other mandates. Most refugees were affiliated with a specific faction and thus were seen as a basis of support that could be transferred across the border in preparation for elections.

The Paris Accords, not the Security Council that authorized the UN operation, assigned UNTAC tasks that fell into six major categories: refugee repatriation; ceasefire and demobilization of 70 percent of each faction's forces; organization and running of an election for a new constituent assembly that would draft a constitution, then transform itself into a legislature; development of a human rights program (which included the investigation of abuses); civil administration, controlling five critical areas of the four factions' administrative structures (negligible though they may have been for all but the Phnom Penh regime) in order to ensure a neutral political environment conducive to elections; and coordination of an international rehabilitation and reconstruction effort to rebuild the country.

The tasks facing UNTAC were daunting. This was not to be just a peacekeeping operation separating combatants who had agreed to stop fighting. The agency was to run Cambodia for a period of eighteen months. It was to resettle 365,000 refugees from the Thai border areas, 170,000 "internal refugees" displaced within Cambodia, and 150,000 demobilized soldiers from the four factions' forces. It was also to supervise and train the civil police forces of each faction. At the time many thought that it was not realistic to expect that one UN operation could effectively rebuild a country from the ground up and then conduct a Western-oriented, free, fair, and democratic election in a country that had no history of free elections or power sharing, for that matter.

By almost any definition the refugee repatriation component of UNTAC's operations was a success. It was surprising that so many refugees wanted to return, particularly given the length of time they had resided outside Cambodia. That they did so, without a single accident or a disruptive incident deliberately triggered by the authorities or the Khmer Rouge, by April 1993, in time to participate in the May 23–28 election, is a tribute to their courage and to the will of the four factions and the international community to bring about a smooth population readjustment.

The logistics of transferring 365,000 refugees to Cambodia's interior were formidable. The refugees had to pass through areas that were heavily malarial. The infrastructure that had impeded the earlier relief effort had not been improved in the ensuing thirteen years. Roads, bridges, and transportation networks were in abysmal condition.

Unlike the relief effort begun in 1979 with no UN coordinator for nine months, responsibility for UNTAC's refugee repatriation was assigned to the UNHCR, which helped to lubricate the cross-border flow. The latter's longstanding relationship with Southeast Asia gave it a procedural and operational head start that meant it was far less hampered by the procurement and logistics difficulties that bedeviled all of UNTAC. Also, UNHCR's institutional ambiguity worked in its favor. It could legitimately claim a degree of independence from UNTAC when it served its interests to do so. This was particularly helpful in dealing with the Khmer Rouge. Sergio Vieira de Mello, UNHCR's special envoy, could quietly praise the Khmer Rouge for its cooperation while the head of UNTAC, Yasushi Akashi, was criticizing Khmer Rouge leaders for their non-cooperation with disarmament. On the other hand, UNHCR could emphasize its relationship to UNTAC when that furthered its purpose.

For the most part the refugees were not prepared for life in Cambodia. As Vieira de Mello noted in an interview in April 1992, "International generosity may have gone too far in terms of the care and maintenance, even the spoon-feeding, of Cambodians in exile in the Thai border camps. . . . So we wonder if the refugees are now capable of reacquiring initiative and independence and of accepting a lowered standard of living and health care."[12] It was unclear whether the refugees had the skills necessary to adapt to a harsher life inside Cambodia. More than two thirds had lived in the border camps beyond ten years. Most were originally farmers, but they had not been farming while in the camps. Better than 90 percent of the refugees were under the age of forty-five, with almost half under the age of fifteen. As a result, many had little memory of Cambodia. There was also a high rate of illiteracy.

The repatriation plan stipulated that the refugees' return was to be accomplished in nine months, that they were to receive land, resettlement assistance, and food for a year or up to a maximum of eighteen months, and that limited reintegration assistance and upgrading of essential services (such as health care, education, banking, telecommunications, and other basic utilities) were to be provided for the refugees through so-called quick-impact projects in areas resettled by the refugees.[13] The repatriation process was expected to take place in three stages. Refugees were to be moved from the border camps to staging areas in Thailand for final registration and boarding of buses and trucks. They would then cross the border to reception centers inside Cambodia, where they would stay for up to one week. Six such centers were built, with a combined capacity of up to 10,700 returnees. From there they would travel in trucks to their final destinations.[14]

The first group of 527 refugees crossed into Cambodia on March 30, 1992; they were met by Prince Sihanouk in Sisophon.[15] By April 8, however, only 2,574 refugees had returned to Cambodia. By then the UN was already reevaluating its working hypothesis of ten thousand returnees per week and acknowledged that the plan, drawn up in July 1991, had seriously underestimated the difficulties involved.

The Promise of Land

As originally designed, the resettlement package the refugees were supposed to receive would get them through twelve months, on average. Their building survival kit was to consist of a simple house frame, tools, mosquito nets, and a water container. They were to receive food, which was stockpiled by the WFP, so the refugees could eat until they harvested their first crop twelve to eighteen months later. Refugees were also to receive two hectares of land (approximately five acres) for an average family of 4.4 persons. This aid package was estimated by the *Washington Post* to be worth more than $570, nearly four times the average Cambodian family's annual income.[16] Although UN officials recognized that the aid had the potential to be a source of friction between the refugees and local villagers, they believed it was necessary to facilitate the refugees' reintegration.

The promise of land for returning refugees was one of the most problematic aspects of an otherwise uncontroversial program. Preliminary satellite surveys identifying potentially suitable, unclaimed land turned out to be seriously flawed, causing the UN to concede as early as April that the offer of land had been too generous. Ground surveys revealed far fewer mine-free areas than originally expected. Getting title to the land was problematic, and where there were prior claims, it was usually too expensive to purchase.

The pressure to find land in the four provinces nearest the Thai border increased UNHCR's difficulties. Eighty percent of the refugees asked to be resettled in those provinces largely because of their proximity to Thailand, even though only 60 percent had lived there before fleeing Cambodia.[17] Moreover, the inability of the leaders in the capital to compel local authorities in some areas to make land available prolonged the dependence of some refugees on food assistance and put off their prospects for attaining self-sufficiency.

In late May, conceding that the promise of land was no longer realistic, UNHCR offered the returnees other options, including cash. Although many refugees wanted land, most (88 percent) opted for cash grants of $50 per adult and $25 per child. The change in policy nonetheless triggered a violent protest at one of the Thai border camps.[18] As of mid-June twenty-seven thousand refugees had been returned to Cambodia, but none had received the originally promised allotment of land.[19]

By September, when about 100,000 refugees had been returned, criticism from both returnees and refugee officials had intensified; they claimed UNTAC and UNHCR were not resettling refugees but merely transporting them back into Cambodia and then leaving them to their own devices. The prospect of refugees taking the money, dashing across the border, and then dropping out of sight alarmed UNHCR officials. The debate over how much the agency should be undertaking in order to help resettle the refugees opened a rift in the organization. On the one hand, criticism that UNHCR failed to deliver what had been promised—specifically, land—was valid. On the other hand, there was serious concern about creating social tensions between returning refugees and local villagers. Even without receiving land, the refugees had been given a leg up economically. One *New York Times* article reported that local officials in Battambang Province said that villagers, who lived at a bare subsistence level, were resentful of the refugees who returned with a package of aid that was far above subsistence.[20]

The Pace of Return Quickens

Despite the inability of UNHCR to make land available to refugees, repatriation continued throughout 1992, peaking at forty thousand monthly in early

1993.[21] (The largest Thai border camp, Site 2, was closed on March 30, 1993.) Unlike with regard to other aspects of the UNTAC program, the Khmer Rouge placed no obstacles in the way of the repatriation effort. Of the 260,000 refugees who had returned by the end of January, 55,000 were from Khmer Rouge camps.[22]

Most refugees returned under UNHCR auspices (the six hundred who refused to be repatriated were informed by the government of Thailand that they would be deported),[23] but untold numbers returned on their own. More than 90 percent of the refugees returned to SOC-controlled areas rather than to those controlled by the resistance factions. Although there had been fears that landless refugees would flood Phnom Penh, that did not happen. In all likelihood refugees returned to areas where they had relatives, and they reintegrated themselves, assisted by UN cash grants.

However, criticism of UNHCR never fully dissipated. Critics charged that repatriation was overfunded and thus excessively costly. The chief error lay in budgeting for problems that did not exist. Unlike most of UNTAC's other components, UNHCR planned for a worst-case scenario. It wrongly expected it would have to move refugees back into areas that continued to be wracked by war. There were other reasons as well to find fault. Sergio Vieira de Mello reflected, "Our mistake was being too paternalistic. . . . We simply had to abandon the imbecilic notion of giving away land and telling people where to go."[24]

Largely thanks to their own determination, the refugees were successfully reintegrated into Cambodian society. Repatriation efforts focused almost exclusively on the border camp refugees largely because of the visibility and clear definition of the task. Since disarmament of the factions' forces did not take place, UNTAC did not have to meet the requirement of reintegrating roughly 150,000 demobilized soldiers, as had been anticipated. Nor was much done about the internally displaced, who largely migrated when and where they chose, without much assistance from UNTAC.

Quick-Impact Projects

The achievement of UNHCR can also be partially attributed to the successful undertaking of quick-impact projects for refugees, funded by the United Nations Development Programme (UNDP) and nongovernmental organizations as well as by UNHCR. Although their number and funding were modest, the quick-impact projects were designed to be labor-intensive and thus served as a source of employment. They not only helped to facilitate the refugees' reintegration but also, by pumping cash into the local economy, rallied the villagers' support for UNTAC. Some of these projects, which included the repair or construction of roads, bridges, hospitals, dispensaries, schools, and latrines and the digging of wells and ponds, were similar to the work done by other agencies of UNTAC, especially in the implementation of the military's civic action plan. The quick-impact projects were not limited to improvement of Cambodia's infrastructure. Start-up loans were offered; vegetable seeds, fishing equipment, mosquito nets, and water jars were distributed; and special assistance through nongovernmental organizations was made available to those who were particularly vulnerable, such as the elderly, female household heads, orphans, and amputees. By the end of January 1993, $3.4 million of the $9 million allotted to such projects had been spent.[25] By June UNHCR had funded a total of eighty projects in all twenty-one provinces, including areas controlled by all factions but the Khmer Rouge.

The quick-impact projects were important for the refugees. They were equally important, if not more so, to the local villagers in areas absorbing resettlement, as a tangible means of confirming the international community's concern about Cambodia. They helped to consolidate support for UNTAC and to inform the population about its mission, particularly in remote areas. Quick-impact projects also served as a bridge between relief aid and longer-term rehabilitation and reconstruction activities. This "hearts and minds" activity helped make repatriation work and provide UNTAC with a major success.

UNHCR did many things right, including initiating a training program for its Cambodian staff to carry out similar work after its own was finished. The agency's activities were also well coordinated with UNTAC's overall mission. Repatriation was included as an important component of the Paris Accords, and it was not handled in isolation from other UNTAC tasks. Cooperation between UNHCR and UNTAC's military and civil police components, in particular, helped to make repatriation a success. An important link between UNTAC, the UNDP, and the WFP, which had responsibilities in the demobilization and cantonment process as well, UNHCR was also a link to other UN agencies such as UNICEF and to nongovernmental organizations, whose work cut across UNTAC mandates.

UNHCR worked hard to establish and maintain its credibility with all parties. In that way it was able to insist that fundamental principles be adhered to by all parties. By providing equal treatment to the populations of all factions and strictly respecting their freedom of choice, those involved in the repatriation effort had an easier time ensuring access to and movement in all factions' areas. Making certain that all factions were apprised of developments in the repatriation process, which entailed endless dialogue and negotiation, helped allay their suspicions and gain their cooperation. Even when ceasefire violations and political violence were rampant, the repatriation effort continued unhindered. Moreover, by de-politicizing repatriation, UNHCR succeeded in preventing the refugees from being viewed as interlopers or fifth columnists. Although the Cambodian population recognized that return of the refugees was an important aspect of its national reconciliation—Sihanouk's personal interest in making repatriation work, as well as his influence over all factions, especially the Khmer Rouge, was critical—UNHCR had an important role to play in raising public awareness.

REHABILITATION AND RECONSTRUCTION

The mandate given UNTAC for rehabilitation and reconstruction of Cambodia was simply to lay the groundwork for the international community to bring the country out of economic isolation. Unlike the other components designed to carry out UNTAC mandates, the rehabilitation office had no implementation capability. UNTAC had several objectives in the area of rehabilitation. The first was to design a plan for Cambodia's rehabilitation and reconstruction, which included determining immediate as well as medium- and long-term needs. UN-TAC was to set priorities for meeting Cambodia's many needs, which included humanitarian relief and resettlement needs, as well as improving its physical infrastructure and promoting economic development. The agency was also to mobilize funds and then coordinate rehabilitation activities that would be un-dertaken directly by international, bilateral, and nongovernmental organizations, often through existing Cambodian institutions. Thus the most important aspect of UNTAC's rehabilitation mandate was that it would catalyze the commitment to Cambodia's reconstruction that had been made in the Paris Accords by UN member nations and the international financial community.

Appeal for Donors

In April 1992 Secretary-General Boutros Boutros-Ghali issued an appeal for $595 million for Cambodian rehabilitation.[26] The secretary-general also made a controversial request of $111.8 million for commodity aid and balance-of-payments support to help stabilize the economic and social situation in the coun-try.[27] These funds were, in essence, to be used to prop up the Phnom Penh regime's administrative structure. This aspect of the plan was bitterly opposed by the Khmer Rouge. Over its opposition the twelve-member Supreme National Council (SNC), which had been established as the interim repository of Cam-bodia's sovereignty and contained representatives of all four factions, adopted the framework outlined by the secretary-general on May 7, 1992.[28]

The Declaration on the Rehabilitation and Reconstruction of Cambodia, one of the three Paris Accords documents, stipulated that particular attention should be given in the rehabilitation phase to food security, health, housing, training, education, the transportation network, and the restoration of Cambodia's basic infrastructure and public utilities.[29] The secretary-general's February 1992 imple-mentation plan categorized the urgent needs to be met as three types: humani-tarian aid (food, health, housing, etc.), resettlement assistance—both for the refugees and for the populations in the villages where the refugees would settle—and physical infrastructure renewal and services.[30]

In defining the nature of Cambodia's infrastructure needs, however, the focus was heavily weighted toward preserving the economic stability of the Phnom Penh regime.[31] "The language of the document equates 'Cambodia' with the Phnom Penh government, fueling Khmer Rouge charges of UNTAC 'de facto recognition' of that party as the country's legitimate representative."[32] When the Khmer Rouge complained to the UNTAC chief, Yasushi Akashi, he waved aside their complaints and pressed forward to seek the funding the UN believed was necessary to keep the country from falling apart.

The Tokyo Donors' Conference, June 1992

On June 20 and 22, 1992, Japan hosted the Ministerial Conference on Rehabilitation and Reconstruction of Cambodia (Tokyo Conference) in response to the secretary-general's appeal. The donors' commitments exceeded Boutros-Ghali's expectations with pledges totaling $880 million.[33] However, in their final statement the donors expressed serious concern about "the difficulties UNTAC is encountering in the implementation of the Agreements, in particular over the refusal of one party to allow the necessary deployment of UNTAC."[34]

In May an SNC-UNTAC Technical Advisory Committee on Rehabilitation, under the chairmanship of the UNTAC director of rehabilitation, had been established to review, with all four factions, all proposals and programs for rehabilitation projects. This Technical Advisory Committee would then recommend to the SNC projects for approval. The Khmer Rouge refused to cooperate with the Technical Advisory Committee on the grounds that many of the proposed projects tended to support the Phnom Penh regime.[35] Akashi pledged on June 22 that "he would insure that funds were distributed 'in an equitable manner' to areas controlled by each of the four factions."[36] He also sent a signal that, unless UNTAC were able to deliver the assistance freely, the Khmer Rouge was not going to receive it.[37]

Approval of Rehabilitation Projects

Although the secretary-general indicated in September 1992 that Khmer Rouge cooperation had increased after the donors' conference, it still posed obstacles to the approval of projects. Six months after UNTAC had begun operations in Cambodia, virtually none of these proposals had been translated into activity on the ground. Most remained at the proposal stage, pending completion of further studies. The slow rate at which actual work was undertaken resulted in criticism of UNTAC for insufficient progress on reconstructing Cambodia's physical infrastructure. That criticism reflected a lack of understanding about UNTAC's role in the rehabilitation process, which gave it responsibility for coordinating reconstruction but no mandate for initiating or undertaking projects itself.

Although it was represented on the Technical Advisory Committee, the Khmer Rouge largely blocked its effective use, causing the director of rehabilitation to fall back on a process of individual discussions with each faction about rehabilitation proposals. That process created problems, causing donors to circumvent the formal procedures, often appealing directly to Sihanouk for project approval, believing that his signature would suffice in place of SNC approval.[38]

Further hampering UNTAC's coordination of rehabilitation activities was less than full cooperation on the part of donors. Some donors requested approval of projects only after they had already signed agreements with Phnom Penh, thus depriving the Technical Advisory Committee of any real chance of amending the projects.[39] There were numerous examples of bilateral aid projects that, for political reasons, were never even submitted to the Technical Advisory Committee for approval.[40]

As the formal mechanisms for approving projects did not work well, neither did the informal process of UNTAC consultation with the factions separately. Most of the assistance was negotiated by donor agencies directly and exclusively with the Phnom Penh administration, leaving out the other three factions. Donors essentially went their own way, arguing that, since it was their money, they should control how it was spent. The result was that of the $880 million pledged, donors directed $85 million to activities not identified by the UN as priority needs or not intended to begin until after the elections were held.[41]

Slow Disbursement of Donor Funds

A more serious problem, however, was that disbursement of assistance by the donors proceeded exceedingly slowly. At the same time the list of approved projects grew even longer.[42] By March 1993, although $540 million of the $880 million pledged had been committed for specific rehabilitation activities, only $100 million had actually been disbursed.[43]

Aid disbursement was hampered by a variety of considerations including donors' greater interest in long-term projects, which were often conditioned on additional studies, than in meeting immediate needs and national rehabilitation. Donor countries preferred larger-scale rehabilitation projects, "possibly for reasons of profile as well as of development philosophy."[44] By contrast, the nongovernmental organizations initiated a large number of projects, many of which were small and simple but effective in the Cambodian context. Underpinning much of the hesitation was a fundamental unwillingness to embark on large-scale aid commitments with the country's political future so uncertain. Political violence had been rising during the fall, peaking in December 1992. In the early months of 1993, it appeared uncertain whether the May 1993 internationally supervised election for a new government would be held at all, despite a remarkably successful voter registration drive that had been completed by February 1993. Roger Lawrence, UNTAC's rehabilitation director, expressed concern that donor nations had been slow to make good on their pledges for fear the peace process would fall apart: "We are in a vicious circle here in which the peace process founders in part because the economic component isn't working—and the economic part is not working because the peace process is perceived as foundering. . . . Whole regions of Cambodia haven't seen any tangible evidence of reconstruction."[45]

Rehabilitation was also hindered by other problems, including donors' tendency to neglect the rural areas in favor of projects to benefit Phnom Penh city dwellers. Five of Japan's nine projects were for Phnom Penh residents, even though 90 percent of Cambodia's population lived in rural areas.[46] The background paper for the February donors' review meeting observed that the donors' concentration on Phnom Penh and the northwestern provinces, where the bulk of the refugees were expected to settle, was leading to an uneven distribution of projects that could adversely affect Cambodia's reconstruction. The lack of clear focus on rural rehabilitation had resulted in the particular neglect of the northeastern provinces. It also contravened the objectives of the Paris Accords, which stipulated that "economic aid should benefit all areas of Cambodia, especially the more disadvantaged, and reach all levels of society."[47]

Donors tended to fund their commitments associated with repatriation and resettlement, but not their pledges related to training and the maintenance of essential social services. In fact, 77 percent of disbursements through mid-December 1992 had gone to repatriation and resettlement activities, with only 5 percent to infrastructure support, 5.8 percent to general education and training, and 6.6 percent to health and sanitation.[48] Nor did disbursements mirror overall pledges, since only one third of the total funds committed were for resettlement activities.[49] After the May elections the success of quick-impact projects as part of the repatriation and resettlement activities was recognized and incorporated into the development strategy.[50]

Donor commitment was once more reaffirmed at the first meeting of the International Committee on the Reconstruction of Cambodia (ICORC) of September 8–9, 1993, in Paris. The establishment of ICORC had been agreed upon at the 1992 Tokyo Conference, but it was not intended to become operational until after the formation of a new Cambodian government. It was to serve as an international mechanism for coordinating, together with the new government, medium- and long-term assistance for Cambodia's reconstruction.[51] By the first meeting of ICORC, donors' efforts had, as a matter of course, shifted from rehabilitation to reconstruction, with a recognition of the need for urgent financial assistance to the newly elected government to provide effective administration throughout the country.[52] A subsequent ICORC meeting in March 1994 reaffirmed the international community's commitment to the reconstruction of Cambodia and increased pledges from contributing countries that raised the total committed since 1991 to $1.7 billion.[53]

Budgetary support for the new government was supposed to come from international financial institutions as well as from direct bilateral aid. Assistance from the multilateral lending institutions had been previously blocked by failure of the four factions to agree on terms for loans. The formation of the new government made possible the start of loan negotiations between Cambodia and the World Bank,[54] as well as a visit by the managing director of the IMF.[55]

UNTAC's Protection of Cambodia's Natural Resources

Early on UNTAC recognized the serious threat posed to Cambodia's environment and to its economic future by overexploitation of natural resources, particularly the rapid depletion of timber stock and gem mines. On May 7, 1992, UNTAC suggested that the SNC consider establishing a mechanism for reviewing the contractual arrangements relating to extraction of natural resources. On July 23 the SNC decided to set up a second Technical Advisory Committee, also chaired by UNTAC's rehabilitation director, to recommend specific measures to deal with the problem. That work, which included the review of a countrywide moratorium on the export of logs from Cambodia, principally into Thailand, laid the groundwork for measures taken against the Khmer Rouge later that year.[56]

On September 22, 1992, the SNC, acting at UNTAC's recommendation, adopted a moratorium on the export of unprocessed logs beginning December 31. When the UN Security Council adopted measures on November 30 designed to force Khmer Rouge compliance with the peace plan, it included the moratorium on the export of logs from Cambodia "to protect Cambodia's natural resources," as well as a ban on oil sales to Khmer Rouge areas.[57] Neither the Thai government, however, nor its military, nor Thai businesspeople had any interest in abiding by the logging provisions of the UN embargo, which jeopardized their lucrative trade with the Khmer Rouge. A moratorium on the export of minerals and gems from Cambodia was adopted by the SNC on February 10, 1993, over Khmer Rouge objections, but this was also ignored by the Thais.[58]

Donor governments' reluctance to disburse funds was not shared by the private sector. There was a remarkable growth in indigenous trade and entrepreneurship, spurred by UNTAC's expenditures as well as foreign private investment, which fostered a general sense of confidence in Cambodia's future. Although this was limited largely to Phnom Penh, it nonetheless had a notable effect on Cambodia's economy.[59]

Many believed that the only way to defuse the Khmer Rouge threat was to reintegrate Cambodia into the international community. Ending Cambodia's diplomatic isolation was important; rebuilding Cambodia economically was equally so. The Khmer Rouge's appeal, they believed, would be rendered less attractive if Cambodians were to see the economic benefits that could flow from Western-style commerce. Thailand's and Japan's backing for such an approach was hardly disinterested. Both moved in quickly (and in Thailand's case, rapaciously), for Cambodia had historically been a source for economic exploitation.

Laying the Groundwork for Rebuilding Cambodia

Unlike repatriation, which was a virtually unqualified success, rehabilitation and reconstruction had a somewhat less favorable outcome. Donors were less forthcoming with their pocketbooks than they were with rhetoric. Moreover, the need to keep the aid flows neutral had an inhibiting effect on development.[60]

Like most of UNTAC's other components, the rehabilitation and reconstruction component was not truly neutral in how it carried out its work. It attempted to keep aid flows distributed fairly, but it was not capable of controlling foreign investment, nor could it prevent donors from directing their aid to support their own particular political clients. Undoubtedly, the preponderance of assistance to urban areas skewed rehabilitation work in the Phnom Penh authorities' favor.

Khmer Rouge objections were vehement, but to no avail. By denying UNTAC access to the areas it controlled, the Khmer Rouge handed UNTAC its most powerful lever: money. Whereas funds flowed, to a greater or lesser extent, into the areas controlled by all three other factions, the Khmer Rouge–controlled areas were denied the economic benefits of both official donor rehabilitation assistance and private foreign investment. Although the Khmer Rouge leaders must have chewed their nails in frustration, they never backed down, undoubtedly fearing that exposure to Western commerce and ideas could erode their political support if they opened their areas even the slightest bit.

Yet for all its problems UNTAC laid the groundwork for Cambodia's eventual reconstruction. It developed a plan, set priorities, established mechanisms for coordinating international assistance, both during its tenure and after the formation of the new government, and sustained donors' interest in rebuilding Cambodia.

LESSONS FROM CAMBODIA

Relief and Maintenance Phases

Undoubtedly, there are likely to be more problems with relief efforts conducted amidst ongoing conflicts than with repatriation and rehabilitation programs during the implementation of an internationally agreed-on peace process. Peace agreements provide parameters within which the involved parties must operate. They also provide an explicit structure for the humanitarian aid effort. Emergency relief efforts, by their very nature, tend to be ad hoc operations. In Cambodia's case the lack of centralized coordination was a key problem during the initial relief effort. Gradually, the endeavor developed into two relief operations: The first, on the Thai-Cambodian border, had to deal with massive influxes of people and their need for not only food but clothing, shelter, and work; the second entailed a program to feed the "starving" population inside Cambodia that had been physically dislocated and ravaged by years of Khmer Rouge rule. That effort was complicated by hostility from the Vietnamese occupiers and the Phnom Penh regime toward outsiders running a program that would, if successfully carried out by the local regime, have earned it some legitimacy as a government. The regime's desire for legitimacy had a number of effects: It restricted the relief effort to provision of food, preferring to handle delivery itself. As a result its government bureaucrats were fed first and the civilian population was left in many instances to fend for itself. Second, it prevented the transformation inside the country from relief to a development program that Cambodia badly needed. Thus the Phnom Penh regime and its Vietnamese occupiers perverted the aid program's objectives and significantly contributed to the duration of the drawn-out maintenance phase.

As the years passed, Vietnamese obstacles and international hostility toward the occupation caused the program within Cambodia to wither. With donors precluded from engaging in rehabilitation and development inside Cambodia as the regime became increasingly diplomatically isolated, the aid program concentrated on the Thai-Cambodian border where the refugees' physical maintenance became the sole function. Military and diplomatic stalemate kept the refugees confined to camps as the resistance factions' forces filtered in and out, siphoning off food and supplies. Maintenance was costly, although it became somewhat more efficiently handled when UNBRO took over. There the problem sat—with the refugees denied resettlement rights within Thailand or entry into third countries. Keeping the camp populations in place served the factions' interests. It also served Thai military interests that had profited enormously from the relief operation.

In Cambodia's case those involved with the relief effort made the best of difficult circumstances. However, they allowed collective guilt for nonaction during the years of Khmer Rouge rule to shape their perceptions of the situation inside Cambodia, thus causing them to overestimate the prospects for starvation. Although malnutrition existed, the more critical problem was distribution. Most of the massive outpouring of aid never made it to ordinary Cambodians, who nonetheless managed to survive.

More unfortunate, Western donors subordinated their concern for the Cambodian people's welfare to their determination to oppose the Vietnamese occupiers. The legitimation of the Khmer Rouge—the originator of the conflict— was the unintended result. In that sense the Western donor governments share equally the blame for perverting the relief operation's objectives and perpetuating the conflict.

Repatriation

Clearly, UNTAC repatriation worked better than the relief operation because it occurred as part of an overall peace process under UN auspices. Repatriation worked because all Cambodian factions and the international community wanted the refugees returned. Repatriation also worked because it was carried out by a single entity: UNHCR as a part of UNTAC. The plethora of agencies—official and nongovernmental—that responded to the border refugee crisis reflected an outpouring of concern, if not guilt, but they tended not to work well together. Coordination was difficult and hindered by political factors. Repatriation was free of many such constraints.

Central to the repatriation's success was UNTAC's information and education campaign. It taught Cambodians about democratic elections and gave returnees confidence that the country was on a new, different track. The agency's civilian quick-impact projects and the military civic-action programs also helped ease the refugees' return with activities that had a tangible economic effect on ordinary Cambodians.

Dealing with dislocated populations is likely to become an increasingly important job for the UN as ethnic and tribal conflicts become more pervasive.

Today's conflicts are causing sudden, massive displacement of populations—from Rwanda, from Bosnia, and from some of the former Soviet republics. Kurds are still displaced; Sudanese are on the move; and Angolans remain unsettled. Increasingly, the UN will be called on not only to feed, clothe, and shelter those displaced but also to move them back when conflict winds down. The UN experience in Cambodia points strongly to the necessity for working actively to depoliticize repatriation efforts by seeking commitments to that effect from the involved parties and by the UN itself maintaining strict neutrality to maximize the participants' cooperation. Deliberate efforts by UNHCR to maintain impartiality, while time-consuming and occasionally torturous, prevented the process from being subverted by any faction. Although it may be difficult to achieve such balance in future repatriation efforts, UNTAC's success suggests that it is possible and worth the effort.

Rehabilitation and Reconstruction

Clearly, UNTAC helped to jump-start Cambodia's economic recovery and laid the groundwork for development projects that had been anticipated. From 1991 to 1993 economic growth ranged between 7 and 8 percent.[61] Some of that growth resulted from money that flowed into Cambodia because of UNTAC's presence, but it also reflected Cambodians' confidence in the future.

Peace, or something approximating it, came to Cambodia because the patrons decided to stop using their surrogates to fight their own battles and instead to concentrate on finding a way for Cambodians to govern themselves. The UN was essential to that effort. The UN engaged in peace-building in Cambodia—an effort that far exceeded that of a simple humanitarian operation. Whether UNTAC's impact will be longer lasting now rests with the Cambodian people.

NOTES

1. Portions of this chapter appeared in Janet E. Heininger, *Peacekeeping in Transition: The United Nations in Cambodia* (New York: Twentieth Century Fund, 1994).

2. Robert H. Miller, "Historical Sources of the Conflict in Southeast Asia: Cambodia at the Vortex," *Conflict* 10, no. 3 (1990): 207.

3. Ibid.

4. William Shawcross, *The Quality of Mercy: Cambodia, Holocaust, and Modern Conscience* (New York: Simon & Schuster, 1984), p. 415. The assessment of the initial relief effort draws heavily on Shawcross's work.

5. Ibid., p. 97.

6. Ibid., p. 373.

7. Ibid., p. 144.

8. Internal U.S. Department of State memorandum dated February 2, 1981, as cited in Shawcross, *The Quality of Mercy*, p. 381.

9. For a description of the shift from relief to maintenance, see Shawcross, *The Quality of Mercy*, pp. 353–54.

10. As quoted in Shawcross, *The Quality of Mercy*, p. 415.

11. The author discusses material in this section on repatriation and in the following section on rehabilitation and reconstruction in *Peacekeeping in Transition*.

12. Quoted in Ron Moreau, "The Perilous Road Home," *Newsweek*, April 13, 1992, p. 37.

13. *Report of the Secretary-General on Cambodia*, UNTAC, S/23613, February 19, 1992, para. 137, p. 23 (Secretary-General's Implementation Plan).

14. Secretary-General's Implementation Plan, para. 138, p. 23; and Moreau, "The Perilous Road Home," p. 36.

15. Philip Shenon, "U.N. Starts Cambodia Refugee Return," *New York Times*, March 31, 1992, p. A12.

16. William Branigin, "U.N. Starts Cambodian Repatriation," *Washington Post*, March 31, 1992, p. A14.

17. Henry Kamm, "Return of Refugees to Cambodia to Take Longer than Planned," *New York Times*, April 12, 1992, sec. 1, p. 22.

18. William Branigin, "Missteps on the Path to Peace," *Washington Post*, September 22, 1992, p. A14.

19. William Branigin, "Khmer Rouge Balks, Halts Peace Process," *Washington Post*, June 13, 1992, p. A15.

20. Kamm, "Return of Refugees to Cambodia."

21. *Fourth Progress Report of the Secretary-General on the United Nations Transitional Authority in Cambodia*, UN Security Council S/25719, May 3, 1993, para. 89.

22. Lois B. McHugh, *United Nations Operations in Cambodia*, CRS Issue Brief IB92096, Congressional Research Service, updated January 25, 1993, p. 7.

23. *Fourth Progress Report*, para. 88.

24. Ron Moreau, "Cambodia: 'This Is My Home,' " *Newsweek*, February 22, 1993, p. 38.

25. U.S. Congress, Senate, Committee on Foreign Relations, *Reform of United Nations Peacekeeping Operations: A Mandate for Change*, 103rd Cong., 1st sess., August 1993, S. Prt. 103-45, p. 29.

26. For an itemization of that figure, see *The Secretary-General's Consolidated Appeal for Cambodia's Immediate Needs and National Rehabilitation*, UNTAC, May 1992, p. i.

27. Ibid.

28. *Report on UNTAC's Activities: The First Six Months, 15 March–15 September 1992*, September 15, 1992, para. 135, p. 29.

29. *Declaration on the Rehabilitation and Reconstruction of Cambodia*, UN Security Council S/23177, October 30, 1991, Annex, sec. IV, para. 10.

30. Secretary-General's Implementation Plan, para. 153, p. 26.

31. For Special Representative Yasushi Akashi's defense of such emphasis, see *Cambodia: An Economic Assessment of Rehabilitation Needs*, UNTAC, June 22, 1992, foreword. The information contained in the report was gathered in March 1992, although the report was not issued until June. It served as the basis for *The Secretary-General's Consolidated Appeal*.

32. William Branigin, "U.N. Peace-Keeping Efforts Criticized in Cambodia, Bosnia: Khmer Rouge Charges Tilt toward Phnom Penh," *Washington Post*, June 19, 1992, p. A30.

33. David E. Sanger, "880 Million Pledged to Cambodia But Khmer Rouge Pose a Threat," *New York Times*, June 23, 1992, p. A2; Philip Shenon, "Most Cambodians See Nothing of Aid," *New York Times*, February 21, 1993, sec. 1, p. 10.

34. *Tokyo Declaration on Cambodia Peace Process*, Ministerial Conference on Rehabilitation and Reconstruction of Cambodia, Tokyo, June 22, 1992, reprinted in *Japan Times*, June 23, 1992, p. 13.

35. *Report on UNTAC's Activities*, paras. 139–40, p. 30; *Second Progress Report of the Secretary-General on the United Nations Transitional Authority in Cambodia*, UN Security Council S/24578, September 21, 1992, para. 52, p. 12.

36. Sanger, "880 Million Pledged to Cambodia."

37. Ibid.

38. United States General Accounting Office (GAO), "Subject: Multilateral and Bilateral Donors Who Have By Passed Approved Channels for Project Endorsement by the SNC," internal memorandum, no date.

39. Ibid.

40. Ibid.

41. *Appendix II: Multilateral Humanitarian and Development Assistance to Cambodia*, document provided to the GAO by Michael Feldstein, desk officer for Indochina, Agency for International Development, dated by GAO October 20, 1992, p. 12. The main report to which the Appendix belongs could not be located by GAO. The $85 million figure was also cited in the donors' review meeting of February 25, 1993, *Rehabilitation and Development in Cambodia: Achievement and Strategies*, a report prepared by UNTAC in collaboration with UNDP and the UN specialized agencies, p. 3.

42. *Third Progress Report of the Secretary-General on the United Nations Transitional Authority in Cambodia*, UN Security Council S/25124, January 25, 1993, para. 86, p. 18.

43. *Report of the Secretary-General on the Implementation of Security Council Resolution 792 (1992)*, UN Security Council S/25289, February 13, 1993, para. 31, p. 8; *Multilateral Humanitarian and Development Assistance to Cambodia*, p. 12.

44. Donors' review meeting of February 25, 1993: *Rehabilitation and Development in Cambodia*, p. 3.

45. Shenon, "Most Cambodians See Nothing of Aid."

46. Ibid.

47. Donors' review meeting of February 25, 1993: *Rehabilitation and Development in Cambodia*, p. 22.

48. Ibid., p. 24.

49. Ibid.

50. *Report of the Secretary-General Pursuant to Paragraph 7 of Resolution 840 (1993)*, UN Security Council S/26090, July 16, 1993, para. 30, p. 6.

51. *Tokyo Declaration on Rehabilitation and Reconstruction of Cambodia*, Ministerial Conference on Rehabilitation and Reconstruction of Cambodia, Tokyo, June 22, 1992, para. 5 and Annex: "Framework of ICORC."

52. "First Meeting of the International Committee on the Reconstruction of Cambodia," press release, Paris, September 9, 1993, para. 17, p. 9, available from the United Nations Conference on Trade and Development (UNCTAD).

53. William Shawcross, *Cambodia's New Deal*, Contemporary Issues Paper no. 1 (Washington, DC: Carnegie Endowment for International Peace, 1994), p. 87.

54. "First Meeting of the International Committee on the Reconstruction of Cambodia," para. 18, p. 9.

55. "IMF Chief Visits Indochina," *Indochina Digest* 6, no. 41 (October 15, 1993): 1.

56. *Second Progress Report of the Secretary-General*, paras. 57–58, p. 13.

57. Trevor Rowe, "U.N. Council Penalizes Khmer Rouge," *Washington Post*, December 1, 1992, p. A32.

58. *Report of the Secretary-General on the Implementation of Security Council Resolution 792 (1992)*, para. 25, p. 7.

59. See *Impact of UNTAC on Cambodia's Economy*, a report prepared by the Economic Adviser's Office, UNTAC, Phnom Penh, December 21, 1992, p. 15.

60. Ibid., p. 14.

61. Shawcross, *Cambodia's New Deal*, p. 77.

8

Humanitarian Aid in the Former Yugoslavia: The Limits of Militarized Humanitarian Assistance

JOSEPH R. RUDOLPH, JR.

On July 11, 1995, two years, two months, and four days after the UN Security Council had declared Srebrenica, Zepa, Bihac, Tuzla, Goradzde, and Sarajevo protected "safe havens" in order to assure the UN's ability to provide humanitarian assistance to the citizens and displaced Bosnian Muslim refugees in those cities, Bosnian Serb forces seized Srebrenica, forcing as many as forty thousand civilians to flee. Within a week, as stories of atrocities circulated concerning the fate of the Bosnian Muslim soldiers captured by the Serbs, Zepa fell and the thirty-five thousand Muslim refugees jammed into that protected area began their trek toward another uncertain sanctuary.

The blatancy of the Serbian attacks, as much as the military action itself, forced the kaleidoscope of countries and international organizations involved with the UN's operation in the former Yugoslavia to reassess their commitments to the operation. Some questioned whether the UN mission in Bosnia could or should be continued. Yet even before these events, there were clear signs that the UN mission in the former Yugoslavia was in trouble (and not just because of operational snafus like the one that had deployed over one thousand essentially unarmed and untrained Bangladeshi peacekeepers in Bihac the previous November). Thus, for example, Serb leaders in Bosnia and elsewhere had repeatedly threatened to retaliate against civilians and UN personnel in the event that NATO air power were to be used against the Serbian artillery attacking the "safe havens." Furthermore, shortly before the assaults on Srebrenica and Zepa, the French commander of the UN forces in Sarajevo had told his officers not "to

accept any more casualties. . . . Under no circumstances . . . engage either warring party [in activities] which might put the life of one of our soldiers in jeopardy."[1]

Somewhere, somehow, something (or several things) had gone seriously awry
in the UN's humanitarian venture in the former Yugoslavia and its largest peacekeeping operation ever.[2]

ANATOMY OF THE CONFLICT

Yugoslavia's decomposition is chronicled briefly in the appendix to this chapter, as is the story of UN and international humanitarian intervention there.
Weaving these tales together are four broad themes. When the federal state that
Tito had forged began to unravel in the late 1980s, it was composed of six
republics, plus two autonomous zones (Vojvodina and Kosovo) in the Serbian
republic. Because of the large numbers of Serbs in many of the states outside of
Serbia, the Serbian leaders controlling the Yugoslav federation and military made
it clear that they would not accept existing internal boundaries as the basis for
the states' seeking independence.[3] It was not an idle warning. When Slovenia,
Croatia, and Bosnia-Herzegovina declared their independence, warfare ensued.

The initial battleground was Slovenia; however, after a short skirmish, probably because of the modest numbers of Serbs in that republic (see Table 8.1),
the federal government withdrew its army from Slovenia and aimed it at Croatia.
A longer war ensued there before a ceasefire officially ended hostilities and the
battle shifted to Bosnia-Herzegovina, where conflict ebbed and flowed for more
than three years before the Bosnian Serbs began seizing the "safe havens" they
had hitherto been besieging. With the subsequent lull in the fighting in Bosnia,
the drama shifted back to Croatia, whose army had utilized the Serbian military's
focus on Bosnia to attack and evict the Serbs living in the self-declared "Independent Serbian Republic" inside Croatia. Throughout, the overall rhythm of
the warfare has been much more that of a meandering than a broadening or
escalating war. Conflict has never been heavy in any two republics at the same
time. Nor have the conflicts as yet spread to the politically sensitive areas of
Montenegro and Kosovo, despite frequent fears that they might. Nor, except for
the international boycott placed on it for aiding the Serbian factions in other
republics, has Serbia itself been a battleground. At the same time each new twist
in the battle zones has generated a need for the involvement of outside parties—
as peacemakers, monitors of ceasefire lines, investigators of the charges of human
rights violations and genocide, and protectors of the tenderers of humanitarian
assistance to the thousands of displaced people inside the former Yugoslavia and
the equivalent numbers pouring into neighboring countries.

Humanitarian Peacekeeping

The "humanitarian crises" of displaced persons that have earmarked the conflict from its outset are largely the product of the "siege warfare" techniques

Table 8.1
The Peoples of the Former Yugoslavia[1]

Republic	Majority Group	% Serbian	Population
Bosnia-Herzegovina	Slovenes (39.5%)[2]	32%	4.1 million
Croatia	Croats (75.1%)[3]	11.5%	4.6 million
Macedonia	Macedonians (67%)	2.3%[4]	1.9 million
Montenegro	Montenegrins (68.5%)	3.3%[5]	600,000
Serbia (Overall)	Serbs	85.4%	9.3 million
Kosovo Region	Albanians (77.4%)	13.2%	1.6 million
Vojvodina Region	Hungarians (19%)	54.4%	2.0 million
Slovenia	Slovenes (90.5%)	2.2%	1.9 million

Notes:
[1] All figures are pre-conflict. Most are based on 1980 census materials, reported in Glenn E. Curtis, ed., *Yugoslavia: A Country Study* (Washington, DC: Library of Congress, 1992), p. 293. The population estimates in the final column were as of 1991.
[2] An additional 7.9 percent of the population in Bosnia-Herzegovina identified themselves as "Yugoslavs."
[3] An additional 8.2 percent in Croatia identified themselves as "Yugoslav." Outside of Bosnia-Herzegovina, Croatia, Serbia (4.8%), and the smaller areas of Montenegro (5.3%) and Vojvodina (8.2%), only approximately 1 percent or fewer claimed "Yugoslav" as their national identity.
[4] The Albanian minority, by contrast, was 19.8 percent.
[5] Montenegro also has a 13.4 percent Muslim minority.

pursued by the Serbian forces. Bosnian and Croatian towns that could not be taken were cut off from power, water, and food, and those inhabitants who sought to relieve their misery often had difficulty penetrating the Serbian lines. As a result, throughout much of the conflict, the boundary between UN "peace operations" (preventive deployment, peacekeeping, peace enforcement) and humanitarian ones has been blurred.[4] Indeed, the UN fundamentally blurred that line in August and September of 1992, when it dispatched thousands of peacekeeping forces to Bosnia as Chapter VII (enforcement) units charged with taking "all necessary actions" to protect the flow of humanitarian assistance. Subsequently, the war in Bosnia has produced a cornucopia of phrases of the "robust self-defense," "preventive peacekeeping," "aggressive peacekeeping," and "muscular peacekeeping" ilk—the lexicon of peacekeeping escalating with the increasing numbers of UN troops in Bosnia-Herzegovina to the point where the humanitarian and peacekeeping missions of the UN have become so intertwined that it is difficult, as a practical matter, to separate them.

Last to Arrive, Last to Leave

The UN became involved in the deteriorating political situation in the former Yugoslavia only after a series of other third parties (the European Union, NATO, the Western European Union, and the Helsinki group) failed to halt the growing conflict among Yugoslavia's constituent regions and nationalities. In part, this development reflected Secretary-General Boutros Boutros-Ghali's philosophy that regional conflicts, as much as possible, should be treated by regional organizations; however, in a broader sense, it fits the habitual pattern of the UN's becoming involved in a dispute only after other parties have failed to resolve the conflict and/or exacerbated it, and after the conflict has escalated in size, complexity, and resistance to diplomatic resolution. Not surprisingly, the UN's record in solving or even managing these conflicts has been a checkered one: In not a single instance has the UN interceded in a communal conflict of the Croatian-Bosnian Muslim-Serb variety and been able to resolve it peacefully. Late in becoming involved, the UN has usually been the last outsider to leave such conflicts (e.g., Lebanon and Cyprus).

Mission Creep

Finally, UN activity has steadily escalated incrementally, from monitoring the ceasefires in Slovenia and Croatia, to launching a large, humanitarian mission (especially in Bosnia), to deploying tens of thousands of peacekeepers to protect the UN's humanitarian programs. In turn, the latter eventually led to the arrival of NATO rapid deployment ground forces (RDF) in July 1995 to protect the UN troops guarding the humanitarian personnel in Bosnia's "safe havens."[5] Finally, NATO forces replaced UN peacekeeping forces and imposed at least a temporary settlement by force of arms on Serb forces in Bosnia.

AGGRESSIVE PEACEKEEPING—AUTOPSY OF THE MISSION

It is easier to trace the escalation of intervention than it is to explain how the UN mission in the former Yugoslavia turned so sour. The UN was not without experience in civil wars. Moreover, from the outset the stories emanating from the field were discouraging, bearing such headlines as "Shelling Greets U.N. in Croatia,"[6] "Frustrated UN peacekeepers threatening to pull out of Sarajevo,"[7] and "Hostility toward U.N. Builds in Sarajevo."[8] Indeed, it is precisely because of its messy experience in both the Congo and Lebanon and its initially negative experience in Croatia and Bosnia that the UN might have been expected to be better prepared for what it later encountered in Bosnia.

In fact, the prospects for the UN's ability to fashion a successful response to the conflicts and crises in Slovenia, Croatia, and Bosnia were never very good, given that the UN was facing other challenges when Yugoslavia began to collapse and given the complexity of the conflict that the UN faced within the former Yugoslavia.

Context, Context, Context

If the three keys to success in business are location, location, location, it may be equally said that the three essential elements in successful policy development and implementation all involve context.

Thus, when Saddam Hussein's army invaded Kuwait, he presented the world with an unmistakable case of international aggression in the heartland of the energy source on which Western civilization runs. In the face of this aggression, the national interests of the United States, its European and Pacific allies, the democratizing states of Central Europe, and many Arab states were generally in harmony, or as nearly so as countries with such diverse interests can be: Halting Saddam's army and controlling Saddam's ambitions was in everyone's interest. In addition, political leaders who considered foreign policy their strong suit occupied the presidencies and prime ministerships of the United States, France, Britain, and Germany, while the Soviet Union, which might previously have vetoed a strong UN Security Council response, had just lost a good part of its former territory and was dependent on Western countries for the funds its democratizing leadership needed to survive.[9]

However, no parallels characterized either the breakup of Yugoslavia or the interests of those actors who responded to the misery, human rights violations, and communal conflict its collapse produced. To the contrary, a host of other interests and endeavors continuously precluded a careful, coordinated response to events in the former Yugoslavia by the international community and continuously diluted the implementation of those policies that did emerge.

At the same time Yugoslavia was collapsing, so too was the Soviet Union.[10] This was a vastly more important event to the United States and its NATO allies, not to mention Russia. Likewise, while Slovene leaders were declaring Yugoslav laws invalid in Slovenia in February 1992, most of the major actors in international relations were engaged in a 100-hour ground and air offensive against Saddam Hussein's army in Iraq. Later, lingering problems with Saddam Hussein forced the United States to deploy troops in Kuwait (August 1992), and to protect Iraqi Kurds and Shiite Muslims from Saddam's army, even as the unraveling of the humanitarian operation in Somalia was forcing the United States to consider a military operation there as well. And so it went. By the summer of 1992, Russia's peacekeeping priorities were being directed toward its own borders, troubled by ethnic conflicts from Moldavia to Central Asia. To the west a suddenly unifying Germany was coming to terms with the economic and social costs of unification, including rising violence inside Germany against its foreign residents and refugees.

Nor were Russia and Germany the only countries whose problems with internal ethnic conflict or breakaway regions deflected their attention from events in Yugoslavia and/or diminished their support for the self-determination efforts of others. The spring-summer of 1992 found Spain concerned that violence in Catalonia or its Basque region would mar the Olympic Games about to be held in Barcelona.[11] Canada—long a mainstay in UN peacekeeping undertakings—was again preoccupied with constitutional reforms to avert a successful Quebec referendum on continuing the union with the rest of Canada. France was facing a resurgence of national violence by the separatists in Corsica and by the French against foreigners in France, who were being scapegoated for most of France's unemployment ills by Le Pen's National Front. Britain was still searching for a means of resolving the conflict in Northern Ireland, where twenty thousand of its troops had been deployed for twenty years, a conflict that had spread to London during Christmas of 1991. And all the while, in 1990–92, the principal countries in Europe were struggling through the difficult negotiations involved with drafting, ratifying, and implementing the Maastricht Accord designed to push European supranationalism to a new level. Meanwhile outside Europe, Nigeria remained deeply mired in the civil war in Liberia, and India was still calculating the costs it had incurred in trying to resolve the Sinhalese-Tamil communal war in Sri Lanka.

Against this backdrop the unfolding events in central Europe were of only secondary or tertiary concern to most of the world's principal powers. Moreover, when these actors did focus on the developments in Croatia and Bosnia, diverse national interests frequently set key players at cross-purposes to one another. The United States sided early with the Bosnian Muslims and their effort to create an independent Bosnia. Germany, though generally committed to the principle of self-determination, for historical reasons tended to support the Croats in their efforts to launch an independent Croatia and in their clashes with both the Serbs and the Bosnian Muslims in Bosnia-Herzegovina. For its part, Russia persistently leaned toward the Serbs, even to the point of occasionally undermining the UN's operation in the former Yugoslavia.[12]

International bodies have similarly had difficulty in responding effectively to developments in the Yugoslav theaters. In addition to their members frequently dividing over the issues confronting them, divergent organizational interests and perspectives have made it difficult for these bodies to collaborate effectively. As Rand analyst James Steinberg has summarized the situation, the CSCE initially placed its emphasis on protecting human rights. In contrast, the European communities were more concerned with conflict resolution, but only insofar as it could be achieved through political mediation and proffered economic rewards. The Western European Union and NATO favored a military response; the UN preferred responses of a peacekeeping and humanitarian aid nature.[13] Occasionally the turf battles and conflicting orientations of these actors resulted in policy paralysis; at other times policy losers in one arena carried *their* priorities to another, as when British and German leaders, unable to gain support in Europe for their peacekeeping proposals, carried them to the UN for action.

If It's December It Must Be Somalia

Lastly, the sudden proliferation of UN peacekeeping operations after 1990 may have prevented the specific missions undertaken from receiving due consideration. On the eve of the war in Bosnia, for example, the UN committed approximately twenty thousand troops to Cambodia under the auspices of the UN transitional authority there, even as it was struggling to continue financing its mission of twenty-two hundred in Cyprus.[14] Concurrently, the collapse of the Soviet Union was generating pressures on the UN to deploy peacekeeping forces to avert or contain conflicts involving the countries emerging from the Soviet empire.

The requests for UN peacekeeping personnel often came from those living in such troubled areas as a South Africa committed to major system change.[15] In some instances—and events in Bosnia and Croatia fall largely into this category—the dangers to the peace posed by rising violence and international conflict have forced the UN to act. Still, to no small degree the sharp increase in UN peacekeeping activities resulted from Secretary-General Boutros-Ghali's determined effort to carve a role for the UN in the post-Soviet world order. Thus, although often speaking of the role of regional organizations in resolving regional conflicts, the secretary-general steadfastly clung to Article 53 of the UN Charter to defend the Security Council's exclusive right to undertake enforcement activities in response to such conflicts.

For whatever reason, UN peacekeeping activity proliferated between 1988 and 1994 at a rate exceeding one new mission every six months. Moreover, the critical months were precisely those in which the decisions were made regarding the war in Bosnia; that is, the fall and winter months of 1992, which begat the operation in Bosnia, the preventive peacekeeping mission in Macedonia, and the humanitarian venture in Somalia, a venture that shortly involved twenty-eight thousand U.S. soldiers augmented by personnel from more than a dozen other countries.

ASSESSMENT: HUMANITARIAN PEACEKEEPING IN THE FORMER YUGOSLAVIA

Alan James has correctly cautioned against assessing peacekeeping operations solely on the basis of whether the conflict is resolved rather than in terms of their achievements across a range of goals, including crisis defusion, truce maintenance, and contribution to the avoidance of broader military confrontations.[16] From this perspective the UN's accomplishments in former Yugoslavia cannot be easily dismissed, especially given the circumstances under which its humanitarian peacekeeping operations had to function there.

Communal conflicts are, persistently, the most difficult of all conflicts to resolve. They can quickly tribalize domestic conflict control arrangements and strip the veneer of civilization away from developed societies no less than developing ones.[17] It was just this type of conflict that confronted the UN mission in the former Yugoslavia.

Measured in human terms, the cost of the conflicts in Slovenia, Croatia, and Bosnia has been enormous to a country formerly containing only approximately twenty million people. In the secretary-general's December 3, 1992, report on the situation in Bosnia and Herzegovina, it was estimated that more than three million people in the former Yugoslavia required humanitarian assistance, most as refugees and displaced persons.[18] Without humanitarian assistance, more than 400,000 Bosnian Muslims were expected to die of starvation and exposure during the winter of 1992–93; over half the prewar Bosnian population was estimated to need outside assistance to ensure sufficient supplies of food, medicine, and shelter for the winter.[19] Most searing, the stories emanating from the conflicts were consistently vile—tales of torture, misery, and horror, of genocidal ethnic cleansing, and of the Serbs using rape, torture, and mass exterminations as tools of warfare and land reclamation.[20]

In responding to this situation, the UN pursued a multipronged blend of humanitarian relief operations, refugee assistance, investigations of human rights violations, ceasefire and conflict resolution negotiations, and even aggressive peacekeeping operations to contain the conflict.[21] Thus, when the initial relief efforts were disrupted by Serbia, Security Council Resolution 770 called on member states to take those measures necessary to assure the delivery of assistance. The resolution eventually led to the creation of the United Nation Protection Force in Bosnia (UNPROFOR II). Similarly, when it was later estimated that still only 25 percent of the humanitarian supplies were reaching their intended recipients, the UN adopted the "no fly zone" policies to better assure their arrival. Along the way UN forces helped to clothe and feed the refugees and the besieged and, in some instances, helped rebuild war-torn areas. Meanwhile, UNPROFOR I in Croatia continued to discharge its noncombatant roles of assuring the delivery of humanitarian relief, protecting released detainees, and implementing ceasefire agreements.[22]

The UN also pursued preventive policies to minimize war-zone atrocities and avert the spread of the conflicts into other areas. Fact-finding contingents were thus dispatched and war crimes tribunals were threatened for the most egregious abusers of human rights, creating a precedent later followed by the UN in responding to events in Rwanda. When an invasion of Macedonia by either the Serbs or Albania seemed a possibility, the Security Council unanimously agreed to dispatch a battalion of U.S.-supplied "preventive" peacekeepers to that republic to deter the spread of war to it.[23]

Unfortunately, it is difficult to measure the UN's success quantitatively in terms of what has not happened, perhaps because of its presence, that is, the number of people who might have died had humanitarian assistance not been tendered, the regions that might have been invaded had it not been for preventive peacekeeping efforts, and the atrocities that might have been committed were UN personnel not watching and thereby steering the process of ethnic cleansing into gentler channels. It becomes particularly difficult to be satisfied with this accounting mechanism when the overall flow of events in the former Yugoslavia has been so persistently discouraging. Legal scholars and practitioners who hoped that strong UN action in Bosnia would lead to prosecution of those committing war crimes have been particularly critical of the UN. Typical is the conclusion of the law professor who argues that "for whatever reason, the Security Council has been worse than ineffective in stopping human starvation used as an intentional strategy of war, intentional shelling and bombing of civilians, mass rape, 'ethnic cleansing,' and other genocidal acts, and outside aggression."[24] Yet even if the focus is on what the UN has affirmatively achieved, for virtually every accomplishment there is a qualification.

The peacekeepers sent to the "safe havens" ultimately failed in their mission when the Serbs chose to attack these towns and use the peacekeepers as hostages in their bargaining with NATO.

Throughout UNPROFOR II's operation UN supplies sent to the besieged were routinely disrupted.

The embargo placed on Yugoslavia for aiding Serbian combatants in Bosnia caused suffering among the citizens of Belgrade and Serbia without ending the war; the arms embargoes placed on all belligerents were porous even before the United States began to reexamine an arms policy that officially denied the Bosnian Muslims the weapons with which to protect themselves.

The more egregious acts of ethnic cleansing and atrocities were ameliorated, but not eliminated, and there is little likelihood that significant numbers of perpetrators will ever be punished.

Massive starvations were averted, but the relievers became a part of the besieged, and the perhaps 500,000 Yugoslav refugees resettled outside their homelands have often become a source of international irritation as the costs incurred by those housing them have steadily increased.[25]

LINGERING QUESTIONS FROM A LINGERING CONFLICT

The Article 2(7) Labyrinth

Beyond the legal community, comparatively little attention has been devoted to the question of the circumstances under which the UN may legitimately undertake humanitarian intervention in a decomposing state, given (a) the prohibition in Article 2(7) of the UN Charter against intervention "in matters which are essentially within the domestic jurisdiction of any state" and (b) the admonitions in the Helsinki Accords against altering borders. The UN was able to sidestep this issue in Yugoslavia by recognizing Croatia, Slovenia, and Bosnia-Herzegovina, thereby turning the (until then) Yugoslav civil war into an international conflict lying within the Security Council's competence. Subsequently,

Croatia's government conveniently *invited* the UN to deploy UNPROFOR I inside its borders, thereby negating any charges of UN intervention in Croatia—but only at the considerable cost of leaving the UNPROFOR operation in Croatia at the pleasure of a government that was itself committed to the goal of ethnic cleansing.

Though hardly satisfactory, such stopgap arrangements suffice in the political world when there is both the will and the physical capability to undertake the type of humanitarian peacekeeping operations mounted in Yugoslavia and Somalia.[26] Nevertheless, to the extent that these operations are supposed to reflect a more rule-of-law world in which human rights enjoy greater protection, humanitarian intervention in civil wars requires a more concrete, legal foundation. In this regard the conflicts in Yugoslavia may have borne fruit, producing new legal justifications for extending the reach of the Security Council to civil wars when the warfare either generates border issues involving adjacent states—as occurred to a very limited extent along Slovenia's border with Austria during the Yugoslavia-Slovenia conflict—or generates such a large exodus of refugees into adjacent states that the war acquires a significant international dimension.[27]

Self-Determination versus Viability

The principal political question is closely related to the legal one discussed herein: Under what circumstances does fidelity to the principle of national self-determination warrant diplomatic (much less military) support of separatist ethno-territorial groups in a multinational state, especially where these movements are likely to be militarily opposed by the central government or where the outcome may be a small country of modest to weak economic viability? The UN did not have to face this issue in Yugoslavia; by the time that country's decomposition affected the Security Council's agenda, a substantial number of states were already in the process of extending diplomatic recognition to Croatia and Slovenia. Nor is Yugoslavia's collapse likely to produce states of marginal economic viability, given the prevailing assumption that the newly democratizing states of Central and Eastern Europe will all, sooner or later, be parts of the European Union and thereby benefit from economies of scale.

Nevertheless, the (at best) borderline irresponsible behavior of Germany and other countries in encouraging Croatia and Bosnia to pursue independence without calculating the consequences or providing them with the tangible support necessary to go their separate ways securely remains one of the more depressing sideshows of the Yugoslav drama. Moreover, with the exception of a few scholarly articles largely written by renowned students of nationalism,[28] there has been very little discussion of what constitutes responsible political behavior when the principle of self-determination clashes with the ability of territorial minorities to go it alone. It remains very much an issue needing to be addressed in a world of multinational states with grieving territorialized minorities.[29]

Managing Interventionary Diplomacy

More immediately, a series of important logistical, tactical, and strategic issues raised by this humanitarian peacekeeping venture requires a careful examination before similar ventures are pursued. These include:

1. the UN's capacity to manage multidimensional peacekeeping ventures at the current level, especially given the multiple problems of coordination that they pose;[30]
2. the UN's ability to secure the United States' increasingly essential support for and involvement in dangerous peacekeeping operations at a time when there is reluctance to expose U.S. ground troops to danger and the Congress is cutting financial commitments to the UN;[31]
3. the UN's ability to recruit enough blue helmets to staff its expanding peacekeeping operations without having to rely on large numbers of troops of questionable experience and qualifications from Third World or Central European states eager to rent them to the UN for hard currency;[32] and
4. the UN's ability to fashion mission definitions and rules of engagement capable of diminishing the vulnerability of peacekeepers without obliterating the self-restraints that separate peacekeeping from enforcement missions.[33]

If the UN can resolve any of these issues, it should become easier to resolve the others. More secure operations, for example, might ease the crunch the UN is facing in raising peacekeeping forces. Yet even if all these issues are resolved, there will still remain two key strategic questions raised by the humanitarian peacekeeping operation in Bosnia: First, is peacekeeping a suitable response to the growing number of communal conflicts in the world? Second, how effective can peacekeepers be in such conflicts?

Peacekeeping and Evil

When Soviet tanks crushed the nationalist revolution in Budapest in 1956, it was suggested that the next time such an intervention occurred, NATO states should flood the invaded country with journalists and Red Cross volunteers. Their watchful eyes, it was posited, would restrain Soviet brutality. Few asked the question that the communal conflict in Bosnia has forced the world to face: What if the aggressor does not care what anyone thinks?

The answer to that question is now clear. Neither monitors nor peacekeepers sent to protect humanitarian programs can deter the carnage, however "aggressive" or "muscular" the peacekeeping may be. Peacekeepers typically require the permission of the host country to operate in its borders and may thus be sent packing whenever the host government demands it. Nor can peacekeepers stop ethnic cleansing by well-armed factions, customarily lacking, as peacekeepers are, in both the mandate and the armor that would be necessary to do so. Peacekeepers function best, as has been persistently noted, where there is a peace to keep.

Where the problem is an ongoing or escalating war, unilateral or NATO-like multilateral military intervention *may* force the belligerents to consider negotiations, but a thin line of blue helmets deployed among military units led by elements opposed to any compromise is incapable of doing so.[34]

The Impossibility of Neutrality

Equally serious, even where men of good will interested in peace lead the warring communities, it is highly unlikely that a peacekeeping operation will contribute to conflict resolution because of the high probability that the peace-keepers will, themselves, become a part of the conflict, unless the peacekeepers appear on the scene with overwhelming force.

Much has been recently written about the de facto absence of impartiality in UN operations.[35] In fact, few multilateral or unilateral peacekeeping missions have been truly neutral. The United States had a definite stake in the outcome of the communal conflict in Lebanon and has similarly had one in mind in Bosnia. The same can be said of Britain in its intervention in Northern Ireland, and India in its intervention in the power struggles between Tamils and Sinhalese and among Tamil factions in Sri Lanka. Even so, it has been particularly difficult to view UN action in Yugoslavia as being neutral, and not just because at the time of its intervention only one of the national actors (the Serbs) was being accused of genocide and of willfully disrupting international humanitarian assistance. By definition UN relief missions were prejudicial to the Serbian strategy of besieging their Croatian and Bosnian Muslim enemies and starving them into submission.

More generally, it may be impossible for peacekeepers to function in a manner likely to be long perceived as neutral in an ongoing civil war. Peacekeeping personnel necessarily define their mission in static terms, either legally (laws or ceasefires requiring enforcement) or militarily (protecting a territorial status quo). In either instance it means identifying with an existing order in a dynamic situation where the legitimacy of the status quo is at issue, and—however inadvertently or indirectly—becoming a part of the combat. Thus although pyramiding peacekeeping personnel on top of humanitarian assistance programs in a communal war may temporarily give those programs greater protection, the long-term cost is likely to entail the peacekeepers' becoming either hostages to the conflict (Bosnia) or combatants in it (the UN in Somalia, India in Sri Lanka).

In the meantime the Yugoslav drama continues, and as this chapter goes to press, the new configuration of the former Yugoslavia after the inevitable departure of NATO forces is most likely to be drawn by military forces in the field and sustained by balance-of-power arrangements weighing Croatia (and perhaps Bosnia) against Serbia-Belgrade, perhaps each with its own set of outside protectors and protagonists. The system *may* even bring a parcel of peace to the combatants. If so, however, it will be packaged in a form much more reminiscent of previous world orders than the new and better, more rule-of-the-law world whose image inspired the UN humanitarian operations in the former Yugoslavia such a relatively short time before.

APPENDIX: THE CONSTRUCTION AND DECONSTRUCTION OF A STATE

Background

1878	Serbia, including Montenegro, achieves independence from Ottoman rule.
1918	Kingdom of the Serbs, Croats, and Slovenes is formed following World War I.
1929	King Alexander I names the country Yugoslavia and assumes near dictatorial powers.
1945	Tito assumes power of postwar Yugoslavia, converting it into a communist state composed of six republics.
1980	Tito dies but the continuing fear of Soviet domination helps temporarily to hold the country together.
1990	Revolutions sweep the Soviet Union and Eastern Europe; four Yugoslav republics elect noncommunist governments.

Disintegration

1991	Western countries encourage Croatia and Slovenia to secede, promising them early diplomatic recognition. Both declare their independence on June 25. War ensues briefly in Slovenia; by winter heavy fighting engulfs Croatia.
January 15, 1992	The EC diplomatically recognizes Croatia and Slovenia.
February 1992	Bosnia-Herzegovina votes for independence; the UN creates a peacekeeping force for Croatia.
March 1992	A ceasefire takes hold in Croatia; the EC proposes a plan for the cantonization of Bosnia.
April 7, 1992	United States recognizes the three breakaway republics and EC recognizes Bosnia; warfare in Bosnia ensues.
May 7, 1992	Serbs and Croats agree to divide Bosnia-Herzegovina without consulting the 44 percent Muslim plurality there.
May 15, 1992	United Nations Resolution 752 demands end of outside interference in Bosnia and noninterference with humanitarian aid.
May 22, 1992	The UN admits Slovenia, Croatia, and Bosnia.
May 30–31, 1992	The UN votes to impose mandatory economic sanctions on Yugoslavia for militarily aiding Bosnian Serbs.

Conflagration

June 4, 1992	At Oslo, NATO agrees to permit its soldiers to operate outside of NATO territory in Europe.
July 1992	The EC negotiator, Lord Carrington, obtains Serb agreement to place heavy weapons under UN auspices.
August–September 1992	London Peace Conference fails to reach an agreement; the UN approves the use of force to deliver aid to Bosnia and threatens to try perpetrators of war crimes; UNPROFOR II is deployed in Bosnia.
September 19, 1992	Security Council votes 12–0 to expel Yugoslavia for supporting Serb aggression in Bosnia.
October 9, 1992	The UN creates initial "no fly" areas, banning military flights over war zones.
December 11, 1992	Security Council votes to deploy a preventive peacekeeping force in Macedonia (Resolution 795).
January 2, 1993	Doomed Vance-Owen Plan for splitting Bosnia-Herzegovina into ten cantons is unveiled in Geneva.
February 22, 1993	Security Council unanimously authorizes an international tribunal to prosecute war crimes.
May 1993	Bosnian Serbs reject Vance-Owen Plan; Security Council creates six "safe havens" in Bosnia.
August 1994	(Muslim) government of Bosnia finally defeats breakaway Muslim faction in Bihac.
September 1994	Croatian and Bosnian Muslim leaders agree to begin constructing a joint federation.
November 1994	War in Bosnia enters third winter with Bosnian Muslims launching a briefly successful counteroffensive.
January 12, 1995	President of Croatia threatens to end the mandate of the twelve thousand UN troops in Croatia.
February 13, 1995	The UN Yugoslav War Crimes Tribunal orders the arrest of twenty-one Bosnian Serbs for committing atrocities.
May 30, 1995	United States agrees to permit the use of U.S. ground forces to protect evacuation or relocation of peacekeepers.
June 1995	France, the United Kingdom, and Holland create an armored RDF to protect peacekeepers in Bosnia.
July 1995	Serbs launch major offensive against safe areas; Srebrenica and Zepa fall; Boutros-Ghali delegates the secretary-general's veto over NATO air strikes to UN field commanders in Bosnia; RDF deployed in Sarajevo.
August 1995	Croatia launches all-out offensive against the rebellious Serb region in Croatia, adding 200,000 Serbs to refugee crisis confronting UN workers; Serb attack on Sarajevo produces sustained NATO air response.

December 14, 1995   Under U.S. auspices, leaders of Bosnia, Croatia, and Ser-
                           bia sign Dayton, Ohio Accord partitioning Bosnia-
                           Herzegovina. A Muslim-Croat federation is awarded 51
                           percent of the land, while Serb separatists are granted 49
                           percent. U.S. forces are deployed to implement the Ac-
                           cord.

1996   Implementation of Accord proceeds slowly, as difficulties
                           surface in the field. Accord-mandated elections in Bos-
                           nia are repeatedly deferred.

NOTES

1. General Hervé Gobilliard, cited in a Reuters dispatch appearing in *The* [Baltimore] *Sun*, May 16, 1995.

2. More than thirty-five thousand UN troops were in the former Yugoslavia as of June 1992–nearly ten thousand more than operated in the Congo at the height of the UN's 1960–64 involvement in that country's civil war, previously the UN's most massive undertaking.

3. For discussions of the background to, and early stages of, the conflict in the former Yugoslavia, see especially Charles Gati, "From Sarajevo to Sarajevo," *Foreign Affairs* 124, no. 4 (1992): 64–78; Sabrina Petra Ramet, "War in the Balkans," *Foreign Affairs* 124, no. 4 (1992): 89–98; and Sabrina Petra Ramet, *Nationalism and Federalism in Yugoslavia, 1962–1991* (Bloomington: Indiana University Press, 1992).

4. Concerning the UN's peace operations, see *Peace Operations: Information on U.S. and U.N. Activities* (Washington, DC: GAO, 1995).

5. Britain, France, and the Netherlands, the three NATO states providing the RDF, collectively accounted for nearly one third of the UN peacekeeping contingent in Bosnia and Croatia. As of May 1995 French personnel numbered 4,603 among the 36,856 UN troops, and British troops 3,516. Jordan and Pakistan were contributing approximately 3,000 troops each, and Canada had slightly over 2,000 troops there. The Netherlands ranked sixth, with 1,684 troops in the field. *Washington Post*, May 31, 1995, p. A24.

6. Associated Press story, reported in the *Washington Post*, March 12, 1992.

7. *The* [Baltimore] *Sun*, August 6, 1992.

8. *Washington Post*, December 31, 1992. By comparison the initial reports involving other recent peacekeeping operations have often been overly optimistic; for example, "Boutros-Ghali Confident on Somali Peace Talks" (*Washington Post*, January 6, 1993).

9. See Michael Mandelbaum, who describes the Gulf War as "the last gasp of a morally and politically clearer age," in "The Reluctance to Intervene," *Foreign Policy* 95 (Summer 1994): 3.

10. See, for example, "Gorbachev Clears Way for Secessions," *Washington Post*, August 27, 1991, reported at approximately the same time Lord Carrington was conducting negotiations aimed at averting a war in Croatia.

11. "Spain Sees Basques' Arrests Reducing Threats to Olympics," *New York Times*, March 31, 1992.

12. See, for example: "Serb, Russian Nationalists Forge Alliance from Wreckage of Bosnian Strife," *Washington Post*, January 3, 1993; and "U.N. Fires Russian for Allegedly Aiding Croatian Serbs," *Washington Post*, April 12, 1995.

13. See James P. Steinberg, "International Involvement in the Yugoslavia Conflict,"

in Lori Fischer Damrosch, ed., *Enforcing Restraint: Collective Intervention in Internal Conflicts* (New York: Council on Foreign Relations Press, 1993), pp. 49–76.

14. "Finances Imperil UN Cyprus Effort," *Washington Post*, April 18, 1992.

15. See "ANC Seeks UN Presence in Africa," *Washington Post*, July 16, 1992.

16. Alan James, "The U.N. Force in Cyprus," *International Affairs* (Summer 1989): 481–500.

17. See Joseph Rudolph, "Intervention in Communal Conflicts," *Orbis* 39, no. 2 (1995): 259–73.

18. UN Doc. A/47/747, 1992, paras. 34–36.

19. "Bosnian Deaths May Top 400,000 This Winter," *The* [Baltimore] *Sun*, November 4, 1992.

20. See, for example, "Bosnians Deported in Sealed Rail Cars," *The* [Baltimore] *Sun*, July 23, 1992; "Serbs Accused of '91 Croatia Massacre," *Washington Post*, January 26, 1993; and "Refugees Tell of Serbian Acts of Terror in Banja Luka," *The* [Baltimore] *Sun*, March 27, 1994.

21. Steinberg, "International Involvement," pp. 43–44.

22. For a discussion of the success of the UNPROFOR contingents in the context of the noncombatant nature and goals of their missions, see Major-General John A. Mac-Innis, Deputy Force Commander for UNPROFOR, "The Rules of Engagement for U.N. Peacekeeping Forces in Former Yugoslavia: A Response," *Orbis* 39, no. 1 (1995): 97–100.

23. Macedonia was later (1994) accorded international recognition and seated in the UN.

24. Jordan J. Paust, "Peace-Making and Security Council Powers: Bosnia-Herzegovina Raises International and Constitutional Questions," *Southern Illinois University Law Journal* 19 (Fall 1994): 131–42.

25. See "Bosnian War Refugees Languish in Slovenia: Goodwill Eroding as Costs of Care Mount," *Washington Post*, January 9, 1993.

26. The UN sidestepped the domestic jurisdiction issue in Somalia by the facile route of determining that there was no government in charge whose jurisdiction it could be usurping.

27. See especially in this context Ruth Gordon, "United Nations Intervention in Internal Conflicts: Iraq, Somalia, and Beyond," *Michigan Journal of International Law* 15 (Winter 1994): 519f; Jost Delbruck, "A Fresh Look at Humanitarian Intervention under the Authority of the United Nations," *Indiana Law Journal* 67 (Fall 1992): 887f; and Steven John Stedman, "The New Interventionists," *Foreign Affairs* 72, no. 1 (1993): 1–15.

28. See especially two articles in *Foreign Affairs*: Michael Lind, "In Defense of Liberal Nationalism," *Foreign Affairs* 73, no. 3 (1994): 87–99; and Gidon Gottlieb, "Nations without States," *Foreign Affairs* 73, no. 3 (1994): 100–112. Also thoughtful are Amitai Etzioni's sharp critique of the national self-determination principle, "The Evils of Self-Determination," *Foreign Policy* 89 (1992–93): 21–35; Michael Walzer, "The New Tribalism: Notes on a Difficult Problem," *Dissent* 49 (Spring 1992): 164–71; and Gerard F. Powers, "Testing the Moral Limits of Self-Determination: Northern Ireland and Croatia," *Fletcher Forum of World Affairs* 14, no. 2 (Summer 1992): 29.

29. Concerning ethnicity, conflict, and international politics, see Charles William Maynes, "Containing Ethnic Conflict," *Foreign Policy* 90 (Spring 1993): 3–21; and Rodolfo Stavenhagen, "Ethnic Conflicts and Their Impact on International Society," *International Social Science Journal* 43 (February 1991): 117–31.

30. Challenges involve coordinating (1) a variety of peacekeeping ventures around the world from New York; (2) a series of peacekeeping activities in a single operation (e.g., UNPROFOR I in Croatia; UNPROFOR II in Bosnia); and (3) a number of peacekeeping units in a single theater of war (e.g., the units from the nineteen different countries operating in Bosnia at the end of 1994). Concerning the breakdown of these coordination efforts in Bosnia, see Peace Operations, esp. p. 23.

31. Circularly (and perversely), U.S. foreign policy has been trying to utilize UN personnel because of the risks of engagement to U.S. troops, even as the Congress has sought to pare contributions to the UN because of the perceived ineffectiveness of its operations. See "Republicans Seek to Curb U.N. Funding: Peacekeeping Efforts Could Be Eliminated," Washington Post, January 23, 1995; and "U.S. Urges U.N. Forces to Remain in Bosnia," The [Baltimore] Sun, July 13, 1995.

32. This problem has grown as Canada and other long-time contributors to international peacekeeping forces have reconsidered their commitments in light of the increasing duration and dangers of recent UN peacekeeping missions. However, except for the hardship the weather worked on Bangladeshi troops ill prepared for it, there are few adverse tales related to mercenaries as peacekeepers in the UNPROFOR missions—certainly nothing to rival the tales of blue-helmeted Bulgarians flying home from Cambodia in an aircraft laden with a diminishing supply of heavy spirits, a number of Cambodian prostitutes, and an excess of souvenir snakes slithering down the aisle, all after the troops were accused of corrupt activities while in Cambodia.

33. See "U.N. Approach to Peacekeeping Undercuts Ability to Protect," Peace Operations: Update on the Situation in the Former Yugoslavia (Washington, DC: GAO, May 1995), sec. 3. On the specific problem of peacekeeping without guidelines in the "conceptual no-man's land" between peacekeeping and enforcement, see John Gerard Ruggie, "The U.N.: Wandering in the Void," Foreign Affairs, 72, no. 4 (1993): 26–32.

34. Concerning the advantages of side-taking over peacekeeping in civil wars involving competing nations, see Rudolph, "Intervention in Communal Conflicts." For a more general discussion of the weakness of the UN in the contemporary world, see Saadia Touval, "Why the U.N. Fails," Foreign Affairs 73, no. 3 (1994): 44–45.

35. See Richard K. Betts, "Delusions of Impartiality: the United Nations and Intervention," Current (February 1995): 27–32; and Betts's more extensive article, "The Delusion of Intervention," Foreign Affairs 73, no. 4 (1994): 20–33.

PART III

Prospects for Future Humanitarian Interventions

9

The United Nations High Commissioner for Refugees in the Post–Cold War Era

GIL LOESCHER

Formally established in 1950 at the height of East-West confrontation, the United Nations High Commissioner for Refugees (UNHCR) was initially charged with protecting and assisting people displaced in the aftermath of World War II and those fleeing Communist persecution in Europe. From the 1960s until recently, the focus shifted away from Europe to the Third World. During the last thirty years most of UNHCR's operations have been centered in Africa, Asia, and Latin America. Although the assistance contributed by the international community has at times been substantial, the pressures created by the presence of large refugee populations and sudden mass exoduses in recent years have been enormous. By the beginning of 1995, the number of people living in exile had increased to twenty million. No continent is now immune from the problem of mass displacement. In addition to new and recurring crises in the Third World, significant refugee movements have recently taken place in the Balkans and throughout the former Soviet Union. Refugee populations in excess of ten thousand can now be found in over eighty different countries around the world.[1]

INTERNAL WARS AND REFUGEES IN THE POST–COLD WAR ERA

The 1990s have ushered in a new era for refugees. During the Cold War, refugee movements were principally caused by wars between states, by the breakup of colonial empires and the creation of multiethnic states, and by the spread of communist regimes.[2] Today, by contrast, refugee movements are likely to be the result of internal ethnic, communal, religious, and secessionist conflicts, fueled by the increasing availability of arms and antipersonnel mines, sharp socioeconomic divisions, human rights abuses, anarchy, and environmental degradation. The UNHCR has been confronted with one refugee emergency following another in rapid, sometimes overlapping succession. Refugee crises in Iraq, Bosnia, Croatia, Sudan, Sierra Leone, Kenya, Somalia, Bangladesh, Nepal, the Caucasus, Tajikistan, Benin, Ghana, Rwanda, Burundi, and elsewhere have strained UNHCR capacities almost to the breaking point. At the same time UNHCR is trying to resolve the longstanding refugee problems of the previous decade, primarily through repatriation in a context of continuing instability and insecurity.

The end of the Cold War has brought about major changes in the general pattern of refugee emergencies and the challenges they pose to the international refugee regime for the provision of relief and protection.[3] Most of the major refugee crises of the 1990s are triggered by internal conflicts in which ethnic identity and secession are prominent elements in both the goals and the methods of adversaries. In such conflicts it is common for civilians to be used as weapons and targets in warfare, and large-scale displacements are perceived as a legitimate political means to claim control over territory.

The current climate is unlike that of previous decades, when the former superpowers provided authoritarian states or their adversaries with arms, resources, and political support. The ending of the Cold War has removed many of the constraints that the United States and the former Soviet Union placed on their former clients. Local conflicts are no longer kept in check by the need to avoid flash points that could lead to direct superpower conflict. The collapse of communism and the breakup of the former Soviet Union, the end of bipolar ideological rivalry, and the reluctance on the part of the remaining major powers to commit their armed forces and their financial expenditures to foreign crises where their national interests are not jeopardized have freed authoritarian leaders to repress their opponents and have allowed minorities and opposition groups to initiate secessionist struggles. Moreover, whereas the former superpowers no longer use the Third World to pursue their geopolitical rivalry, other states do. For various reasons they have stepped into the breach to provide support to one side or the other in most internal wars. In addition, arms continue to be easily acquired on the world market by virtually all parties. Consequently, reduced tensions between Moscow and Washington have paradoxically been followed by growing violence and larger numbers of forcibly displaced people in the developing countries, parts of the former Soviet Union, and the Balkans.

As the numbers of wars involving secession and state formation have become more frequent and destructive in the aftermath of the Cold War, governments and international organizations have begun to try to influence countries whose policies and internal conditions have created massive refugee flows. The goal of the international actors is to enable those who have fled to return home. Unfortunately, the international community lacks experience in devising policies to affect the internal affairs of governments that are unable or unwilling to protect their own citizens. As a result, the most difficult political and humanitarian issues confronting the international community in the mid-1990s are how governments and international organizations can intervene to prevent refugee flights within countries or across international borders, and how they can provide assistance and protection to internally displaced people when their governments or opposition movements object to such intervention or when (as in Somalia, Liberia, or Afghanistan) it is impossible to determine the legitimate government or authority in the country. The more immediate short-term problem for international agencies at present is to determine when and how repatriation and reintegration are most appropriate, particularly when the conflicts, which originally caused the population displacements, are not yet fully resolved.

THE CHALLENGES FACING UNHCR: INSTITUTIONAL CONSTRAINTS AND POTENTIAL PROBLEMS

Throughout the Cold War UNHCR approached the refugee problem in a reactive, exile-oriented, and refugee-specific manner.[4] The agency worked with people primarily after they had fled across borders to neighboring countries, where they required protection and assistance. Staff concentrated their activities on assisting refugees in camps and on negotiating with host governments for support. UNHCR focused exclusively on the consequences of refugee flows rather than on the causes and paid little or no attention to preventing or averting refugee movements. It placed primary responsibility for solving refugee problems on states that received refugees rather than on states that caused refugees to flee. Hence, UNHCR emphasized local settlement and third-country resettlement over repatriation.

The agency also concentrated almost exclusively on people who were deemed to fall within the 1951 UN Refugee Convention definition or those who were forced into exile because of war or related causes. Internally displaced persons were aided only insofar as the home government accepted it.

Since the end of the Cold War, UNHCR faces new challenges for which traditional approaches are inadequate. Now the organization focuses on meeting the immediate needs of refugees, returnees, and internally displaced people who live amidst conditions of intercommunal violence, shifting borders, and ongoing conflict. In countries of asylum across the world, UNHCR has extensive experience in aiding refugees on the basis of its mandate and well-defined international refugee instruments. But in countries undergoing civil wars, UNHCR staff find themselves not only working with governments but also with opposition groups, guerrilla forces, and political factions. In Bosnia, for example, UNHCR has had to negotiate not only with the Bosnian government ministries but also with Bosnian Serb political and military officials. The organization's staff are also engaged alongside UN peacekeeping forces in anarchic and unstable countries that lack viable national and local structures. Their duties include protecting civilians against reprisals and forced displacement, relocating and evacuating civilians from conflict areas, and assisting besieged populations, such as those in Sarajevo, who choose not to move from their homes. Frequently, however, UNHCR lacks any firm institutional and legal basis for this work.

THE CHALLENGES OF WORKING IN INTERNAL CONFLICTS

In the post–Cold War era responding to conflicts and crises before they escalate has become a policy imperative for governments and international organizations alike. Such a policy includes providing early warning, practicing preventive diplomacy, and ensuring respect for human rights. Initiatives in this direction have been undertaken by UNHCR itself, which has started to develop strategies and approaches to address the root causes of refugee flows before they start and to reduce or contain refugee flows that have already begun.[5] The challenge of assisting and protecting people within their own countries raises difficult questions concerning UNHCR's mandate and fundamental principles. This shift to a preventive strategy, moreover, cannot be accomplished easily or quickly. Working in countries of origin differs substantially from working in countries of asylum. The agency is ill-equipped to respond to the needs of refugees, internally displaced people, and returnees who live amid conditions of intercommunal violence and ongoing conflict. For example, UNHCR staff experience serious difficulties in gaining access to displaced people, especially in areas contested by governments and armed opposition groups, and many UNHCR staff lack prior experience in working with internally displaced people. Furthermore, most staff are not recruited or trained to work in the cross-fire of internal conflicts where the internally displaced and returnees are often viewed as the enemy, and UN assistance as biased and as favoring one side to the disadvantage of the other. In situations like Bosnia, the Caucasus, or Tajikistan, UNHCR is using techniques closely akin to the work of the ICRC, but its staff lacks the special training, skills, and experience of ICRC staff members.

A major obstacle to taking a more active role in refugee protection in countries of origin derives from the nature of UNHCR itself. The agency was designed to appear to be nonpolitical and strictly humanitarian, a strategy employed to receive permission to work in host countries and to secure funding from donor governments. As it is presently structured, UNHCR is not mandated to intervene politically against governments or opposition groups, despite documentation of human rights violations. In addition, UNHCR staff are often unfamiliar with human rights and humanitarian law and are uncertain of how governments and opposition groups will react to their interventions using these protection norms.

In many internal wars relief assistance operations are also vulnerable to political manipulation by the warring parties, who perceive humanitarian assistance as one of several weapons of warfare. In most internal conflicts food assistance is used as a political weapon. Adversaries sometimes divert assistance from the proper recipients for military or political goals, and they deny assistance to certain populations and geographical areas by blocking access by international agencies. If UNHCR is to respond effectively to these new internal conflict situations, there is an urgent need both to reorganize the staffing, training, and operations of the agency to reflect its new roles and to give it the necessary resources, tools, and mandate to do the job effectively.

LONG-STANDING INSTITUTIONAL CONSTRAINTS

In addition to political factors, several long-standing institutional constraints inhibit UNHCR action. In particular, the absence of an autonomous resource base and the limited mandates and competencies of UNHCR and other international humanitarian agencies continue to restrict the international community in its response to most post–Cold War refugee crises, just as they have done for most of the past forty-five years.

INADEQUACY OF EXISTING RESOURCE BASE

The 1990s have presented UNHCR with several new emergencies, and its overall expenditures have therefore grown significantly. The sums required for UNHCR operations have risen from around $550 million in 1990 to about $1.5 billion in 1995.

In addition to facing the increased costs incurred in responding to refugee crises, internal displacements, and repatriations, humanitarian missions today are likely to be protracted affairs with no clear outcome. In the former Yugoslavia, for example, UNHCR has committed approximately one quarter of its staff and one third of its total resources worldwide to providing assistance and protection to nearly four million people.[6] The agency is now in danger, not only of overextending itself because of its involvement in vicious and intractable conflicts, but also of exhausting the political interest of donor governments in continuing to fund such protracted operations, even in high-profile situations like Bosnia.

One of UNHCR's most significant weaknesses is its dependence on *voluntary* contributions to carry out existing and new programs. Annual budget projections are based on existing and anticipated refugee case loads, whereas ad hoc or special appeals are issued to meet sudden emergencies. The flow of assistance from donor governments is neither reliable nor always in the most appropriate form. In addition, funding is frequently provided late and is often earmarked for particular uses with political or geostrategic overtones. In the past donor governments have often made funding contingent upon external political factors. Today, however, these governments are less influenced politically by refugee situations, which they view as local or regional problems of little if any direct foreign policy or security value. Without compelling strategic and ideological motivations, funding for refugee operations is being cut back in favor of the domestic priorities of the industrialized states. Indeed, the increasing number of humanitarian emergencies during the past six years has coincided with falling foreign aid budgets in many of the important donor states, particularly in the United States. The major powers are reluctant to provide funds for humanitarian programs when internal conflicts in aid-recipient countries continue unabated. Thus despite the clear link in situations involving displacement and regional security, such as in the Caucasus and Central Asia, there is weak donor interest in funding a comprehensive strategy for dealing with refugees and internally displaced people. In 1992, for example, the UN was unable to raise $100 million for the reconstruction of Afghanistan from states that, during the previous decade, are estimated to have spent over $10 billion on its destruction. It is a tragic irony that major Western donors appear to have lost political incentive for providing generous support to new programs just at the moment when some of the political barriers to effective humanitarian action have disintegrated.

INADEQUACY OF EXISTING MANDATES AND INTERNATIONAL HUMANITARIAN LAW

Although there is a clear mandate for the protection and provision of humanitarian assistance to refugees, existing political, diplomatic, economic, and legal mechanisms are not sufficiently developed to cope with the increasingly complex and volatile population movements of the post–Cold War period. In particular, no specific international organizations are mandated to protect and assist the internally displaced.[7] Although more numerous than refugees, internally displaced persons do not normally qualify for comparable legal protection because they have not crossed an international border. In addition, the political issues involved, particularly state sovereignty and nonintervention in domestic affairs, make the question of the internally displaced one of the most challenging problems confronting the international community in the 1990s.

Furthermore, existing human rights and humanitarian laws offer internally displaced persons inadequate protection. They also do not adequately cover forcible displacements and relocations, humanitarian assistance and access, the right to food, and the protection of relief workers.[8] In particular, situations of public emergency and internal violence fall outside the scope of the Geneva Conventions of 1949 and Additional Protocol II of 1977. As a result many human rights provisions are suspended when an emergency threatens the national security of a state. It is precisely in these conditions that internal displacement often occurs. As the maltreatment and targeting of civilian populations in internal wars has become a more established international concern, efforts to strengthen the norms and mechanisms for dealing with humanitarian assistance and human rights protection have gained new urgency.

THE SEARCH FOR SOLUTIONS REQUIRES NEW ALLIANCES AND NEW ACTORS

Hindered both by its dependence on voluntary contributions to carry out its programs and its need to obtain the acquiescence of host governments before intervening, the UNHCR alone cannot resolve the problems of refugees, returnees, and internally displaced people. More attention needs to be focused on the range of agencies, in addition to the traditional relief organizations, which in the future must be involved in the effort to find solutions.[9] These include development agencies, human rights networks, and peacekeeping and conflict resolution mechanisms—all of which must be involved in innovative approaches and collaborations to resolve conflicts and their accompanying displacements.

Interagency cooperation is the key to a more effective response to the problems of displacement. If UNHCR has any hope of ensuring that it is not alone in working toward a solution to displacement and that it will be able to shift potentially long-term humanitarian operations in the future to other, more suitable agencies, it must continue to work at improving coordination with those who deal with issues such as human rights, sustainable development, and peacekeeping and peacemaking, with particular focus on strategic planning and on making legal and institutional arrangements.

DEPARTMENT OF HUMANITARIAN AFFAIRS

Making the system work better requires a more effective division of labor among the many actors involved in responding to the humanitarian, political, and security dimensions of internal conflicts. In December 1991 the UN General Assembly created the office of Emergency Relief Coordinator with the role of providing a central focal point with which governments and intergovernmental and nongovernmental organizations could negotiate concerning UN emergency relief operations. In early 1992 the Emergency Relief Coordinator was given the higher status of under-secretary-general, heading the newly formed United Nations Department of Humanitarian Affairs (DHA). The new UN department is an important first step toward assigning responsibilities to UN agencies in complex emergencies, especially in situations where mandates overlap or where no entity has a clear mandate to act. The DHA will make quick decisions on the best coordinating mechanisms at the field level and negotiate access to all requisite agencies in an emergency, without waiting for a formal government request. The donor states influential in the creation of the DHA would like the new department to gather data and manage information, mobilize resources and orchestrate field activities, negotiate a framework of action with the political authorities, and provide overall leadership to humanitarian aid efforts.[10]

Unfortunately, lack of adequate staff strength in the field and the rapid succession of humanitarian crises in the post–Cold War period have caught the DHA unprepared and have made it impossible for the department to cover its planned lead role in most recent emergencies. The DHA has been called upon to coordinate the humanitarian response to these emergencies at a time when the mechanisms for interagency coordination are still being established and remain largely untested. Perhaps the greatest difficulty confronting the DHA is that the specialized agencies, including the UNHCR, have a high degree of constitutional autonomy and independence and have resisted any attempt by the DHA to impose strong authority. In recent years the DHA has presented consolidated appeals for humanitarian emergencies to donor governments on behalf of the entire UN community. The response of governments to date has been disappointing, and the appeals, themselves, have often been a collection of individual agency requests rather than a consolidation of requests previously screened to establish priorities and to avoid overlapping or competing activities.[11]

Despite the practical difficulties, there is widespread agreement that, for the DHA to bring about improvements in the UN's response capacity, the office's coordination role needs to be recognized by the other UN agencies; further, the DHA needs to be given sufficient resources, politically and financially, to effectively undertake the tasks assigned to it. Coordination cannot, of course, be arbitrarily imposed from above; the challenge confronting the DHA is how to get UN agencies to function more effectively as a system rather than as a loose collection of independent actors, each with separate mandates, finances, and programs.

COORDINATING RELIEF AND DEVELOPMENT

The international community needs to take adequate account of the relationship between underdevelopment and displacement. Interventions for purposes of relief and development are now viewed as ends of a continuum rather than as separate and discrete activities.[12] Humanitarian aid activities should be conducted in ways that not only provide relief of life-threatening suffering but also reduce local vulnerability to recurring disasters, enhance indigenous resources and mechanisms, empower local leadership and institutions, reduce dependence on outside assistance, and improve prospects for long-term development. Experts believe that relief and development activities that involve local participation generally prove more successful than those that do not.[13]

Closer coordination between UN development and refugee agencies represents a key solution to situations involving refugees, returnees, and the internally displaced. Cooperation between UNHCR and UNDP already takes place in quick impact projects, or "QIPs," that are aimed at assisting a variety of displaced groups in Central America, Mozambique, and Cambodia. In addition, in recent years the two agencies have established joint management structures to create preventive zones and cross-mandate programs to stabilize and prevent displacement in border areas in the Horn of Africa.

Although great efforts have been made at coordination between UNHCR and development and financial institutions like the UNDP and the World Bank, far more effective interagency planning, consultation, and implementation are required. The roles and responsibilities of refugee and development agencies in such efforts continue to be determined on an ad hoc, situation-by-situation basis. In most countries emergency relief aid is administratively and programmatically divorced from development concerns. Unlike refugee and relief-oriented organizations, development agencies usually work on the basis of long-term plans and programs, making it difficult to respond to unexpected events such as refugee movements or repatriation programs.[14] Thus a "development gap" exists between short-term humanitarian relief assistance and long-term development. Through QIPs, which are small-scale development projects, such as the digging of wells, that lead to the immediate rehabilitation of communities, UNHCR and UNDP have recently undertaken some emergency development in countries with large returnee and displaced populations. However, because of their small size and limited nature, QIPs have only partially filled the gap between immediate assistance and longer-term development. In addition, UNHCR is not a development agency, and the task of the overall rehabilitation of these communities has to be carried out by UNDP, the World Bank, or other UN agencies that can more appropriately deal with reconstruction and development. This requires a full transfer of responsibility from UNHCR to the development agencies after the immediate emergency relief phase is over, but this is something UNDP, in particular, consistently resists because it views itself as having a development, not an emergency, focus.

Interagency coordination is especially important in the large-scale repatriations UNHCR is planning for the mid- to late 1990s. Internal conflicts have been highly destructive of physical infrastructures and human capital. Ceasefires and repatriations usually require new financial and political commitments from the international community. In countries such as Afghanistan, Angola, Ethiopia, Cambodia, and Mozambique, a precondition for successful returns is development aid and reintegration assistance aimed at alleviating extreme poverty in countries of origin.[15] Experience in many of these countries has demonstrated that the governments of many war-torn societies are simply not able to assume full responsibility for reintegrating returning refugees and other displaced populations. Without improved economic prospects for returnees and for foreign aid and investment in rebuilding the physical infrastructure in these countries, political instability and new displacements are likely to occur, resulting in renewed need for humanitarian relief. A focus on safety of return and successful reintegration will require rethinking the roles and mandates of international organizations and NGOs: shifting their operational priorities from receiving countries to countries of return, training agency staff to work in conditions involving development as well as relief assistance, and fostering closer cooperation and coordination between development and refugee agencies on the one hand, and human rights and refugee agencies on the other.

LINKING HUMAN RIGHTS AND REFUGEES

Greater development assistance alone is not enough to create safe conditions for those returning home; international cooperation must also ensure democratization and respect for human rights. However, neither good governance nor respect for human rights falls within UNHCR's domain. The existing UN human rights machinery needs to be strengthened and applied more effectively to deal with refugees, returnees, and the internally displaced.[16] Despite the close connection between the refugee problem and the protection of human rights, the international community has until recently maintained a sharp distinction between the two issues. This division was a consequence of the reactive and exile-oriented approach to the problem of refugees that characterized the international refugee regime's activities during most of the Cold War.[17] Mainly because it dealt with refugees only after they had fled from a country where they were persecuted and sought asylum in another state, UNHCR had almost no effect on human rights conditions in countries of origin. The causes of refugee flows were considered to be a separate concern, falling outside the organization's humanitarian and nonpolitical mandate. This rigid separation of UN refugee and human rights agencies and compartmentalization of tasks limited the opportunities to address the underlying causes of conflicts and to encourage respect for human rights.

Despite this long-standing neglect of refugee issues, the UN human rights system has in recent years demonstrated its *potential* capabilities to respond quickly to a select number of human rights emergencies involving the internally displaced. Since 1992 the UN Commission on Human Rights has convened exceptional sessions to discuss urgent human rights situations in the former Yugoslavia and Rwanda, and since 1991 it has regularly discussed the protection needs of internally displaced persons.

At the same time the UN Human Rights Center, through its advisory services, has been associated with a number of UN peacekeeping or peace enforcement missions, providing significant technical assistance and cooperation to the UN human rights presence in the field, for example in El Salvador, Haiti, and Somalia, and now in Cambodia and Rwanda, under the leadership of the new high commissioner for human rights. These actions underscore the key potential role of the UN human rights machinery as well as the Security Council's growing involvement in humanitarian matters; they also highlight the recognition that the promotion and protection of the human rights of refugees, returnees, and the internally displaced are an integral part of UN peacemaking.[18]

Despite growing recognition that the UN human rights machinery needs to become directly involved in refugee protection, many of the traditional constraints on the international human rights regime have not disappeared with the passing of the Cold War. At present the UN human rights program is grossly understaffed and underfunded. At a time when billions of dollars have been poured into emergency relief programs and peacekeeping operations, virtually no extra funds have been provided for the UN human rights regime, despite its potential to strengthen civil society, promote democratic and pluralistic institutions and procedures, and thereby prevent human rights abuses and avert mass displacements.

If the UN hopes to respond more effectively to the global problem of refugees, it must strengthen its capacity to monitor developments in human rights issues. A greater protection role in the field should be granted to UN human rights personnel. At present the UN Human Rights Centre has country expertise but no field presence. Typically, the centre dispatches special rapporteurs, usually on a selective basis, to trouble spots to report back to the commission on alleged human rights abuses. In the short-term the Centre can strengthen its coverage in the field by the continued expansion of its advisory services and technical cooperation to undertake activities that strengthen institutions that sustain democracy and civil society. In addition, by offering services such as training judges, strengthening electoral commissions, establishing ombudsmen, training prison staff, and advising governments on constitutions and legislation regarding national minorities and human rights, the commission is likely to be more successful in its activities and less threatening to governments than in more straightforward human rights monitoring.

In recent years there has been much discussion about the creation of special human rights machinery for the internally displaced.[19] At its 1995 session the UN Human Rights Commission reappointed the special representative on the internally displaced to monitor developments and to help sustain a positive dialogue with a view to achieving solutions with governments. The special representative, however, must be given proper political support and funding in order to carry out his tasks effectively. A General Assembly resolution confirming the role and mandate of the special representative is now required to institutionalize this office further. A significant first step toward trying to deal with the problem would be to designate a permanent representative for the internally displaced. This representative could undertake fact-finding missions, intercede with governments, publish reports, and bring violations to the attention of human rights bodies and the Security Council.

Recently, attempts have been made to create closer linkages between UN refugee and human rights organs. UNHCR and the Centre for Human Rights have agreed to cooperate on information sharing and the training of personnel and are planning joint action with regard to the problem of stateless people. Despite these improvements, there remains an urgent need to develop a coherent and integrated approach to the defense of human rights, the protection of the forcibly displaced, and the resolution of the global refugee problem. Unfortunately, this will continue to be an uphill struggle as long as states continue to guard their sovereignty and remain fundamentally opposed to international human rights monitoring and intervention.

PEACEKEEPING AND OUTSIDE MILITARY FORCES AND REFUGEES

As part of the international community's increasing focus on preventive action, UN agencies and UN peacekeeping forces now place greater emphasis on the problem of displacement in the country of origin. For example, they now help to provide assistance to victims of ethnic conflict as close to their homes as possible, create havens or secure areas where displaced persons can get help in relative safety, deploy troops to prevent the expulsion of civilians in some areas, and protect relief workers who are caught in the cross-fire between opposing sides. In addition to greater pressures to provide in-country assistance and protection, there is greater emphasis on repatriation, which involves organizing the return moves, providing logistical assistance for the actual moves, setting up on-site reception centers at the resettlement locations, and furnishing help in re-integrating refugees. Many refugees will be returning home before the very problems that caused them to flee, including violence and persecution, have been resolved. The danger is that premature returns will result in considerable human rights violations.

Under these circumstances UN and outside military forces frequently work alongside UNHCR and relief agencies to meet humanitarian exigencies in conflict zones. The military brings logistics skills and resources that can meet immediate needs of civilian populations at risk in humanitarian emergencies, including such activities as protecting relief shipments, creating safety zones, prepositioning supplies, and relocating or evacuating civilians.[20]

Although recent experiences have demonstrated that the military has unrivaled access to a range of material and logistical resources which are simply not available to UNHCR and other humanitarian organizations, relief operations in Iraq, Somalia, Bosnia, and Rwanda have also underscored some of the difficulties of military-civilian cooperation in providing relief in situations of continuing conflict. The objectives and working methods of the two groups of actors are different and, in some cases, contradictory. Military staff are often unfamiliar with the mandates and priorities of relief organizations, lack knowledge of human rights norms and international humanitarian law, and demonstrate little appreciation or understanding of local customs and institutions. Military forces rarely, if ever, have a purely humanitarian agenda, and they are generally unwilling to work under external direction, even in operations conducted under UN auspices.

Recent experiences in Bosnia also demonstrate that the provision of military security for relief operations can compromise the neutrality of humanitarian aid agencies and can even threaten the delivery of humanitarian assistance. In the former Yugoslavia UNHCR has had difficulty in carrying out its mandate as a result of its close association with UN military forces on the ground and also, more generally, with the punitive and economic actions taken by the UN Security Council. United Nation troops, mandated to ensure humanitarian access to civilian populations, were not given sufficient means and political backing to carry out their tasks. As a consequence UNPROFOR and UNHCR were criticized for not providing adequate protection to civilians in their own communities and for not being able to rescue them when their lives were threatened. Moreover, sanctions imposed by the Security Council on the Federal Republic of Yugoslavia imposed great hardship on civilians and undermined the credibility of UNHCR to act impartially in a civil war context.

Military and humanitarian intervention can also sometimes have an adverse impact on the resolution of conflicts. In the struggle to provide aid to the displaced and other war victims, the resolution of the root causes of the conflict can easily become increasingly peripheral. In Bosnia, for example, inadequate humanitarian and military action, combined with selective sanctions and ineffective diplomatic initiatives, impeded more robust political and military pressures for most of the conflict. Thus it is likely that, in future relief operations, if humanitarian action is not accompanied by the necessary political will or action to resolve interethnic conflicts, military forces and relief agencies will become bogged down in longstanding, protracted humanitarian operations.

FUTURE INTERNATIONAL COOPERATION AND THE GLOBAL REFUGEE PROBLEM

The refugee emergencies of the post–Cold War era highlight the fact that combating the causes of forced migration cannot proceed solely within the mandate of international humanitarian organizations like UNHCR. The global refugee problem is not a humanitarian problem requiring charity; it is a political problem requiring political solutions, and, as such, it cannot be separated from other areas of international concern such as migration, human rights, international security, and development assistance. Such an approach raises complex questions of harmonization of efforts, coordination, determination of institutional responsibilities, and allocation of resources. Thus the challenge for the international community will be not only to respond to the immediate humanitarian problems of displaced people but also, in the long run, to confront the conditions that lead to these dislocations. These are political tasks that require a more active role from national policy makers and a greater willingness to fully utilize the UN and regional mechanisms on security, peacekeeping and peacemaking, and human rights in order to anticipate as well as react effectively to refugee incidents around the world.

A more comprehensive and effective international response to refugee problems will require that adequate resources be available at short notice. The UNHCR, the Office of the Emergency Relief Coordinator, and other UN agencies cannot accomplish their missions unless the major donor states, including the United States, are prepared to bear a greater financial burden, albeit one that is hardly substantial when compared to the money spent on defense during the Cold War.

Greater interagency cooperation, financial support, and reinforcement of existing institutional mechanisms are the only effective ways for the international community both to manage interdependent issues like refugee movements and to ensure long-term global strategic stability.

NOTES

1. UNHCR, *The State of the World's Refugees, 1993: The Challenge of Protection* (New York: Penguin Books, 1993).

2. Aristide Zolberg et al., *Escape from Violence: Conflict and the Refugee Crisis in the Developing World* (New York: Oxford University Press, 1989); and Gil Loescher, *Beyond Charity: International Cooperation and the Global Refugee Problem* (New York: Oxford University Press, 1994).

3. Loescher, *Beyond Charity*; and Larry Minear and Thomas G. Weiss, *Mercy under Fire: War and the Global Humanitarian Community* (Boulder, CO: Westview Press, 1995).

4. UNHCR, *The State of the World's Refugees, 1995: The Search for Solutions* (Oxford: Oxford University Press, 1995).

5. Office of the United Nations High Commissioner for Refugees, Inter-Office Memorandum no. 78/92, *The Report of the UNHCR Working Group on International Protection* (Geneva: UNHCR, July 31, 1992).

6. Author's interviews with UNHCR staff in Geneva.

7. Francis Deng, *Protecting the Dispossessed: A Challenge for the International Community* (Washington, DC: Brookings Institution, 1993).

8. Norwegian Refugee Council and Refugee Policy Group, *Human Rights Protection for Internally Displaced Persons* (Washington, DC: Refugee Policy Group, 1993).

9. For a more detailed discussion of the short- and long-term policies for dealing with the global refugee problem, see Loescher, *Beyond Charity*.

10. Jacques Cuenod, "Coordinating United Nations Humanitarian Assistance," *RPG Focus* (Washington, DC: Refugee Policy Group, June 1993).

11. Minear and Weiss, *Mercy under Fire*.

12. Mary Anderson and Peter Woodrow, *Rising from the Ashes: Development Strategies at Times of Disaster* (Boulder, CO: Westview Press, 1989).

13. Minear and Weiss, *Mercy under Fire*.

14. Leon Gordenker, *Refugees and International Politics* (New York: Columbia University Press, 1987).

15. A study that examined some of the possibilities and problems of repatriation and reconstruction in the early 1990s is Anthony Lake et al., *After the Wars: Reconstruction in Afghanistan, Indochina, Central America, Southern Africa, and the Horn of Africa* (New Brunswick, NJ: Transaction Publishers, 1991).

16. Roberta Cohen, *United Nations Human Rights Bodies: An Agenda for Humanitarian Action* (Washington, DC: Refugee Policy Group, 1992); and *Refugees and Human Rights* (Washington, DC: Refugee Policy Group, 1995).

17. UNHCR, *The State of the World's Refugees, 1995*.

18. Alice Henkin, ed., *Honoring Human Rights and Keeping the Peace: Lessons from El Salvador, Cambodia, and Haiti* (Washington, DC: Aspen Institute, 1995).

19. Deng, *Protecting the Dispossessed*.

20. Leon Gordenker and Thomas G. Weiss, eds., *Soldiers, Peacekeepers, and Disasters* (Basingstoke, England: Macmillan, 1991).

10

Conflict and Cooperation: Humanitarian Action in a Changing World

Thomas G. Weiss

The euphoria surrounding the end of the Cold War was short-lived. Today, the hopefulness of 1989 already seems like ancient history.

Optimism about the possibilities for democratization and multilateral conflict resolution—captured prematurely by President Bush's "new world order" and by President Clinton's "assertive multilateralism"[1]—have ceded to more sober assessments about the precarious state of international security and the UN. Democratization has spread, but accompanied by the plague of micro-nationalism and fragmentation. Rather than the tabula rasa of the "end of history," the demise of East-West tensions permitted the brutal expression of grievances. The spread of Western-style democracy has been more painful than Francis Fukuyama predicted.[2]

The outset of the post–Cold War era reinvigorated the UN Security Council and heralded enhanced prospects for international conflict management and humanitarian intervention. In spite of recent setbacks, some observers remain buoyant, as suggested by the title of the January 1995 report from the Commission on Global Governance, *Our Global Neighbourhood*.[3] In any event, the earlier positive atmosphere and the bullishness of successful international efforts to thwart aggression in the Persian Gulf have changed rather dramatically to a mood of pessimism following UN flops or quasi-failures in Bosnia, Croatia, Somalia, Haiti, and Rwanda, along with less visible ones in Angola, Afghanistan, and the Sudan. Observers usually point to Somalia as the turning point, when Pollyannaish notions about intervening militarily to thwart aggression or stop thugs were replaced by more realistic estimates about the limits of such actions.[4]

Where are we, then, after the fiftieth anniversary of the world organization? Over the last few years there have been numerous efforts to address conflict and cooperation in order to improve humanitarian action in the post–Cold War era. This chapter takes stock of the UN's strengths and weaknesses and suggests a few ways to remedy the latter.

DOMINANT TRENDS

Two mega-trends dominate the UN's handling of post–Cold War crises. The most significant feature of international responses in the last years has been the growing willingness of the international community to address, rather than ignore, emergencies within the borders of war-torn states that are emerging as the dominant security challenges of our times.[5] Of the eleven new security operations begun since the first-ever, head-of-state summit of the Security Council in January 1992, all except two have been deployed in civil wars. Of the eighty-two conflicts that have broken out since the fall of the Berlin Wall, seventy-nine were intrastate conflicts; and, in fact, two of the three remaining ones, namely, Nagorno-Karabakh and Bosnia, could also be considered civil wars.[6]

Although the language about absolute state sovereignty in UN Charter article 2(7) remains intact, humanitarian imperatives have led governmental organizations, intergovernmental organizations (IGOs), and nongovernmental organizations (NGOs) to redefine when it is possible "to intervene in matters which are essentially within the domestic jurisdiction of any state." Sometimes there is no sovereign (the case of collapsed states like Somalia), and sometimes sovereignty is overridden in the name of higher norms (the case of assisting the Kurds in northern Iraq).[7]

The second trend relates to an ever-burgeoning demand for helping hands from UN soldiers. Secretary-General Boutros Boutros-Ghali wrote in January 1995 that "this increased volume of activity would have strained the Organization even if the nature of the activity had remained unchanged."[8] After stable levels of about ten thousand troops in the early post–Cold War period, their numbers have jumped rapidly. In the last few years seventy to eighty thousand blue-helmeted soldiers have been authorized by the UN's annualized "military" (peacekeeping) budget that now approaches $4 billion.

These figures represent just the additional costs of deployment and not the real costs to troop-contributing countries. And they only hint at the magnitude of related problems. In recent years peacekeeping debts and arrears, along with shortfalls in the regular budget, have often been about three times the annual regular budget of the world organization.

IS THERE AN AGENDA FOR PEACE?

In January 1992 members of the Security Council requested that the then newly elected Secretary-General assess the promise of the UN in a changed world. No other recent international public policy document has generated so much discussion—by practitioners and scholars—as *An Agenda for Peace* since its June 1992 publication.[9] Boutros-Ghali's report has framed the debate and contains many intriguing suggestions, but it is at its most ambitious in defining the UN's potential security role.[10]

The deployment of outside military personnel under UN command could be expanded usefully, as the secretary-general proposes, in several areas similar to those in which they have been used effectively in the past. With the consent of the parties and using force only as a last resort and in self-defense, such deployments would include supervising confidence-building measures related to military downsizing, fact-finding, staffing early warning centers, and acting as buffers in either interstate or intrastate conflicts when belligerents agree. Regarding these activities, the secretary-general makes concrete recommendations for improving personnel, logistics, information, and above all, financing.

For many other activities there is no UN track record. If there is, it is lackluster or worse, with no consensus among member states. The protection of UN civilian and humanitarian personnel is perhaps the most obvious. The experience of the UN Guards contingent in Iraq—the secretary-general's principal illustration—provides a poor guide to thinking about the future. The presence of the guards was helpful for a time, but not because of their pistols and blue baseball caps. They were based in a country whose population and military had been defeated and temporarily subjugated; Iraq found them initially less odious than Western troops; and NATO air power was in nearby Turkey to underline the fact that the guards were not helpless. The use of more numerous, but not significantly more effective, UN soldiers in Bosnia was an extension of wishful thinking.

An Agenda for Peace explored significant departures from past practice, including coercive economic and military sanctions under Chapter VII. The most significant was the proposal to create peace enforcement units. Ceasefires would be guaranteed by UN soldiers when warring parties no longer agreed to respect a negotiated halt to carnage. The secretary-general underscored that these soldiers would be required to be more heavily armed than yesterday's peacekeepers. The experience in several situations—with at least thirty ceasefires for Bosnia and various agreements for Somalia and Rwanda—suggests how much these departures exceeded the expectations of governments and the abilities of the UN.

In a progress report issued in January 1995 to mark the UN's fiftieth anniversary, *Supplement to "An Agenda for Peace,"* the secretary-general came to the same conclusion and trimmed his sails. He retreated and recommended caution because of phenomena that had been partially or totally unforeseen in 1992. Among them are precisely the two trends that were discussed—the intensity and ugliness of internal conflicts and the quantitative and qualitative changes in the UN system's efforts to deploy multifunctional operations. The new document is mainly a call for reduced expectations and UN activities; and this new reticence vis-à-vis multilateral military efforts has a direct bearing on the possibilities for humanitarian action in a changing world.

CONCEPTUAL PROBLEMS

The dramatic increase in UN operations in the post–Cold War period has catalyzed analyses.[11] Yet discussions in UN circles are still characterized by confusion about traditional peacekeeping and coercion, and the gray areas in between.[12]

The literal position of UN troops is dangerous and awkward. Many analysts, diplomats, and UN staff stumble more figuratively when they fail to distinguish clearly old-style "peacekeeping"—the interposition of neutral forces when warring parties have agreed to a ceasefire, or, at least, to putting one in place. They employ the same term, even if it is qualified by adjectives, for example, "wider" peacekeeping by Whitehall or "aggravated" peacekeeping by the Pentagon, for a variety of situations where consent is absent or problematic and where military capacity outranks moral authority. The confusion is even greater when an operation shifts from Chapter VI to VII (Somalia and Rwanda) or combines the two (the former Yugoslavia).

The UN has demonstrated for several decades that it can manage Chapter VI military operations. Peacekeeping is often called "Chapter six-and-a-half," former UN Secretary-General Dag Hammarskjöld's clever indication that this UN invention was not foreseen by the Charter's framers. But peacekeeping is really an extension of Chapter VI rather than a would-be Chapter VII. Management and financial reforms undoubtedly could improve peacekeeping because each operation is still put together from scratch ad hoc, based on best-case scenarios with inadequate resources.

At the same time the UN has also demonstrated its inability to handle Chapter VII, which the secretary-general has now recognized in his *Supplement*: "[N]either the Security Council nor the Secretary-General at present has the capacity to deploy, direct, command and control operations for this purpose."[13] The inability to manage enforcement cannot be wished away, nor can it be overcome by tinkering. The world organization's diplomatic and bureaucratic structures are inimical to initiating and overseeing military efforts when serious fighting rages, where coercion rather than consent is the norm.

Part of the problem is that the UN has relied too heavily on the experience of past operations when coping with post–Cold War crises instead of delineating distinct new characteristics. Peacekeeping should be reserved for consensual missions, which is where the UN secretariat has a comparative advantage. Otherwise, peacekeeping becomes an infinitely elastic concept without operational significance. It is not a cure-all for the chaos of ethnonationalism but, rather, a discrete tool for conflict management when consent among belligerents is present, and diplomatic, rather than military, expertise is required from the UN side.

In his first press conference of 1995 the secretary-general straightforwardly recognized "that the United Nations does not have the capacity to carry out huge peace endorsement operations, and that when the Security Council decides on a peace enforcement operation, our advice is that the Security Council mandate a group of Member States, [those which] have the capability."[14] In his *Supplement* he notes that peacekeeping and enforcement "should be seen as alternative techniques and not as adjacent points on a continuum."[15]

Conceptual clarity is also absent from many considerations of "intervention."[16] This term covers the spectrum of possible actions—from making telephone calls to dispatching military forces—that are intended to alter internal affairs in another country. As such, it is almost synonymous with the state practice of international relations, which in the post–Cold War period has witnessed more significant outside intrusions into domestic affairs than previously.

Specifically, what concerns us here is Chapter VII decisions by the Security Council to enforce international decisions through economic and military sanctions. Both have consequences for victims and humanitarians. Talk-show hosts, academic conference-goers, politicians, and the proverbial person in the street are preoccupied with what the editor of *Foreign Affairs* described, prematurely, as the "Springtime for Interventionism."[17] They are hesitating at a fork in the road about using military force in support of humanitarian objectives. One route leads back toward traditional peacekeeping and the other toward the measured application of superior military force in support of more ambitious international decisions, including the enforcement of human rights.[18]

The present balance of opinion favors the former, and the Somalia and Bosnia experiences are critical.[19] Military reticence about the prospects for humanitarian intervention ironically joins the negativism of critics who see U.S. dominance in multilateral military efforts as a continuation of U.S. hegemony.[20]

Two unlikely apologists for outside military forces, Alex de Waal and Rakiya Omaar, have observed: "Humanitarian intervention demands a different set of military skills. It is akin to counterinsurgency."[21] This realization will not be comforting to the Pentagon and others still recovering from the "Vietnam syndrome."[22] Yet lessons from the United Kingdom's efforts in Malaysia undoubtedly are more relevant in developing strategies for intervention in failed states than the experience of Operation Desert Storm. As such, the ability of a relatively small number of well-trained soldiers, with adequate political support at home, who were able to stay the course is more salient than high-tech weaponry applied to overwhelm an enemy as quickly as possible.

Dissenters from "military humanitarianism" are numerous.[23] They include many developing countries clinging to the notion that state sovereignty does not permit outside intervention, which, in their view, serves to protect them against major power bullying.[24] They also argue, and perhaps rightfully, that intervention is messy and that it is easier to get in than to get out. At the same time the Security Council's definition of what constitutes "threats" to international peace and security is undergoing expansion, covering virtually any subject, while the Security Council remains unpredictably selective in applying that definition to specific threats.

Developing countries are joined by others whose reasoning is less ideological but based on a static interpretation of international law. In an anarchical world, according to this argument, states require reciprocal rules to mitigate inevitable competition. A further refinement is that outside military forces make more problematic the task of the affected country's own civilian authorities. Abandoning nonintervention, it is argued, leads to further instability and weakens democratic tendencies and institutions.

Other critics of robust intervention are civilian humanitarians working in the trenches. For them "humanitarian war" is an oxymoron.[25] More numerous than Quakers or Mennonites, they argue that humanitarian initiatives are strictly consensual, premised on impartiality and neutrality. Although these civilian humanitarians are protected by the international law of armed conflicts, of which the ICRC is the custodian, they must of necessity rely on political authorities involved in armed conflicts for access to and respect of civilians. Under such circumstances military intervention not only raises the levels of violence and complicates the lives of civilian humanitarians in the short run but also makes reconciliation more difficult in the longer run.

Yet with one in every 130 people on earth forced into flight from war, humanitarian intervention may sometimes be the only way to halt genocide, massive abuses of human rights, and starvation.[26] Thus partisans of the other route at the fork in the road, including this author, are open to the option of outside military forces to assist civilians trapped in wars. When consent cannot be extracted, economic and military coercion can be justified in operational *and* ethical terms. When there is sufficient political will, an effective humanitarian response may include military backup that goes far beyond the minimalist use of force in self-defense by traditional UN peacekeepers. Rather than suspending relief and withdrawing, the international community can use enough force to guarantee access to civilians, protect aid workers, and keep thugs at bay.

Humanitarian intervention is not an end in itself, but a last-ditch effort to create enough breathing room for the reemergence of local stability and order, which are ultimately prerequisites for the conduct of negotiations that can lead to consent—about humanitarian "space" and, eventually, about lasting peace as well. The Commission on Global Governance proposed "an appropriate Charter amendment permitting such intervention but restricting it to cases that constitute a violation of the security of people so gross and extreme that it requires an international response on humanitarian grounds."[27]

On the UN's fiftieth anniversary it is worth recalling that the UN was supposed to be different from its defunct predecessor, the League of Nations. There should be no illusion about the world organization's acting automatically as a fire brigade in humanitarian crises. But the provisions for enforcement in the UN Charter permit action to stop atrocities in such places as Somalia, Bosnia, Rwanda, northern Iraq, and Haiti when there is sufficient political will.

PROBLEMS IN UN OPERATIONS

A fundamental difficulty in evaluating UN operations is the ambiguity of "success" and "failure" resulting from imprecision about timeframes and the durability of results. Have efforts in the former Yugoslavia been successful because they have saved lives and avoided a wider conflict in Europe, or a failure because the international community delayed standing up to aggression, genocide, and the forced movement of peoples? Were short-term efforts in Somalia successful because death rates dropped in 1993, or a long-term failure because billions were spent to stop the clock temporarily, only to witness the country prepare to revert to banditry and chaos in 1995? Were efforts in Cambodia a short-term success because Cambodians went to the polls and permitted the return of King Norodom Sihanouk, or a long-term failure because the Khmer Rouge remain poised to return to civil war? Were efforts in El Salvador successful because peace was negotiated and elections held, or a failure because the root causes of the civil war remain—mainly, unequal land distribution and limited participation in decision-making? Without greater precision about the expectations of comprehensive operations, analysts can agree on the facts and yet have totally different evaluations about the utility of a particular operation.

Whatever the criteria for success and failure, however, three major operational shortcomings have been manifest in recent years. First, the UN has been unable to address what has entered the social science vocabulary as "imploded" or "failed states."[28] The evaporation of state sovereignty has created a vacuum in local authority and public services. Recent civil wars have witnessed the massive looting and destruction of infrastructure and the killing or flight of many trained persons from the public and private sectors. There has been no meaningful attempt, external or internal, to get these failed societies back on their collective feet.

Of course, the difficulties of nation-building should not be ignored. The hubris symbolized by U.S. efforts in Vietnam or Soviet ones in Afghanistan should give pause. The citizens of post-conflict countries must ultimately take responsibility for the reconstitution of viable civil societies, but they require buffers and breathing space after protracted civil war, or even after a short but particularly brutal one.

Second, traditional deficiencies in UN command and control have worsened. On the purely technical side, communications are notoriously difficult because of multiple languages, procedures, and equipment, such difficulties being exacerbated by the lack of common training for individual contingents. Operations also suffer from multiple chains of command within a theater and between the military and the civilian sides of the UN secretariat. The normal tendency for contingents to seek guidance from their own capitals is intensified with complexity and danger.

The dearth of military professionalism, especially when combat conditions prevail, is serious and unlikely to improve. The UN secretariat has not kept pace with the dramatically increased demand. The means to plan, support, and command peacekeeping, let alone enforcement, is scarcely greater now than during the Cold War, or, in one analyst's view, "The U.N. itself can no more conduct military operations on a large-scale on its own than a trade association of hospitals can conduct heart surgery."[29]

Modest progress in establishing a situation room in New York and some consolidation in UN administrative services are hardly sufficient to make the militaries of major or middle powers feel at ease about placing the UN in charge of combat missions.[30] The assertive multilateralism trumpeted, especially by Madeleine K. Albright, the then permanent UN representative from the United States, at the outset of this administration became untenable as a result of Somalia. Alain Destexhe, the secretary-general of Médecins Sans Frontières, linked this development with the international community's unwillingness to react to genocide in Rwanda: "[T]he intervention fiasco in Somalia and the deaths of more than 30 professional soldiers so shocked the American public that the Clinton administration had to rethink its foreign policies."[31] With the UN and its member states bogged down in civil wars—scarcely imagined by the founders and certainly not where successes have been common—there are, increasingly, political, economic, and military pressures in Western capitals to avoid engagement.

Third, the comprehensiveness of recent UN operations itself creates new problems.[32] The side-by-side deployment of international personnel within "multifunctional operations" requires professional knowledge within each unit as well as the institutional means to ensure coordination. This routinely involves military, civil administration (including election and human rights monitoring and police support), and humanitarian expertise with an overlay of political negotiations and mediation.

For example, a lesson from the former Yugoslavia is that when the humanitarian and military aspects of a UN operation cannot be separated—because they are both linked to Security Council decisions—they should be integrated. Greater efforts are required to spell out these relationships in advance to avoid the kind of ill-defined relationships into which drifted the main humanitarian organization, UNHCR, and UNPROFOR.

When UN forces are providing humanitarian support directly, UN organizations must develop a better understanding of precisely how military structures operate and what priorities motivate military decisions at both the micro and macro levels in order to help guide the military. If such organizations intend to work with UN military forces in the future—and this is likely to be the norm—they must also take steps to orient, train, and exchange information with military personnel. The recruitment of ex-military officers might go a long way toward determining how individual UN organizations could influence the military and make better use of the capabilities potentially at the disposal of humanitarian organizations.

No word is used more frequently in international organizations and governments than "coordination." But no other word connotes more things to more people. Everyone is for it, but no one wishes to be coordinated. The two existing "models" for coordination—the lead agency that UNHCR played in the former Yugoslavia and the more systemwide overview provided by DHA in Rwanda—have supporters and detractors.[33]

The authority and responsibilities associated with the lead agency role have never been fully or formally defined. United Nations humanitarian organizations operate the way that the rest of the system does, as a loose association. Each organization has its own set of priorities, governing board, and fund-raising strategy. The absence of a systemwide response and the accompanying lack of guidance for NGOs is unfortunate, to say the least, when so many lives are at stake and resources in such short supply.

The structural problems of DHA are well known to most observers of the humanitarian arena—very limited budget, little field presence, inexperience, and no leverage over the various moving parts of the UN system. The creation of DHA was supposed to rectify the numerous operational problems criticized by donors during the international response to the crises in the Persian Gulf.[34] However, DHA has made little difference to leadership or performance, although information sharing has improved. The structural weaknesses are obvious when one considers that coordinators have no real budgetary authority and do not outrank the heads of subordinate units. Erskine Childers and Sir Brian Urquhart have argued that the need to establish a division of labor within the UN system and between it and NGOs "remains seriously neglected in the continued jockeying and jostling of UN-system organizations vis-à-vis each other and the intrinsically weak new DHA 'Coordinator.' "[35] There is no more urgent priority than the establishment of a better international division of labor and a more coherent structure to exploit the resources and energies of all humanitarians.

THREE POLICY SUGGESTIONS

Certainly this section cannot present the entire gamut of reforms to cure the UN's ills as it pursues the primary task of maintaining international peace and security and addresses humanitarian crises. A number of proposals for comprehensive reforms has been put forward—not only by Childers and Urquhart but also by such groups as the Commission on Global Governance and the Independent Working Group on the Future of the United Nations.[36] They range from altering the composition of the Security Council to revitalizing the professional staff to overcoming the dismal financial picture of the world organization.

The purpose here is not to pick and choose among these proposals but, rather, to develop three ideas that address the three key shortcomings discussed earlier. The first concerns failed states. In spite of the preoccupation with civil wars, the state is hardly obsolete.[37] The appearance of imploded states, and others so obviously on the brink, suggests that "inadequate stateness" may be the overriding weakness in many areas where civil war is raging. There is no need to be nostalgic about the repressive national security state in order to argue that a minimal ability to guarantee law and order and a functioning economy is a necessary, if insufficient, condition for civil society without civil war.

In spite of the past experience of the UN in the Middle East over five decades and more recently in Cambodia,[38] there is little evidence that the world organization could or would routinely be permitted to be involved in substituting itself for state authority. The UN is reluctant to assume such an assignment, but the need is painfully obvious. In the new breed of internal conflicts, the functions of government—including social services, police, the judiciary, and other related state activities—are not merely suspended: The assets of the state are also looted and destroyed, while officials are routinely killed or forced to flee.

A modified system of trusteeship is required. Since 1994, when the last trust territory (Palau in the South Pacific) became independent, the Trusteeship Council, one of the six primary organs of the UN, has been essentially without a portfolio. Could this organ not be transformed to handle temporarily the problems of states that have ceased to function and to provide a modicum of breathing space to permit the reconstitution of civil society?

Proposals calling for recolonizing countries unable to govern themselves are implausible, to say the least,[39] but similar proposals continue to surface in the policy literature and debate.[40] Local populations would not tolerate the imposition of external paternalism, and former colonial powers are hardly in a queue to resume the white man's burden. But the UN certainly could be called upon selectively to assume temporary control or governorship.

There is, of course, no quick fix, and the record of the various types of international trusteeship and administration is mixed. As Adam Roberts has noted, "Iraq and Rwanda, both of which were under trusteeship for substantial periods in the first half of this century, serve as reminders that trusteeship is no simple cure-all."[41] As the sensibilities of states that have been independent for only three decades or less are bound to be offended by the suggestion, such functions are more likely to be added piecemeal to UN mandates than through a new overall system of trusteeship. However, if the city of Boston could turn over the administration of its public schools to a private university, perhaps failed states could follow a similar logic in calling temporarily upon the UN.

The second suggestion addresses the military inadequacies of the UN. Experience suggests that UN decisions should trigger interventions that will be subcontracted to coalitions of major states. Regional powers (e.g., Nigeria within West Africa and Russia within the erstwhile Soviet republics) could be expected to take the lead combined with larger regional (i.e., the Economic Community of West African States and the Commonwealth of Independent States) or global coalitions. The pursuit of the Gulf War and the creation of safe havens for Kurds are perhaps the best illustrations of this procedure. Perhaps only when regional powers cannot or will not take such a lead should more global-level powers be expected to do so (e.g., France in Rwanda or the United States in Somalia). However, blocking humanitarian intervention, with which some powers are willing to proceed even when others are reluctant to get involved (e.g., the United States vis-à-vis Rwanda between early April and late June 1994), should be ruled out.

In light of the "strategic overstretch" of the type that Paul Kennedy attributes to empires,[42] alternatives to UN command and control of serious military operations must be found. Three Security Council decisions between late June and late July 1994 indicated the growing relevance of military intervention by major powers in regions of their traditional interests: a Russian scheme to deploy troops in Georgia to end the three-year-old civil war there, the French intervention in Rwanda to help stave off genocidal conflict, and the U.S. plan to spearhead a military invasion to reverse the military coup in Haiti.

One analyst commented that "the increasing sense that peacekeeping is so ineffective a tool for resolving crises like Somalia or Bosnia [suggests] that it might well be better to scrap it altogether and leave the policing of the world's trouble-spots to great powers or regional hegemons."[43] In his first press conference of 1995 the secretary-general himself agreed to acknowledge the meeting of pragmatism and principle.[44]

The decision in Budapest in December 1994 by the Conference (now Organization) on Security and Cooperation in Europe (OSCE) to authorize three thousand troops, of whom less than half would be Russian, after a ceasefire in Nagorno-Karabakh is another illustration of the pertinence of military subcontracting. These experiments indicate that the evident gap between international capacities and increasing demands for help could be filled by regional powers or even hegemons operating under the scrutiny of a wider community of states that would hold the interveners accountable for their actions.[45]

Charles William Maynes's "benign realpolitik" straightforwardly recognizes this reality, which amounts to a revival of spheres of influence with UN oversight.[46] The Security Council is experimenting with a type of great power politics that the UN was originally founded to end but that is increasingly pertinent for a feasible doctrine for humanitarian intervention, as it recognizes the inherent difficulties of multilateral mobilization and management of military force.[47] As Boutros-Ghali has written, "[T]hey may herald a new division of labour between the United Nations and regional organizations, under which the regional organization carries the main burden but a small United Nations operation supports it and verifies that it is functioning in a manner consistent with positions adopted by the Security Council."[48]

The third suggestion concerns the problems of humanitarian action by civilians in war zones.[49] Military forces have an important logistic capacity in the most dire of circumstances; but most human needs should continue to be the responsibility of civilians. Governments resist considering new entities, but one should be created to deliver emergency aid in active war zones with Chapter VII economic or military sanctions. This specialized cadre would be a truly "international" ICRC.[50] The volunteers should not be part of the common UN staff system because they would have to be appropriately insured and compensated. In many ways these persons could well be more in harm's way than soldiers.

In December 1994 the General Assembly recognized the vulnerability of soldiers and civilians in humanitarian operations and approved the text of a treaty for ratification by states. It requires signatories to protect UN staff and to arrest those responsible for crimes against them.

The effective protection of the new category of humanitarian workers would be enhanced by the implementation of an international decision to treat attacks against all humanitarian personnel as an international crime. This procedure would build upon the logic of earlier precedents in which the effective prosecution of terrorists and airplane hijackers is less subject to the vagaries of national legislation or the extraditional whims of host countries.

Resources and capable relief specialists could also be siphoned from existing humanitarian agencies with distinguished records in armed conflicts—like UNHCR, UNICEF, and the WFP. Under this arrangement, the UN's humanitarian agencies themselves would be absent when Chapter VII is in effect. If a peacekeeping operation changed to enforcement, they would withdraw.

The politicization of humanitarian action—or the perception of its politicization, which has the same impact—in Bosnia, Somalia, and Rwanda has altered civilian humanitarian orthodoxy. London's International Institute for Strategic Studies suggested some possible new principles that were based on an internal UN memorandum about humanitarian action when outside military forces are involved. The new bottom line was the recommendation that civilian humanitarians "should not embark on humanitarian operations where, over time, impartiality and neutrality are certain to be compromised"; and "[i]f impartiality and neutrality are compromised, an ongoing humanitarian operation should be reconsidered, scaled down or terminated."[51]

This argument would have been anathema to humanitarian practitioners only a few years ago, when the unquestioned imperative was to respond to every manmade tragedy. But it has emerged as a new reality, which means, as I have argued elsewhere, that the "age of innocence is over."[52] The conclusion to the most comprehensive evaluation to date of Somalia prescribes "tough love"—the desirability of having left the Horn when it became obvious that looting, corruption, and extortion of assistance was effectively fueling the war. Although it may seem callous to walk away from suffering, it may prove to be the most humane option: "it would likely have led either to improved protection allowing the continuation of aid or to an opportunity, with departure from Somalia, to channel scarce aid resources to other countries' emergencies."[53]

Thus like the military forces deployed for a humanitarian intervention, the proposed civilian delivery unit should form an integral part of a unified command that would report directly to the Security Council and not to the secretary-general. The non-UN troops authorized by the council and staff from the new humanitarian unit together would comprise a core of soldiers and civilians in possession of expertise and body armor—a "HUMPROFOR," or Humanitarian Protection Force.

The new UN humanitarian entity should also have ground rules for mounting and suspending deliveries. An essential element, for example, would be the explicit agreement by troop contributors that the UN-blessed interventionary forces would be bound by the Geneva Conventions and Additional Protocols. Instead of using customary international law and its incorporation into national military law, they would submit themselves to an international prosecution mechanism devised for the purpose.

This new unit's members would no doubt be more comfortable than the staffs of most UN organizations with the inevitable consequences for vulnerable civilians of imposing either economic or military sanctions as part of a political strategy. Assistance would go to refugees and internally displaced persons without regard to juridical status. The new unit might well be dominated by retired military personnel who would not reject out of hand the necessity to subordinate themselves and work side by side with military protection forces within a hierarchical and disciplined structure. They should, in any case, be experienced in working with military forces and able to bridge the military-civilian cultural divide that has impeded effectiveness in many war zones. Moreover, a single structure, instead of the decentralized UN model, would make buck-passing, a standard clause in job descriptions, more difficult in active war zones.

Attaching this unit to the Security Council would insulate the office of the UN's chief executive from Chapter VII's finger-pointing and call to arms. The UN secretary-general should be kept available for more impartial tasks, and an especially important one would be administering failed states. This new unit attached to the Security Council would be a humanitarian adaptation of the precedent set by Rolf Ekeus. As executive chairperson of the Special Commission on Disarmament and Arms Control in Iraq, he was appointed by, and reports to, the Security Council rather than to the secretary-general. As part of the Chapter VII enforcement governing the terms of the ceasefire after the Gulf War, Ekeus was the Security Council's emissary. Boutros-Ghali remained a potential interlocutor for even a pariah regime or its successor.

Moreover, insulating purely humanitarian efforts would help reduce politicization. Most UN organizations are ill-equipped to function efficaciously when bullets are flying, and all are uncomfortable about their association with enforcement, which, by definition, contradicts the principles of impartiality and neutrality. United Nations humanitarian agencies should devote their limited human and financial resources to what they do better, namely, emergency aid after natural disasters or ceasefires as well as reconstruction and development.

CONCLUSION

The danger of prescription for contemporary history is evident. But the risk of not trying is even more perilous for a planet grappling with the debris of micronationalism when major powers refuse to exercise leadership.

The results of the November 1994 elections in the United States complicate relations between UN political and humanitarian authorities and the world organization's most powerful member state. With the UN bogged down in civil wars, there are political, economic, and military pressures in Washington and other Western capitals to avoid new engagements and to pull back from multilateralism.

The May 1994 Presidential Decision Directive (PDD) 25 was a harbinger of this reticence. This document about U.S. participation in UN military efforts signaled the Clinton administration's policy retreat from multilateralism. Only three years separate the bullish optimism that guaranteed survival to the Kurds in northern Iraq and the utter indifference that not only ignored Rwanda's genocide in April 1994 but also prevented other states from acting to halt the tragedy. The initial proposals from the 104th Congress—in particular, the House's National Security Revitalization Act (H.R. 7) and the Senate's Peace Powers Act of 1995 (S. 5)—suggest the further deterioration in Washington's attitudes toward the UN, as do more recent battles between the president and Republican presidential hopefuls over financing the RDF in Bosnia. Congressional reactions to Boutros Boutros-Ghali's successor offer hopes of more positive support for the UN's agenda.

Vigorous efforts contradict the military doctrines originally articulated by Secretary of Defense Caspar Weinberger and subsequently embroidered by General Colin Powell, former chairman of the joint chiefs of staff, and others. According to post-Vietnam logic, the United States should not intervene unless it is committed to total victory with full support from the public and Congress for situations where massive firepower ensures attainable objectives, minimal U.S. casualties, and a clear exit timetable. These are hardly characteristics of the threats of our turbulent times, when the unpredictable interplay of political fragmentation and cheap weapons makes chaos commonplace. In the words of a leading student of media coverage, "The new generation of conflicts can never be of the short, sharp, overwhelming kind that politicians and military planners now believe is vital to sustain a public consensus for involvement."[54]

The challenge is daunting—for the Clinton administration in Washington's Beltway and for the UN in New York's Turtle Bay. For the world organization's fiftieth anniversary even many confirmed internationalists were deeply pessimistic. However depressed by the problems and prospects for humanitarian action in a changing world, they should take solace from Dag Hammarskjöld, who wisely described the UN as an institution created "not in order to bring us to heaven but in order to save us from hell."

NOTES

1. For contrasting views see Warren Christopher, "America's Leadership, America's Opportunity," and Bob Dole, "Shaping America's Global Future," *Foreign Policy* 98 (Spring 1995): 6–27 and 29–43.

2. Francis Fukuyama, *The End of History and the Last Man* (New York: Free Press, 1992).

3. Commission on Global Governance, *Our Global Neighbourhood* (Oxford: Oxford University Press, 1995).

4. See Thomas G. Weiss, "Overcoming the Somalia Syndrome—'Operation Rekindle Hope'?" *Global Governance* 1, no. 2 (1995): 171–87.

5. See Michael E. Brown, ed., *Ethnic Conflict and International Security* (Princeton, NJ: Princeton University Press, 1993); and Ted Robert Gurr and Barbara Harff, *Ethnic Conflict in World Politics* (Boulder, CO: Westview Press, 1994).

6. Charles William Maynes, "Relearning Intervention," *Foreign Policy* 98 (Spring 1995): 108.

7. Jarat Chopra and Thomas G. Weiss, "Sovereignty Is No Longer Sacrosanct: Codifying Humanitarian Intervention," *Ethics and International Affairs* 6 (1992): 95–117. See also a set of essays in Gene M. Lyons and Michael Mastanduno, eds., *Beyond Westphalia? National Sovereignty and Intervention* (Baltimore: Johns Hopkins University Press, 1995).

8. Boutros Boutros-Ghali, *Supplement to "An Agenda for Peace": Position Paper of the Secretary-General on the Occasion of the Fiftieth Anniversary of the United Nations*, January 3, 1995, UN Doc. A/50/60, S/1995/1, para. 77.

9. Boutros Boutros-Ghali, *An Agenda for Peace* (New York: United Nations, 1992).

10. For a critique see Thomas G. Weiss, "New Challenges for UN Military Operations: Implementing 'An Agenda for Peace,' " *Washington Quarterly* 16, no. 1 (1993): 51–66.

11. The best examples of the growing analytical literature are William J. Durch, ed., *The Evolution of UN Peacekeeping: Case Studies and Comparative Analysis* (New York: St. Martin's Press, 1993); Paul Diehl, *International Peacekeeping* (Baltimore: Johns Hopkins University Press, 1993); Mats R. Berdal, *Whither UN Peacekeeping?* Adelphi Paper no. 281 (London: International Institute for Strategic Studies, 1993); John Mackinlay, "Improving Multifunctional Forces," *Survival* 36, no. 3 (1994): 149–73; and Steven R. Ratner, *The New UN Peacekeeping* (New York: St. Martin's Press, 1995).

12. See John Mackinlay and Jarat Chopra, "Second Generation Multinational Operations," *Washington Quarterly* 15, no. 2 (1992): 113–31; and *A Draft Concept of Second Generation Multinational Operations, 1993* (Providence, RI: Watson Institute, 1993).

13. Boutros-Ghali, *Supplement*, para. 77.

14. Boutros Boutros-Ghali, "Transcript of Press Conference," January 5, 1995, UN Press Release SG/SM/5518, p. 5.

15. Boutros-Ghali, *Supplement*, para. 20.

16. For a wide-ranging collection of essays, see *Interventionism: Current Controversies* (San Diego: Greenhaven Press, 1995).

17. James F. Hoge, Jr., "Editor's Note," *Foreign Affairs* 73, no. 6 (1994): v. For a wide-ranging collection of essays, see Paul Winters, ed., *Interventionism*.

18. See Adam Roberts, "The Crisis in Peacekeeping," *Survival* 36, no. 3 (1994): 93–120; and Thomas G. Weiss, "Intervention: Whither the United Nations?" *Washington Quarterly* 17, no. 1 (1994): 109–28.

19. For detailed discussions by the author, see Thomas G. Weiss, "Rekindling Hope in UN Humanitarian Intervention," in Walter Clarke and Jeffrey Herbst, eds., *Revisiting Somalia: The Lessons of U.S./U.N. Intervention* (Boulder, CO: Lynne Rienner, forthcoming) and "Collective Spinelessness: UN Actions in the Former Yugoslavia," in Richard H. Ullman, ed., *The World and Yugoslavia's Conflicts* (New York: Council on Foreign Relations Press, forthcoming).

20. For example, see articles "On Intervention" by Noam Chomsky, Christopher Hitchens, Richard Falk, Carl Conetta, Charles Knight, and Robert Leavitt, *Boston Review* 18 (1993–94): 3–16.

21. Alex de Waal and Rakiya Omaar, "Can Military Intervention Be 'Humanitarian'?" *Middle East Report*, nos. 187–88 (1994): 7.

22. See Richard A. Melanson, *Reconstructing Consensus: American Foreign Policy since the Vietnam War* (New York: St. Martin's Press, 1991).

23. Thomas G. Weiss and Kurt M. Campbell, "Military Humanitarianism," *Survival* 33, no. 5 (1991): 451–65.

24. For a reasoned presentation of some negative arguments, see Ernst B. Haas, "Beware the Slippery Slope: Notes toward the Definition of Justifiable Intervention," in Laura W. Reed and Carl Kaysen, eds., *Emerging Norms of Justified Intervention* (Cambridge, MA: American Academy of Arts & Sciences, 1993), pp. 63–87. See also Marianne Heiberg, ed., *Subduing Sovereignty: Sovereignty and the Right to Intervene* (London: Pinter, 1994).

25. Adam Roberts, "Humanitarian War: Military Intervention and Human Rights," *International Affairs* 69 (1993): 429–49.

26. For these and other gruesome statistics see UNHCR, *The State of the World's Refugees, 1993: The Challenge of Protection* (New York: Penguin, 1993) and *The State of the World's Refugees, 1995: The Search for Solutions* (Oxford: Oxford University Press, 1995).

27. Commission on Global Governance, *Our Global Neighbourhood*, p. 90.

28. Gerald B. Helman and Steven R. Ratner, "Saving Failed States," *Foreign Policy* 89 (Winter 1992–93): 3–20.

29. Michael Mandelbaum, "The Reluctance to Intervene," *Foreign Policy* 95 (Summer 1994): 11.

30. For a review of these concerns, see Frank M. Snyder, *Command and Control: The Literature and Commentaries* (Washington, DC: National Defense University, 1993); *U.N. Peacekeeping: Lessons Learned in Recent Missions* (Washington, DC: GAO, December 1993), Doc. GAO/NSIAD-94-9; and *Humanitarian Intervention: Effectiveness of U.N. Operations in Bosnia* (Washington, DC: GAO, April 1994), Doc. GAO/NSIAD-94–156BR.

31. Alain Destexhe, "The Third Genocide," *Foreign Policy* 97 (Winter 1994–95): 10. See also his *Rwanda: Essai sur le génocide* (Brussels: Editions Complexe, 1994).

32. See Thomas G. Weiss, ed., *The United Nations and Civil Wars* (Boulder, CO: Lynne Rienner, 1995).

33. This is a major theme in Thomas G. Weiss and Larry Minear, *Mercy under Fire: War and the Global Humanitarian Community* (Boulder, CO: Westview Press, 1995); and in Larry Minear and Thomas G. Weiss, *Humanitarian Politics* (New York: Foreign Policy Association, 1995).

34. See Larry Minear and Thomas G. Weiss, "Groping and Coping in the Gulf Crisis: Discerning the Shape of a New Humanitarian Order," *World Policy Journal* 9, no. 4 (Fall 1992): 755–88.

35. Erskine Childers with Brian Urquhart, *Renewing the United Nations System* (Uppsala: Dag Hammarskjöld Foundation, 1994), p. 114.

36. Independent Working Group on the Future of the United Nations, *The United Nations in Its Second Half-Century* (New York: Ford Foundation, June 1995).

37. See Robert H. Jackson, *Quasi-States: Sovereignty, International Relations, and the Third World* (Cambridge: Cambridge University Press, 1990); and Mohammed Ayoob, *The Third World Security Predicament: State-making, Regional Conflict, and the International System* (Boulder, CO: Lynne Rienner, 1995).

38. See Jarat Chopra, *UN Transition Authority in Cambodia*, Occasional Paper no. 15 (Providence, RI: Watson Institute, 1994); Janet E. Heininger, *Peacekeeping in Transition:*

The United Nations in Cambodia (New York: Twentieth Century Fund, 1994); and Ratner, *The New UN Peacekeeping*, pp. 37–206.

39. Paul Johnson, "Colonialism's Back—and Not a Moment Too Soon," *New York Times Magazine*, April 18, 1993. See also William Pfaff, "A New Colonialism? Europe Must Go Back into Africa," *Foreign Affairs* 74, no. 1 (1995): 2–6.

40. See, for example, Helman and Ratner, "Saving Failed States," and Peter Lyon, "The Rise and Fall and Possible Revival of International Trusteeship," *Journal of Commonwealth and Comparative Politics*, no. 31 (1993): 96–110.

41. Adam Roberts, "A More Humane World?" draft study for the Commonwealth Secretariat, dated December 1994, p. 20.

42. Paul Kennedy, *The Rise and Fall of the Great Powers* (New York: Random House, 1987).

43. David Rieff, "The Illusions of Peacekeeping," *World Policy Journal* 11, no. 3 (1994): 3.

44. Boutros Boutros-Ghali, "Transcript of Press Conference," UN Press Release SG/SM/5518, January 5, 1995.

45. See also Michael Barnett, "The United Nations and Global Security: The Norm Is Mightier than the Sword," *Ethics and International Affairs* 9 (1995): 37–54.

46. For an extended discussion see Jarat Chopra and Thomas G. Weiss, "Prospects for Containing Conflict in the Former Second World," *Security Studies* 4, no. 3 (1995): 552–83.

47. Charles William Maynes, "A Workable Clinton Doctrine," *Foreign Policy* 93 (Winter 1993–94): 3–20.

48. John Mearsheimer, "The False Promise of International Institutions," *International Security* 19, no. 3 (1994–95): 5–49.

49. Boutros-Ghali, *Supplement*, para. 86.

49. This was originally suggested in Weiss, "Overcoming the Somalia Syndrome."

50. For a discussion of expanding and making greater use of the ICRC, see James Ingram, "The Future Architecture for International Humanitarian Assistance," in Thomas G. Weiss and Larry Minear, eds., *Humanitarianism Across Borders: Sustaining Civilians in Times of War* (Boulder, CO: Lynne Rienner, 1993), pp. 171–93.

51. International Institute for Strategic Studies, "Military Support for Humanitarian Operations," *Strategic Comments*, no. 2 (February 22, 1995). The ICRC is increasingly preoccupied by this subject. See Umesh Palwankar, ed., *Symposium on Humanitarian Action and Peace-Keeping: Report* (Geneva: ICRC, 1994).

52. See Thomas G. Weiss, "Military-Civilian Humanitarianism: The 'Age of Innocence' Is Over," *International Peacekeeping* 2, no. 3 (1995).

53. John G. Sommer, *Hope Restored? Humanitarian Aid in Somalia, 1990–1994* (Washington, DC: Refugee Policy Group, 1994), p. 116. See also Kenneth Allard, *Somalia Operations: Lessons Learned* (Washington, DC: National Defense University, January 1995).

54. See Nik Gowing, *Real-Time Television Coverage of Armed Conflicts and Diplomatic Crises: Does It Pressure or Distort Foreign Policy Decision?* (Cambridge, MA: Harvard University Press, 1994).

11

By Way of Conclusion

LEON GORDENKER

International humanitarian operations and the politics associated with them are too complex to be susceptible of summing up in a convenient phrase. The very term itself, "humanitarian operations," evokes a host of examples, explanations, experiences, issues, and concepts. That is amply demonstrated in this volume, both in the specific case studies and in the more general chapters. Furthermore, the entire notion of some apparatus interfering in the realm of a state, whether functioning or faltering, in order to protect or preserve human life has only rather recent origins. Yet as the foregoing studies demonstrate, humanitarian operations resulting from some (often broad) international cooperation have their place in the contemporary world.

The question of why they exist poses difficulties in description as well as in explanation. Humanitarian impulses, as Thomas G. Weiss points out, may underlie some of them. Presumably, humankind cares for its suffering fellows at least at some times and in some places. Perhaps the imperative precepts of a religion underlie some humanitarian impulses. No doubt modern communications have also broadened the willingness of those who encounter shocking images to extend a helping hand. But do any of these factors explain why governments, some of them not particularly tender with their own nationals, prove willing to support humanitarian ventures? For example, the UN's involvement in the wake of the Soviet invasion and subsequent withdrawal from Afghanistan evoked at least rhetorical backing from governments that had records of ugly human rights violations.

With such queries in view, the humanitarian emergencies and interventions taken up in this volume can all be characterized as having political causes and political and/or legal consequences. In most instances, especially where large numbers of people are displaced in their own countries or become refugees abroad, violations of international law are evident. The use of force in international relations, furthermore, is generally forbidden in the UN Charter. Violations of human rights, accepted as real by all governments and defined in legally binding instruments ratified by most of such governments, accompany illegal or inhumane governmental actions. Even if, as David Forsythe argues, the basis of a right to humanitarian assistance has gradually accreted, international responses cannot yet be expected as a matter of course: They require explicit political decisions by governments.

The conventional all-purpose explanation for what happens in international affairs relies on a ranking of the power of participating parties. Governments, it is said, exercise power over weaker ones in order to further their own national interests. Eric Belgrad raises the question whether governments can justify ventures in humanitarian intervention purely for purposes of securing their own national interests. Recent history might suggest that an upsurge of popular sentiment (in countries where governmental policies are responsive to popular sentiment) impels a governmental definition of national interest that includes responses to humanitarian emergencies. Yet it is doubtful that any government has steadily held to such an approach for all humanitarian emergencies, despite what may be enduring and widespread popular support for the concept. Whatever the explanation for humanitarian assistance, it clearly involves social as well as governmental decisions and processes.

Consequently, domestic political factors pertaining to the causes of and reactions to humanitarian emergencies have to be taken into account. Ethnic and other social rivalries in what passed for the polity had a strong causal role in the emergencies in Yugoslavia, Somalia, Rwanda, and the Middle East, taken up in case studies herein. All of these produced a large number of migrants. They and earlier immigrants may constitute quite real political factors in their host countries. Certainly echoes of old ethnic origins have sounded in the political discussions in the United States concerning humanitarian issues in the Middle East and in Yugoslavia. Similarly, the presence of displaced Cambodians in Thailand has had significant overtones in Bangkok's policies.

Beyond humane, ethical, and ethnic factors in responding to humanitarian emergencies, a broader population than that which is most directly responsive to such emergencies is necessarily affected in the financial donor countries. Their contributions derive from taxation, which is an eternal political issue almost everywhere. Furthermore, as the financial donors usually have well-developed economies and large defense establishments, they are the likely sources, if there are going to be any, of a substantial technical and military workforce. Whereas technical personnel can often be recruited as volunteers from the ranks of scientists, academics, and industrialists from NGOs in the civic society, peacekeepers and enforcers require explicit governmental orders. Such orders make up a controversial agenda, indeed, especially in the United States and Western European countries where important sectors of public opinion are suspicious of governmental programs.

Many of the international responses to humanitarian emergencies taken up in this volume were caused by ethnic war or warlike conflict, both of which are usually justified as the pursuit of self-determination. Some of the incidents, as in Somalia or in the former Yugoslavia, also involved failed or foundering states. Others, as in Cambodia, had to do with the reconstruction of a severely damaged state and with the revival of normal life for its subjects. Some others grew out of international wars of the kind that the UN was originally organized to prevent. Whatever the precise causes, all of them involved decisions and actions—or failures to act—on the part of governments. Such decisions included armed action or other pressure on jurisdictions beyond their borders; defensive action to absorb or limit such pressure; and resistance or accommodation to intervention by third parties, such as international organizations.

Governmental decisions and actions that cause humanitarian emergencies can also be described and evaluated in legal terms. They touch on one of the bases of international society, that is, the rules that generally govern the activities of governments in relation to each other. The international intervention, approved by the UN Security Council, to protect the Kurds of northern Iraq forms the basis of a legal argument for the permissibility of forceful intervention in case of a humanitarian emergency. The incident thus constitutes a precedent for treating humanitarian intervention as permissible under international law and UN practice.

AIMS AND RESULTS OF HUMANITARIAN OPERATIONS

The first, immediate aim of every international humanitarian operation is to prevent the loss of yet more life. Thus in every case discussed here, considerable loss of life or threats to life had become manifest prior to intervention. Understandably, therefore, the first responses had an emergency character and, more often than not, were improvised. Beyond that the goals of humanitarian operations vary according to local circumstances, political context, developments in the course of the operation, changing perceptions, and competition engendered from areas outside the scope of the intervention. Furthermore, not every disastrous human situation summons an international aid effort.

Although such humanitarian goals as organizing assistance from those who have means to those who are deprived is simply stated, in fact, implementation has usually resulted in unforeseen complications. The most overtly politically motivated of these, in the relatively short term, are made clear in the chapters by Alan James and Jim Whitman. As humanitarian demands often emerge from warlike situations, one response that almost always figures on the UN agenda incorporates peacekeeping as either an element or an instrument of the operation. As James points out, peacekeepers must rely on a reputation for impartiality. If, incidentally or by direction, they offer humanitarian assistance, one side or the other in the armed conflict may regard their actions as assisting the enemy and thereby abandoning impartiality. Even without that outcome associated with peacekeeping, as Whitman states, the political commitment of governments furnishing peacekeepers or enforcers is substantially affected by the difficulties of translating humanitarian policies into military activity.

The durability of political commitment conditions the eventual outcome of any humanitarian operation whether or not peacekeeping is involved. The studies here directly and indirectly raise the question as to whether the quick, short-term operation—the severely limited commitment—to provide food, shelter, safety, and health care ever has more than a temporary palliative effect. This line of reason derives from the underlying logic in humanitarian emergencies, especially those caused by fighting: If those involved in the causes deem their rationale for fighting more persuasive than the need to preserve lives, the application of temporary palliatives hardly resolves the basic controversy; it may, in fact, inhibit the achievement of longer-term solutions by casting doubt on the impartiality of the assisting organizations.

Yet long-term action raises numerous difficulties. If it involves any sort of enforcement of international policies, such as orders by the Security Council to "use all means," it can cost assisting governments dearly in terms of casualties and financing. Such costs can quickly sap commitment, especially if it was made in the expectation of a tidy, quick operation. Joseph Rudolph's chapter on Yugoslavia provides the obvious example.

Both the Yugoslav and Rwanda operations discussed here also suffered from incorrect or disregarded political analysis. In retrospect, in neither case do the actions of the Security Council appear to have been based on a firm appreciation of the situation on the ground. At the same time no humanitarian emergency that is short of the finality of mass death has a static character. In Yugoslavia and Rwanda, as in the Middle East, outside forces and the endogenous activities of the people who were to be assisted had serious consequences both for them and for the application of humanitarian programs.

Fear, panic, disinformation, and distortion of interpretations all have a share in producing displaced persons and refugees, as discussed by Gil Loescher. And displacement, as well as the accompanying hunger and disease, looms large among the factors that impel a humanitarian action. In Yugoslavia and Rwanda whole populations fled from their homes, and often across state boundaries, out of fearful uncertainty about what would follow the victory of advancing armed forces. A similar flight gave rise to UN concern with the Palestinians, discussed in the chapter by Nitza Nachmias. No humanitarian program could stem such flight unless it were coupled with guarantees of security. But to obtain workable, believable guarantees, as the history of the UN-protected areas in Yugoslavia illustrates, requires more than tents and verbal formulas.

In most of the cases referred to here, with UNTAC in Cambodia perhaps the exception, the early emergency steps had a strong influence on what developed later. Developments in the field, sometimes in response to humanitarian assistance, drove attempts to adapt policy. This reveals lack of a long-term strategy into which initial humanitarian efforts could be fitted. Without such a strategy the policy responses could hardly surpass sheer expediency. As Thomas Weiss points out, without such a strategy, it is hardly possible to follow up emergency aid with development. Mandates are likely to become confused, as was the case in Yugoslavia. As Janet Heininger makes clear, a strategy was put into place in Cambodia, but only after much diffuse effort to deal with the political disintegration and genocide there, and then only because no other way of caring for the large number of displaced persons would be effective. The strategy allowed for tactical adjustments and sponging out of some of the effects of the earlier half-measures.

ORGANIZATIONAL AWKWARDNESS

Both the unexpected developments in the field and the need for long-term strategies challenge international machinery. Policy makers and administrators must be expected to adapt their approaches proficiently to changing situations. Moreover, such adaptation must take place in a world where—as all but the most naive know—reliable forecasting of social phenomena is hardly available and where military surprise ranks as a favorite tactic.

In this volume all the case studies and most of the references cited are linked with what is loosely called the UN system. Decisions by the Security Council precede the deployment of peacekeepers and enforcers. The UN General Assembly bears ultimate responsibility for UNHCR. WFP is related to FAO but, in fact, functions autonomously within the UN system. Other actors in humanitarian operations, such as WHO, and actors in development, such as the World Bank and UNDP (which also has monitoring duties in connection with refugees and human emergencies), are part of the UN system. Human rights at the international level is one of the more glorious inventions of the UN: The UN secretary-general figures in much humanitarian work as the controller of the loudest tocsin and of a staff that has accumulated relevant experience.

Two glaring weaknesses in this "system" stand out in humanitarian affairs. First, the organs that must approve and later adjust policy are intergovernmental. The Security Council, for instance, has, in addition to its permanent members (whose occasional unanimity sets off jubilation among those who favor an ordered political atmosphere), ten others selected for their geographical location. This membership resembles only in lesser degree the randomness of the 180-plus General Assembly. Such intergovernmental organs have difficulty enough in designing the original mandates for humanitarian operations. Changing those mandates to conform to exigencies of field conditions can turn difficulty into paralysis or, at least, obscurity. The Security Council mastered the arts of paralysis or obscurantism in the cases of Yugoslavia and Rwanda. The General Assembly did not even address the fundamental problem with respect to the Palestinian refugees, where, as Nachmias shows, policy was driven by UN executives, not by deliberate intergovernmental decisions. Such inconstancy or indifference reflects the difficulties described by Whitman in bridging the gap between national determination and international commitment in relation to peacekeeping. This gap is perhaps closely related to the diplomatic tone, which is not treated explicitly in the contributions here but nevertheless exemplifies the decisional process in international organizations. Decisions in these organizations formally reflect the process of bargaining between and among instructed representatives. Their cautious, conventional outlook in undertaking commitments is dominated by interpreting a range of issues as somehow involving "security." The resulting state-centric approach pervades the policy organs of the UN system.

The second weakness relates to the unreliability of the policy organs and can be read in the very general mandates pursuant to which the secretary-general and his staff carry out the day-to-day burden. On the one hand, secretariats operate with an eye on the intergovernmental mandate-setters. On the other hand, it is they who have to face the miseries of trying to deal with heart-wrenching emergencies without sufficient resources. They can expect every instruction and every shortcoming to be subjected to second-guessing by national representatives who are also involved in the national process of securing financial contributions. Of these critics, the first in line are the large financial donors, among whom the rule of thumb may be a magnification of monitoring that is directly proportional to the size of the contribution. If this close monitoring is also paired with attempts to influence or even micro-manage, the UN's burden only becomes heavier when soldiers are involved.

As Weiss notes, the demand for "coordination" is ever-present in UN operations. The term masks the effects of two levels of policy-making and execution. The first has to do with the nature of the UN system. As specific tasks in a humanitarian operation involve several existing UN organizations, efficient practice demands that their work be brought together in a pattern; but these organizations have mandates that go beyond emergencies, relate to their own constituencies, and govern the conduct of programs that are already underway in member countries. As is usual in the UN system, they also have slender financial reserves on which to draw.

Such organizations as the WFP, the WHO, and the World Bank have an intergovernmental legal basis that is independent of the UN General Assembly. Even such creations of the General Assembly as UNRWA, UNHCR, and UNICEF have their own supporting publics within governments and without. They accept no hierarchical commands from the General Assembly or the Economic and Social Council. In fact, what passes for instructions to them—in the form of requests from the General Assembly—is negotiated with their officials or actually derived from these officials. In organizational logic, before they subscribe to such instructions, these senior officers can be expected to demand knowledge of what they are expected to do, what the limits may be, how they relate to the rest of the UN system, and how they will finance humanitarian responses designed in the Security Council, the General Assembly, or the office of the secretary-general. Financing a humanitarian operation may also involve a heavy dose of coordination, for appeals to governments for contributions cannot be made without elaborate preparations to safeguard against failure and against interference with already planned appeals.

Furthermore, the immediate needs of a humanitarian operation run roughshod over the phased programs that are characteristic of development projects. From the origination of such a project to its operational beginning, the recipient government and the international development agency may have spent several years of planning. Finances and execution of individual projects extend over periods of several years. The officials involved on both the governmental and international agency sides of development activity will quite likely have tuned their expectations to such deliberate procedures. The immediate, exigent demands of humanitarian operations at the policy level and in the field can seem, in this context, an unwarranted interference with a hard-won pattern of work.

The nonhierarchical nature of the UN system foreshadows difficulties in coordinating policies. Even when overall policies are agreed upon, coordination issues develop from the field operations. But, as Weiner and Nachmias relate in regard to Rwanda, coordination can be and was achieved at the field level for a short-term project. Similar coordination was the daily fare in Cambodia. Yugoslavia and Somalia disclosed once again, however, that sheer on-site needs do not resolve coordination issues, especially when unexpected developments in the theater of operation or more general political considerations dictate adjustments. Yet it is difficult to avoid the impression that the operatives in humanitarian operations have fewer difficulties with coordination than do the directors of policy in the UN system.

The second level of coordination of policy is located within the member governments of the UN system. This level is even more opaque than the bureaucratic bargaining in UN organizations. Each government has its own arrangements for determining policy and participation in an international humanitarian effort. The component agencies of the UN system connect with different publics and different ministries within governments. For example, the UN works primarily with the foreign affairs ministries, whereas WHO has links with health ministries. The specific links vary greatly over different governments, and in the large ones, the lines of decision-making and authority may be both specialized and complicated. By their very nature, though, humanitarian emergencies cross over organizational boundaries and may be approached differently at the international and national levels. This difference can sow confusion and induce field operatives' strident demands for better coordination. Given the complex interrelationships among national ministries and international organizations, only when a security factor is present, as in peacekeeping and enforcement, is national cooperation in a UN effort likely to be a matter primarily for the political top of government, where concentrated attention can encourage coordination of policy.

Whether a government can develop a policy that receives a coordinated response to a humanitarian emergency can hardly be forecast from the organizational setup contemplated by the government's policy proposal. The broader the humanitarian response, the more political interests will be touched. Pressure groups of various sorts will react. Financial provisions may excite controversy. Policy leadership from top political figures may or may not be engaged. If a reasonable level of coordination can be achieved, patterned instructions can be delivered to representatives at the various organizations of the UN system. If not, representatives from the same capital might be observed taking opposed or inharmonious positions in different organizations of the UN system. In UN history, this is no uncommon occurrence.

Nongovernmental organizations constitute another factor in the coordination tangle. Some NGOs operate as lobbying and advocacy groups at international as well as local levels. Others serve as contractors and as independent service organizations at national and local levels. They appear, for instance, in the Weiner and Nachmias account of activities in Rwanda. If any single qualifying remark can be made about NGOs, it is that they shun hierarchical deals with governments and other organizations. Consequently, coordination with them goes forth under constraints similar to those at the UN center, where organizational independence shapes all negotiations.

Certainly, the contributors here make clear that coordination among organizations poses problems of varying significance in humanitarian operations but does not necessarily dominate them. It can be argued that organizational competition and fragmentation have the valuable function of making doctrinaire mistakes less likely. This is probably so because instead of throwing all organizational resources into a single, hierarchically administered policy, some other alternatives must be considered and could be simultaneously followed. The case of Yugoslavia provides a counterargument: There, the organizational groping that characterized relationships between UN peacekeepers, assistance providers, the European Union and NATO clearly contributed to a confused outcome.

POLICY RECOMMENDATIONS

Humanitarian emergencies force governments, their international organizations, and NGOs into a problem-solving or crisis management mode. They have to react quickly in order to save lives and prevent a broadening crisis. In doing so they develop the policies, practices, and procedures referred to in the chapters here. These have a more abstract quality at headquarters level than on the site of the emergency; but even so, they remain attached primarily to the emergency. A broader context is furnished by the organizational responsibilities that come into play, the legal constraints and opportunities of constitutional mandates, and the moral assumptions that underlie some responses.

Yet as the contributors to this volume make clear, the international experience with humanitarian emergencies raises issues that go beyond mere management techniques. Recommendations for dealing with these issues could be divided into those that imply a rather fundamental reordering in political outlooks and those that have a more organizational tone.

One common political issue involves the inadequate performance of states, acutely illustrated in the chapters that treat Cambodia and Yugoslavia and demonstrated in Somalia, Angola, and Mozambique. Such cases, as well as other instances of humanitarian emergencies, elicit far-reaching, long-term recommendations from the writers in this volume. With regard to the desirable general approaches, these include the following:

- Humanitarian disasters should be treated not as incidents of a short-term character but as protracted tragedies.
- The slow buildup of a right for all persons to humanitarian assistance should be assisted, especially by rich countries.
- A more solid legal foundation should be built for humanitarian intervention.
- Humanitarian missions must maintain impartiality and keep apart from the use of force.
- The approach of international trusteeship should be revived and adapted to situations where extreme weakening of the state is related to humanitarian disasters.

Other suggestions apply mainly in operational situations:

- Humanitarian missions should avoid tendencies to become permanent and should instead foster the revival of local and state political responsibility.
- International mechanisms for developing and administering humanitarian policies need sturdier support from governments.

Recommendations involving less fundamental changes in commitments of those governments and organizations active in humanitarian emergencies have a more specific, shorter-term character. They include the following:

- Subcontract military duties out of the UN structure and assign tasks to regional organizations.
- Use an existing or form a new organizational entity to carry out humanitarian duties in war zones, and exclude the UN from such zones.
- Treat refugees as evidence of wide-ranging disturbances, requiring development, human rights, and other assistance.
- Hand over UNRWA functions to new Palestinian administrative units and terminate UNRWA.

CONCLUSION

The chapters in this volume sometimes touch only lightly and implicitly on profound causal factors in humanitarian emergencies. Reorganizing a failing state or putting a territory under trusteeship may mask the more fundamental issues of the application of self-determination in multiethnic states. The recent increase in ethnic conflicts within states raises basic questions about whether a global order can ever be achieved when states believe they can justify any acts by invoking the principle of self-determination. If that is so, a concomitant issue involves the present boundaries of many states that either divide ethnic groups or include them against their will. The permanence of such states, too, may be called into question by humanitarian disasters that grow out of ethnic conflict.

If responses to humanitarian emergencies in the last decade can be taken to prove anything at all, it is that the interconnection of people in miserable, threatening situations paired with political, economic, social, and legal breakdown has long-term implications. These cannot be wished out of the way with tidy, limited relief efforts that efficiently deliver supplies. Rather, they plunge to the heart of political issues that range from the village fire to the capital and from there to majestic diplomatic gatherings, such as the UN General Assembly. At the same time, as this volume makes clear, the difficulty of gaining support from national governments for long-term efforts that include economic and social development and reconstruction of state authority stands in the way of applying effective measures to avoid humanitarian disasters. In this sense, then, responses to humanitarian emergencies challenge easy assumptions about international politics as short-term questions of national self-interest.

Selected Bibliography

BOOKS AND MONOGRAPHS

Acheson, Dean. *Present at the Creation*. New York: New American Library, 1969.
———. *This Vast External Realm*. New York: W. W. Norton & Co., 1973.
Allard, Kenneth. *Somalia Operations: Lessons Learned*. Washington, DC: National Defense University, 1995.
Anderson, Mary, and Peter Woodrow. *Rising from the Ashes: Development Strategies at Times of Disaster*. Boulder, CO: Westview Press, 1989.
Anstee, Margaret J. "The Experience in Angola: February 1992–June 1993." In Jim Whitman and David Pocock, eds. *After Rwanda: The Coordination of United Nations Humanitarian Assistance*. London: Macmillan, 1996.
Archibong, Victor Eno-obong. "The Organization of American States and the Organization of African Unity on Issues of Peace and Security: A Comparative Analysis of Selected Disputes." Ph.D. diss., University of Kansas, 1987.
Ayoob, Mohammed. *The Third World Security Predicament: State-making, Regional Conflict, and the International System*. Boulder, CO: Lynne Rienner, 1995.
Bennett, Jon. *Meeting Needs: NGO Coordination in Practice*. London: Earthscan, 1995.
Berdal, Mats R. *Whither UN Peacekeeping?* Adelphi Paper no. 281. London: International Institute for Strategic Studies, 1993.
Best, Geoffrey. *War and Law since 1945*. New York: Oxford University Press, 1994.
Blechman, Barry M., and Stephen S. Kaplan. *Force Without War: U.S. Armed Forces as a Political Instrument*. Washington, DC: Brookings Institution, 1978.
Boutros-Ghali, Boutros. *An Agenda for Peace*. New York: United Nations, 1992.

Brown, Michael E., ed. *Ethnic Conflict and International Security*. Princeton, NJ: Princeton University Press, 1993.

Brownlie, Ian, ed. *Basic Documents on Human Rights*. 3d. ed. New York: Oxford University Press, 1993.

Buehrig, Edward H. *The UN and the Palestinian Refugees*. Bloomington: Indiana University Press, 1971.

Bugnion, François. *Le Comité International de la Croix-Rouge et la Protection des Victimes de la Guerre*. Translated by David P. Forsythe. Geneva: ICRC, 1994.

Childers, Erskine, and Brian Urquhart. *Renewing the United Nations System*. Uppsala: Dag Hammarskjöld Foundation, 1994.

Chopra, Jarat. *UN Transition Authority in Cambodia*. Occasional Paper no. 15. Providence, RI: Watson Institute, 1994.

Claude, Inis L. "The Central Challenge to the United Nations: Weakening the Strong or Strengthening the Weak?" In Inis L. Claude, *States and the Global System: Politics, Law, and Organisation*. London: Macmillan, 1988.

————. "Commitments and the Problem of Order." In *States and the Global System: Politics, Law, and Organisation*. London: Macmillan, 1988.

Cohen, Roberta. *Refugees and Human Rights*. Washington, DC: Refugee Policy Group, 1995.

————. *United Nations Human Rights Bodies: An Agenda for Humanitarian Action*. Washington, DC: Refugee Policy Group, 1992.

Commission on Global Governance. *Our Global Neighbourhood*. Oxford: Oxford University Press, 1995.

Conetta, Carl, and Charles Knight. *Vital Force: A Proposal for the Overhaul of the UN Peace Operations System and for the Creation of a UN Legion*. Project on Defence Alternatives Research Monograph no. 4. October 1995.

Cossali, Paul, and Clive Robson. *Stateless in Gaza*. London: Zed Books, 1986.

Cuenod, Jacques. "Coordinating United Nations Humanitarian Assistance." In *RPG Focus*. Washington, DC: Refugee Policy Group, 1993.

Dawkins, Richard. *The Selfish Gene*. New York: Oxford University Press, 1976.

DeMars, William. "Seeds of Sovereignty: Humanitarion Organizations and War in the Horn of Africa." In Chatfield, Charles, et al., eds. *Solidarity beyond the State: The Dynamics of Transnational Social Movements*. Syracuse, NY: Syracuse University Press, forthcoming.

Deng, Francis. *Protecting the Dispossessed: A Challenge for the International Community*. Washington, DC: Brookings Institution, 1993.

Destexhe, Alain. *Rwanda: essai sur le génocide*. Brussels: Editions Complexe, 1994.

Diehl, Paul. *International Peacekeeping*. Baltimore: Johns Hopkins University Press, 1993.

Durch, William J., ed. *The Evolution of UN Peacekeeping: Case Studies and Comparative Analysis*. New York: St. Martin's Press, 1993.

Ellwood, David W. *Italy, 1943–45*. Leicester, England: Leicester University Press, 1985.

Findlay, Trevor. *Cambodia: The Legacy and Lessons of UNTAC*. SIPRI Research Report no. 9. Oxford: Oxford University Press, 1995.

Forsythe, David. *United Nations Peacemaking*. Baltimore: Johns Hopkins University Press, 1972.

Fukuyama, Francis. *The End of History and the Last Man*. New York: Free Press, 1992.

Gaddis, John Lewis. *The United States and the Origins of the Cold War, 1941–47*. New York: Columbia University Press, 1972.

Gilmour, David. *Lebanon: The Fractured Country*. London: Sphere Books, 1983.

Gilpin, Robert. *War and Change in World Politics*. Cambridge: Cambridge University Press, 1981.

Goldstein, Judith, and Robert Keohane, eds. *Ideas and Foreign Policy: Beliefs, Institutions, and Political Change*. Ithaca, NY: Cornell University Press, 1993.

Gordenker, Leon. *Refugees and International Politics*. New York: Columbia University Press, 1987.

Gordenker, Leon, and Thomas G. Weiss, eds. *Soldiers, Peacekeepers, and Disasters*. Basingstoke, England: Macmillan, 1991.

Gow, James. "Nervous Bunnies: The International Community and the Yugoslav War of Dissolution, The Politics of Military Intervention in a Time of Change." In Lawrence Freedman, ed. *Military Intervention in European Conflicts*. Oxford: Political Quarterly Publishing Co., 1994.

Gowing, Nik. *Real-Time Television Coverage of Armed Conflicts and Diplomatic Crises: Does It Pressure or Distort Foreign Policy Decision?* Cambridge: Harvard University Press, 1994.

Gurr, Ted Robert, and Barbara Harff. *Ethnic Conflict in World Politics*. Boulder, CO: Westview Press, 1994.

Haas, Ernst B. "Beware the Slippery Slope: Notes toward the Definition of Justifiable Intervention." In Laura W. Reed and Carl Kaysen, eds. *Emerging Norms of Justified Intervention*. Cambridge, MA: American Academy of Arts and Sciences, 1993.

Heiberg, Marianne, ed. *Subduing Sovereignty: Sovereignty and the Right to Intervene*. London: Pinter, 1994.

Heininger, Janet E. *Peacekeeping in Transition: The United Nations in Cambodia*. New York: Twentieth Century Fund, 1994.

Henkin, Alice, ed. *Honoring Human Rights and Keeping the Peace: Lessons from El Salvador, Cambodia, and Haiti*. Washington, DC: Aspen Institute, 1995.

Henkin, Louis. *The Age of Rights*. New York: Columbia University Press, 1990.

Huntington, Samuel. *The Third Wave*. Norman: University of Oklahoma Press, 1988.

Independent Working Group on the Future of the United Nations. *The United Nations in Its Second Half-Century*. New York: Ford Foundation, 1995.

Ingram, James. "The Future Architecture for International Humanitarian Assistance." In Thomas G. Weiss and Larry Minear, eds. *Humanitarianism Across Borders: Sustaining Civilians in Times of War*. Boulder, CO: Lynne Rienner, 1993.

Jackson, Robert H. *Quasi-States: Sovereignty, International Relations, and the Third World*. Cambridge: Cambridge University Press, 1990.

James, Alan. *Britain and the Congo Crisis, 1960–1963*. Basingstoke, England: Macmillan, 1996.

———. *Interminable Interim: The UN Force in Lebanon*. London: Centre for Security and Conflict Studies, Institute for the Study of Conflict, 1988.

———. *Peacekeeping in International Politics*. Basingstoke, England: Macmillan, in association with the International Institute of Strategic Studies, 1990.

———. "Peacekeeping, Peace-Enforcement, and National Sovereignty." In Ramesh Thakur and C. A. Thayer, eds. *UN Peacekeeping in the 1990s*. Boulder, CO: Westview Press, 1995.

Johnston, Douglas, and Cynthia Sampson, eds. *Religion, the Missing Dimension of Statecraft*. New York: Oxford University Press and the Center for Strategic Studies, 1994.

Kennan, George F. *Russia and the West under Lenin and Stalin*. New York: Mentor, 1960.

———. *Russia Leaves the War*. Princeton, NJ: Princeton University Press, 1956.

Kennedy, Paul. *The Rise and Fall of the Great Powers.* New York: Random House, 1987.

Khouri, Fred J. *The Arab-Israeli Dilemma.* Syracuse, NY: Syracuse University Press, 1968.

Lake, Anthony, et al. *After the Wars: Reconstruction in Afghanistan, Indochina, Central America, Southern Africa, and the Horn of Africa.* New Brunswick, NJ: Transaction Publishers, 1991.

Latter, Richard. *Coordinating U.N. Peace Support Operations.* Cambridge: University of Cambridge, Royal Institute Global Security Programme, 1994.

Lauren, Paul Gordon. *Power and Prejudice: The Politics and Diplomacy of Racial Discrimination.* Boulder, CO: Westview Press, 1988. 2d ed. forthcoming.

Lecky, William E. H. *History of European Morals.* 3d ed. New York: D. Appleton & Co., 1913, Vol. 1.

Liu, F. T. "Peacekeeping and Humanitarian Assistance." In Leon Gordenker and Thomas G. Weiss, eds. *Soldiers, Peacekeepers, and Disasters.* Basingstoke, England: Macmillan, in association with the International Peace Academy, 1991.

Loescher, Gil. *Beyond Charity: International Cooperation and the Global Refugee Problem.* New York: Oxford University Press, 1994.

Lovejoy, Arthur O. *Reflections on Human Nature.* Baltimore: Johns Hopkins University Press, 1961.

Lyons, Gene M., and Michael Mastanduno, eds. *Beyond Westphalia? National Sovereignty and Intervention.* Baltimore: Johns Hopkins University Press, 1995.

Lyons, Terrence, and Ahmed I. Samatar. *Somalia: State Collapse, Multilateral Intervention, and Strategies for Political Reconstruction.* Washington, DC: Brookings Institution, 1995.

Mackinlay, John, and Jarat Chopra. *A Draft Concept of Second Generation Multinational Operations, 1993.* Providence, RI: Watson Institute, 1993.

Mcdermott, Anthony, and Kjell Skjelsbaek. *The Multinational Force in Beirut, 1982–1984.* Miami: Florida International University Press, 1991.

Melanson, Richard A. *Reconstructing Consensus: American Foreign Policy since the Vietnam War.* New York: St. Martin's Press, 1991.

Meron, Theodore. *Human Rights and Humanitarian Norms as Customary Law.* Oxford: Clarendon Press, 1989.

Miller, James Edward. *The United States and Italy, 1945–50: The Politics and Diplomacy of Stabilization.* Chapel Hill: University of North Carolina Press, 1986.

Minear, Larry, and Thomas G. Weiss. *Humanitarian Action in the Former Yugoslavia: The UN's Role, 1991–1993.* Watson Institute Occasional Paper no. 18. Providence, RI: Brown University, 1994.

———. *Humanitarian Action in Times of War: A Handbook for Practitioners.* Boulder, CO: Lynne Rienner, 1993.

———. *Humanitarian Politics.* New York: Foreign Policy Association, 1995.

Morgenthau, Hans J. *Politics Among Nations.* 5th ed. New York: Alfred A. Knopf, 1973.

Mueller, John. *Retreat from Doomsday: The Obsolescence of Major War.* New York: Basic Books, 1989.

Murphy, Robert. *Diplomat among Warriors.* London: Collins, 1964.

Nolan, Cathal. *Principled Diplomacy: Security and Rights in U.S. Foreign Policy.* Westport, CT: Greenwood Press, 1993.

Norwegian Refugee Council and Refugee Policy Group. *Human Rights Protection for Internally Displaced Persons.* Washington, DC: Refugee Policy Group, 1993.

Nye, Joseph. *Bound to Lead: The Changing Nature of American Power*. New York: Basic Books, 1990.

Oraa, Jaime. *Human Rights in States of Emergency in International Law*. New York: Oxford University Press, 1992.

Palwankar, Umesh, ed. *Symposium on Humanitarian Action and Peace-Keeping: Report*. Geneva: ICRC, 1994.

Peace Operations: Information on U.S. and U.N. Activities. Washington, DC: GAO, 1995.

Peters, Joan. *From Time Immemorial*. New York: Harper & Row, 1984.

Pictet, Jean S., ed. *Commentary on the Geneva Conventions of 12 August 1949: IV Geneva Convention Relative to the Protection of Civilian Persons in Time of War*. Geneva: ICRC, 1958.

Pineda, Ana Marie, and Robert Schreiter, eds. *Dialogue Rejoined: Theology and Ministry in the United States Hispanic Reality*. Collegeville, MN: Liturgical Press, 1995.

Quinlan, Robert J. "The Italian Armistice." In *American Civil-Military Decisions: A Book of Case Studies*. A Twentieth Century Fund Study edited by Harold Stein. Birmingham: University of Alabama Press, 1963.

Ramet, Sabrina Petra. *Nationalism and Federalism in Yugoslavia, 1962–1991*. Bloomington: Indiana University Press, 1992.

Ratner, Steven R. *The New UN Peacekeeping*. New York: St. Martin's Press, 1995.

Reitzel, William, Morton A. Kaplan, and Constance G. Coblentz. *United States Foreign Policy 1945–1955*. Washington, DC: Brookings Institution, 1956.

Riasanovsky, Nicholas V. *A History of Russia*. 5th ed. Oxford: Oxford University Press, 1993.

Rosenau, James N. *Turbulence in World Politics: A Theory of Change and Continuity*. Princeton, NJ: Princeton University Press, 1990.

Rothstein, Robert L. *Alliances and Small Powers*. New York: Columbia University Press, 1968.

Russett, Bruce. *Grasping the Democratic Peace: Principles for a Post–Cold War World*. Princeton, NJ: Princeton University Press, 1993.

Schiff, Benjamin. "Assisting Palestinian Refugees." In Emanuel Adler and Beverly Crawford, eds. *Progress in Postwar International Relations*. New York: Columbia University Press, 1991.

Shawcross, William. *Cambodia's New Deal*. Contemporary Issues Paper no. 1. Washington, DC: Carnegie Endowment for International Peace, 1994.

———. *The Quality of Mercy: Cambodia, Holocaust, and Modern Conscience*. New York: Simon & Schuster, 1984.

Singer, J. David. *The Correlates of War*. Vols. 1 and 2. New York: Free Press, 1979, 1980.

Singer, Max, and Aaron Wildavsky. *The Real World Order: Zones of Peace, Zones of Turmoil*. Chatham, NJ: Chatham House, 1993.

Snyder, Frank M. *Command and Control: The Literature and Commentaries*. Washington, DC: National Defense University, 1993.

Sommer, John G. *Hope Restored? Humanitarian Aid in Somalia, 1990–1994*. Washington, DC: Refugee Policy Group, 1994.

Steinberg, James P. "International Involvement in the Yugoslavia Conflict." In Lori Fischer Damrosch, ed. *Enforcing Restraint: Collective Intervention in Internal Conflicts*. New York: Council on Foreign Relations Press, 1993.

United Nations High Commissioner for Refugees. *The State of the World's Refugees, 1993: The Challenge of Protection*. New York: Penguin Books, 1993.

———. *The State of the World's Refugees, 1995: The Search for Solutions*. Oxford: Oxford University Press, 1995.

———. *A UNHCR Handbook for the Military on Humanitarian Operations*. Geneva: UNHCR, 1995.

United States Department of State. *Foreign Relations of the United States*. Vol. 3. Washington, DC: GPO, 1947.

Urquhart, Brian. *Hammarskjöld*. London: The Bodley Head, 1972.

Viorst, Milton. *Reaching for the Olive Branch: UNRWA and Peace in the Middle East*. Washington, DC: Middle East Institute, 1989.

———. *UNRWA and Peace in the Middle East*. Washington, DC: Middle East Institute, 1984.

von Laue, Theodore H. *The World Revolution of Westernization: The Twentieth Century in Global Perspective*. New York: Oxford University Press, 1987.

Weiss, Thomas G. "Collective Spinelessness: UN Actions in the Former Yugoslavia." In Richard H. Ullman, ed. *The World and Yugoslavia's Conflicts*. New York: Council on Foreign Relations Press, forthcoming.

———. "Rekindling Hope in UN Humanitarian Intervention." In Walter Clarke and Jeffrey Herbst, eds. *Revisiting Somalia: The Lessons of U.S./U.N. Intervention*. Boulder, CO: Lynne Rienner, forthcoming.

———, ed. *The United Nations and Civil Wars*. Boulder, CO: Lynne Rienner, 1995.

Weiss, Thomas G., David P. Forsythe, and Roger Coate. *The United Nations and Changing World Politics*. Boulder, CO: Westview Press, 1994.

Weiss, Thomas G., and Larry Minear. *Mercy Under Fire: War and the Global Humanitarian Community*. Boulder, CO: Westview Press, 1995.

Whitman, Jim, and David Pocock, eds. *After Rwanda: The Coordination of United Nations Humanitarian Assistance*. London: Macmillan, 1996.

Winters, Paul, ed. *Interventionism: Current Controversies*. San Diego: Greenhaven Press, 1995.

Woodward, Susan L. *Balkan Tragedy: Chaos and Dissolution after the Cold War*. Washington, DC: Brookings Institution, 1995.

Zacher, Mark. "The Decaying Pillars of the Westphalian Temple." In James N. Rosenau and Ernst-Otto Czempiel, eds. *Governance Without Government: Order and Change in World Politics*. Cambridge: Cambridge University Press. 1992.

Zolberg, Aristide, et al. *Escape from Violence: Conflict and the Refugee Crisis in the Developing World*. New York: Oxford University Press, 1989.

JOURNAL ARTICLES

Abernethy, Virginia. "Optimism and Overpopulation." *Atlantic Monthly* 274, no. 6 (1994): 84.

Barnett, Michael. "Partners in Peace? The UN, Regional Organizations, and Peace-Keeping." *Review of International Studies* 21, no. 4 (1995): 411–33.

———. "The United Nations and Global Security: The Norm Is Mightier than the Sword." *Ethics and International Affairs* 9 (1995): 37–54.

Bettati, Mario. "L'ONU et l'action humanitaire." *Politique Etrangère* 58, no. 3 (1993): 641–59.

Betts, Richard K. "Delusions of Impartiality: The United Nations and Intervention." *Current* (February 1995): 27–32.

————. "The Delusion of Intervention." *Foreign Affairs* 73, no. 4 (1994): 20–33.

Bolton, John R. "Wrong Turn in Somalia." *Foreign Affairs* 73, no. 1 (1994): 57–66.

Burgers, Jan. "The Road to San Francisco: The Revival of the Human Rights Idea in the Twentieth Century." *Human Rights Quarterly* 14, no. 4 (1992): 447–77.

Chomsky, Noam, Christopher Hitchens, Richard Falk, Carl Conetta, Charles Knight, and Robert Leavitt. "On Intervention." *Boston Review* 18 (1993–94): 3–16.

Chopra, Jarat. "Back to the Drawing Board." *Bulletin of the Atomic Scientists* (March-April, 1995).

Chopra, Jarat, and Thomas G. Weiss. "Prospects for Containing Conflict in the Former Second World." *Security Studies* 4, no. 3 (1995): 552–83.

————. "Sovereignty Is No Longer Sacrosanct: Codifying Humanitarian Intervention." *Ethics and International Affairs* 6 (1992): 95–117.

Christopher, Warren. "America's Leadership, America's Opportunity." *Foreign Policy* 98 (Spring 1995): 6–27.

Crocker, Chester A. "The Lessons of Somalia: Not Everything Went Wrong." *Foreign Affairs* 74, no. 3 (1995): 2–8.

Delbruck, Jost. "A Fresh Look at Humanitarian Intervention under the Authority of the United Nations." *Indiana Law Journal* 67 (Fall 1992): 887.

Destexhe, Alain. "The Third Genocide." *Foreign Policy* 97 (Winter 1994–95): 10.

de Waal, Alex, and Rakiya Ommar. "Can Military Intervention Be 'Humanitarian'?" *Middle East Report*, nos. 187–88 (1994): 7.

Dole, Bob. "Shaping America's Global Future." *Foreign Policy* 98 (Spring 1995): 29–43.

Eban, Abba. "The U.N. Idea Revisited." *Foreign Affairs* 74, no. 5 (1995): 51.

Etzioni, Amitai. "The Evils of Self-Determination." *Foreign Policy* 89 (1992–93): 21–35.

Forsythe, David P. "Democracy, War, and Covert Action." *Journal of Peace Research* 29, no. 4 (1992): 385–95.

————. "Human Rights and the U.N.: An Incremental but Incomplete Revolution." *Global Governance* 1, no. 3 (1995).

————. "Human Rights, the United States, and the Organization of American States." *Human Rights Quarterly* 13, no. 1 (1991): 66–98.

————. "Politics and the International Tribunal for the Former Yugoslavia." *Criminal Law Forum* 5, no. 2–3 (1994).

Gati, Charles. "From Sarajevo to Sarajevo." *Foreign Affairs* 124, no. 4 (1992): 64–78.

Gordon, Ruth. "United Nations Intervention in Internal Conflicts: Iraq, Somalia, and Beyond." *Michigan Journal of International Law* 15 (Winter 1994): 519.

Gottlieb, Gidon. "Nations without States." *Foreign Affairs* 73, no. 3 (1994): 100–112.

Guillot, Philippe. "France, Peacekeeping, and Humanitarian Intervention." *International Peacekeeping* 1, no. 1 (1994): 40.

Helman, Gerald, and Steven R. Ratner. "Saving Failed States." *Foreign Policy* 89 (Winter 1992–93): 3–20.

Hoge, James F., Jr. "Editor's Note." *Foreign Affairs* 73, no. 6 (1994).

Huntington, Samuel. "The Clash of Civilizations." *Foreign Affairs* 72, no. 3 (1993): 22–49.

International Institute of Humanitarian Law. "The Evolution of the Right to Assistance." Reprint. *International Review of the Red Cross*, no. 297 (1993): 519–25.

International Institute for Strategic Studies. "Military Support for Humanitarian Operations." *Strategic Comments*, no. 2 (February 22, 1995).

James, Alan. "Peacekeeping in the Post–Cold War Era." *International Journal* 1 (Spring 1995): 244.

———. "The U.N. Force in Cyprus." *International Affairs* (Summer 1989): 481–500.

Jorgensen, Dan. "Cargo Cult: Strange Stories of Desire from Melanesia and Beyond." *Pacific Affairs* 67, no. 4 (1994).

Kennan, George F. "Sources of Soviet Conduct." *Foreign Affairs* 25, no. 4 (1947): 566–82.

Kennedy, Paul, and Bruce Russett. "Reforming the United Nations." *Foreign Affairs* 74, no. 5 (1995).

Lind, Michael. "In Defense of Liberal Nationalism." *Foreign Affairs* 73, no. 3 (1994): 87–99.

Lyon, Peter. "The Rise and Fall and Possible Revival of International Trusteeship." *Journal of Commonwealth and Comparative Politics*, no. 31 (1993): 96–110.

Macalister-Smith, Peter. "Protection of the Civilian Population and the Prohibition of Starvation as a Method of Warfare." *International Review of the Red Cross*, no. 284 (1991): 440–57.

MacInnis, John A. "The Rules of Engagement for U.N. Peacekeeping Forces in Former Yugoslavia: A Response." *Orbis* 39, no. 1 (1995): 97–100.

Mackinlay, John. "Improving Multifunctional Forces." *Survival* 36, no. 3 (1994): 149–73.

Mackinlay, John, and Jarat Chopra. "Second Generation Multinational Operations." *Washington Quarterly* 15, no. 3 (1992): 113–31.

Mandelbaum, Michael. "The Reluctance to Intervene." *Foreign Policy* 95 (Summer 1994): 3, 11.

Mansfield, Edward, and Jack Snyder. "Democratization and War." *Foreign Affairs* 74, no. 3 (1995): 79–97.

Maynes, Charles William. "Containing Ethnic Conflict." *Foreign Policy* 90 (Spring 1993): 3–21.

———. "Relearning Intervention." *Foreign Policy* 98 (Spring 1995): 108.

———. "A Workable Clinton Doctrine." *Foreign Policy* 93 (Winter 1993–94): 3–20.

Mearsheimer, John. "The False Promise of International Institutions." *International Security* 19, no. 3 (1994–95): 5–49.

Miller, Robert H. "Historical Sources of Conflict in Southeast Asia: Cambodia at the Vortex." *Conflict* 10, no. 3 (1990): 207.

Minear, Larry, and Thomas G. Weiss. "Groping and Coping in the Gulf Crisis: Discerning the Shape of a New Humanitarian Order." *World Policy Journal* 9, no. 4 (Fall 1992): 755–88.

Nachmias, Nitza, and Eric A. Belgrad. "Five Decades of Humanitarian Aid: The Case of UNRWA." *Towson State Journal of International Affairs* 29, no. 2 (1994): 1–13.

Nolan, Cathal. "The United States, Moral Norms, and Governing Ideas in World Politics." *Ethics and International Affairs* 7 (1993): 223–39.

Parks, W. Hays. "Air War and the Law of War." *Air Force Law Review* 32, no. 1 (1990): 1–226.

Paust, Jordan J. "Peace-Making and Security Council Powers: Bosnia-Herzegovina Raises International and Constitutional Questions." *Southern Illinois University Law Journal* 19 (Fall 1994): 131–42.

Peace, Kelly-Kate S., and David P. Forsythe. "Human Rights, Humanitarian Intervention, and World Politics." *Human Rights Quarterly* 15, no. 2 (1993): 290–314.

Pfaff, William. "A New Colonialism? Europe Must Go Back into Africa." *Foreign Affairs* 74, no. 1 (1995): 2–6.

Powers, Gerard F. "Testing the Moral Limits of Self-Determination: Northern Ireland and Croatia." *Fletcher Forum of World Affairs* 16, no. 2 (Summer 1992): 29.

Ramet, Sabrina Petra. "War in the Balkans." *Foreign Affairs* 124, no, 4 (1992): 89–98.

Rieff, David. "The Illusions of Peacekeeping." *World Policy Journal* 11, no. 3 (1994): 3.

Roberts, Adam. "The Crisis in Peacekeeping." *Survival* 36, no. 3 (1994): 93–120.

———. "Humanitarian War: Military Intervention and Human Rights." *International Affairs* 69, no. 3 (1993): 429–49.

Rudolph, Joseph. "Intervention in Communal Conflicts." *Orbis* 39, no. 2 (1995): 259–73.

Ruggie, John Gerard. "The U.N.: Wandering in the Void." *Foreign Affairs* 72, no. 4 (1993): 26–32.

Smith, John Maynard. "The Evolution of Behavior." *Scientific American* 239, no. 3 (1978): 176–92.

Sommaruga, Cornelio. "Assistance to Victims of War in International Humanitarian Law and Humanitarian Practice." *International Review of the Red Cross*, no. 289 (1992): 376–77.

Stavenhagen, Rodolfo. "Ethnic Conflicts and Their Impact on International Security." *International Social Science Journal* 43 (February 1991): 117–31.

Stedman, Steven John. "The New Interventionists." *Foreign Affairs* 72, no. 1 (1993): 1–15.

Touval, Saadia. "Why the U.N. Fails." *Foreign Affairs* 73, no. 3 (1994): 44–45.

Walzer, Michael. "The New Tribalism: Notes on a Difficult Problem." *Dissent* 49 (Spring 1992): 164–71.

Weiss, Thomas G. "Humanitarian Conflict Management: Less than the Millenium." *Security Studies* 5, no. 2 (1995–96).

———. "Intervention: Whither the United Nations?" *Washington Quarterly* 17, no. 1 (1994): 109–28.

———. "Military-Civilian Humanitarianism: The 'Age of Innocence' Is Over." *International Peacekeeping* 2, no. 3 (1995).

———. "New Challenges for UN Military Operations: Implementing 'An Agenda for Peace.' " *Washington Quarterly* 16, no. 1 (1993): 51–66.

———. "Overcoming the Somalia Syndrome—'Operation Rekindle Hope'?" *Global Governance* 1, no. 2 (1995): 171–87.

———. "The United Nations at Fifty: Recent Lessons." *Current History* 94, no. 592 (1995): 223–28.

Weiss, Thomas G., and Kurt M. Campbell. "Military Humanitarianism." *Survival* 33, no. 5 (1991): 451–65.

Whitman, Jim, and Ian Bartholomew. "Collective Control of UN Peace Support Operations: A Policy Proposal." *Security Dialogue* 25, no. 1 (1994): 77 92.

Index

About the Editors and Contributors

THE EDITORS

ERIC A. BELGRAD, Professor and Chairman, Department of Political Science, Towson University, Towson, Maryland.

NITZA NACHMIAS, Lecturer, Haifa University, Israel.

THE CONTRIBUTORS

DAVID P. FORSYTHE, Professor and Chairman, Department of Political Science, University of Nebraska, Lincoln, Nebraska.

LEON GORDENKER, Professor Emeritus, Center of International Studies, Princeton University, Princeton, New Jersey.

KENNETH F. HACKETT, Executive Director, Catholic Relief Services–United States Catholic Conference, Baltimore, Maryland.

JANET E. HEININGER, Associate Professor, American University, Washington, D.C.

ALAN JAMES, Research Professor, Keele University, Keele, United Kingdom.

GIL LOESCHER, Professor, Joan B. Kroc Institute for International Peace Studies, University of Notre Dame, Notre Dame, Indiana.

SIR MICHAEL ROSE, General, Former Commander of UN Forces in Bosnia-Herzegovina.

JOSEPH R. RUDOLPH, JR., Professor, Department of Political Science, Towson University, Towson, Maryland.

THOMAS G. WEISS, Associate Director, Thomas J. Watson Jr. Institute for International Studies, Brown University, Providence, Rhode Island.

JIM WHITMAN, Professor, Global Security Programme, Cambridge University, Cambridge, United Kingdom.

MICHAEL WIENER, Brigadier General (Ret.), Former Surgeon General, Israel Defense Forces, Tel Aviv, Israel.

ISBN 0-275-95273-8

HARDCOVER BAR CODE